IMAGES
of Rail

RAILROAD DEPOTS OF EAST CENTRAL OHIO

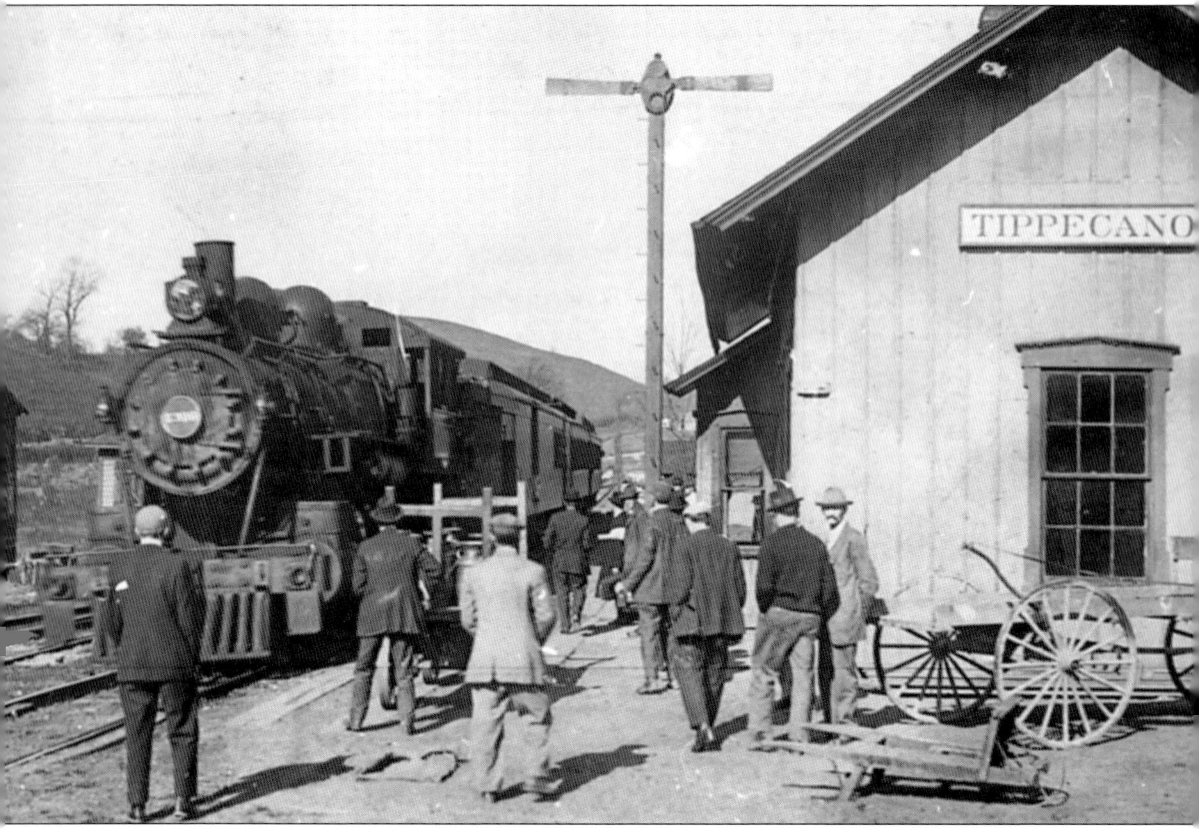

The small-town depot was the connection to the outside world for many communities. This Cleveland, Lorain & Wheeling Railway, later the Baltimore & Ohio Railroad (B&O), depot in Tippecanoe of Harrison County serves as a typical example of the activity when the train chugs into town. Passengers and traveling salesmen arrive and depart, local hacks transport people to a local hotel, local boys peddle newspapers and snacks, baggage, parcels, and mail is transferred, the engine crew see to the needs of the locomotive, and the conductor checks tickets and passes. (Author's collection.)

On the Cover: An Erie Railroad section crew takes a break from track-work to pose for the photographer at the depot in Polk, Ashland County. This style of a combined passenger and freight depot was repeated at many communities along the Erie Railroad from Chicago to the Atlantic coast. (Ashland County Historical Society collection.)

IMAGES
of Rail

Railroad Depots of East Central Ohio

Mark J. Camp

ARCADIA
PUBLISHING

ISBN 978-1-4671-2939-8

Published by Arcadia Publishing
Charleston, South Carolina

Printed in the United States of America

Library of Congress Control Number: 2018931621

For all general information, please contact Arcadia Publishing:
Telephone 843-853-2070
Fax 843-853-0044
E-mail sales@arcadiapublishing.com
For customer service and orders:
Toll-Free 1-888-313-2665

Visit us on the Internet at www.arcadiapublishing.com

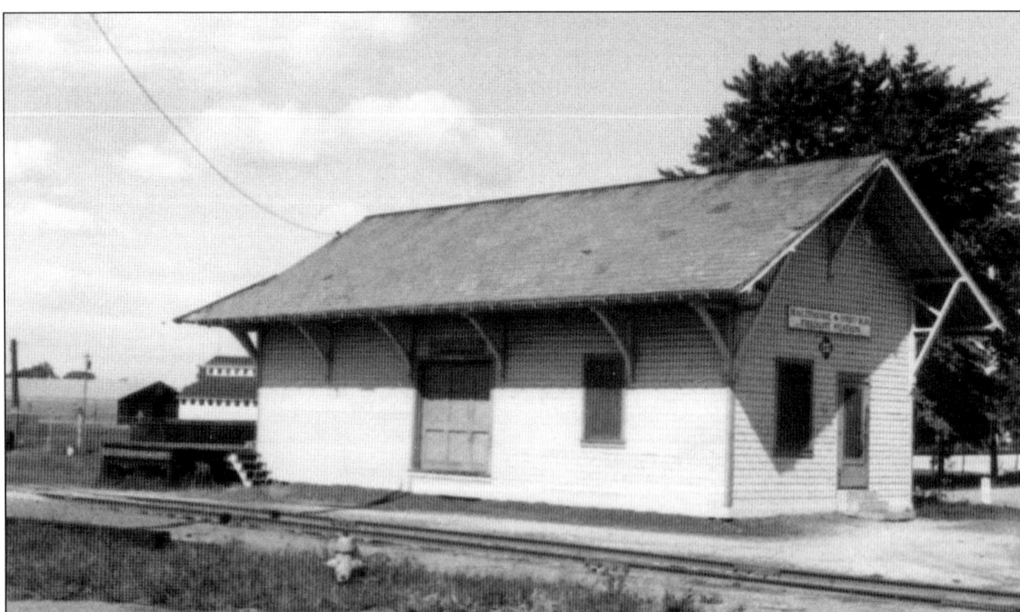

The Millersburg branch of the Baltimore & Ohio Railroad leaves the main line at Lodi and proceeds south to Millersburg by way of Wooster. The only B&O depot to survive until 2017 is this one at Wooster, now in commercial use. At one time, the B&O maintained 10 depots and passenger shelters along this branch. This image was captured in 1967. (Author photograph.)

Contents

Acknowledgments

Although I have photographed widely across Ohio beginning in the early 1960s, I started too late to record even 50 percent of the railroad depots that served this part of the state. Since I have chosen to present vintage views of as many depots as possible, it has been necessary to rely on the works of early photographers, many unfortunately unknown. It is to these itinerant photographers, postcard makers, railroad company photographers, and railfans, now and then, that I owe my thanks. Without their work, much of this would be lost to history.

The next step is for these photographs, postcards, and other data to end up preserved and curated by historical societies, museums, and libraries for the use of future generations. I have spent many hours in such institutions and cannot come close to expressing my gratitude for their fortitude in preserving the past and for all their help in collecting and assembling data. I am especially grateful for the courtesies extended by the Allen County Historical Society, Ashland County Historical Society, Special Collections of the Michael Schwartz Library of Cleveland State University, the Massillon Museum, the Local History Department of the Toledo Lucas County Public Library, the Tuscarawas County Historical Society, and the Walhonding Valley Historical Society. I have also used the Internet resources of Dan West's Existing Ohio Railroad Stations, the Dennison Railroad Depot Museum, East Liverpool Historical Society, Holmes County Historical Society, Orrville Railroad Heritage Society, Stark County Historical Society, Steubenville Historical Society, Wayne County Historical Society, and the Wayne County Public Library.

Additional information has been found in several excellent books including Wayne A. Coles's *Rails of Dreams* (PL&W/Y&S); John B. Corns's *The Wheeling and Lake Erie Railway Volume 1 and 2*; R.L. Hoover's *Railroad Stations of Coshocton, Ohio*; John A. Rehor's *The Nickel Plate Story;* James E. Sharp's *Wally The Story of the Walhonding Valley Railroad;* William S. Snyder's *The Rattlesnake and the Ramsey: The History of the Lorain, Ashland, and Southern Railroad*; Howard V. Vorley Jr. and William N. Poellot Jr.'s *The Pittsburgh & West Virginia Railway;* and various histories of Ashland, Belmont, Columbiana, Coshocton, Carroll, Harrison, Holmes, Jefferson, Knox, Mahoning, Stark, Tuscarawas, and Wayne Counties.

INTRODUCTION

Heading south from Lake Erie, the terrain of eastern Ohio becomes increasingly higher forested uplands dissected by streams and a few major rivers all trying to reach the level of the Ohio River. Initially, commerce followed the bottomland. Canals were then built to provide smoother passages from the Ohio River to the lake, but about the same time, railroads were becoming the new favored method of transportation and replaced a short-lived love affair with canals. Building rail lines through the Alleghany Plateau, however, posed problems not encountered in crossing the flatlands of western Ohio. To maintain acceptable grades, railroads had to cut and fill, tunnel, and bridge many watercourses. This added greatly to construction costs and is the reason for a number of lines to begin as narrow gauge. Narrow-gauge lines were able to operate with sharper curves and steeper grades than traditional standard-gauge operations and equipment and operation were less expensive. The reality was though that these narrow-gauge lines were forced to convert to standard gauge to successfully complete and efficiently interchange with the main lines.

Talk of railroads in this area began in the 1830s, but actual construction did not begin until the late 1840s. Main lines of railroads seeking Chicago and St. Louis were surveyed through the eastern hills. However, the plateau was a relatively untapped resource of coal, iron ore, and ceramic-quality clay. Mansfield and Pittsburgh were connected in 1853 by a line passing through Wooster, Massillon, Canton, Alliance, and Salem. Carrollton and Oneida were joined in 1853. A line connecting Cleveland and Pittsburgh, by way of Alliance and Wellsville, was opened in 1854, along with a branch to New Philadelphia. Steubenville and Newark were connected in 1855. In 1864, a broad-gauge line opened through the region, connecting Akron with Ashland. Massillon, Dover, New Philadelphia, and Uhrichsville were connected in 1873. Another line connected Orrville with Columbus in 1873. A line, originally intended to be built to Wheeling, West Virginia, stretched from Cleveland to Canton and terminated in Mineral City in 1882. The section from Toledo to Zoar Station was connected in 1882, and by 1889, Martins Ferry was reached. Another line stretching from Cleveland south to Minerva Junction, Canton, Beach City, and Coshocton dated to 1883. Coshocton and Loudonville were connected in 1893. The year 1899 saw a connection between Ashland and near Shreve. The year 1902 saw the final construction of a line connecting Alliance with Dillonvale. In 1904, a highline shortcut (built on a high fill to keep the track even in hilly terrain) was opened between Pittsburgh Junction, passing through Hopedale, Smithfield, and Mingo, to Pittsburgh.

By the early 1900s, railroads crisscrossed the hills and valleys of east central Ohio, putting many a community on the map for the first time. At the center of each community served by a railroad was the depot—a structure designed to handle the local business of the railroad. It provided shelter for passengers and their baggage; housed outbound and inbound freight, mail, and parcels; and served as a local office for railroad employees overseeing railroad passenger and freight business. Locals also found the depot the place to receive the latest in newsworthy events and local happenings that came in over the telegraph. The depot was a remarkably efficient building in small-town America. Technically, these were combination depots and were built to standard plans usually designed by company engineers. Usually, there was a set of plans, each a modification of the other, so that depots could be tailored to fit the business volume, population, and importance of a town. A typical combination depot consisted of a passenger waiting room on one end separated from a freight storage room on the other end by a railroad office area where tickets were sold, paperwork completed, telegraph messages sent and received, and train movements recorded. The central office area often included a bay window or vestibule for ease of viewing up and down the track. An orderboard, an elevated signal device, was also often attached to this part of the depot. By means of lanterns or position of a semaphore blade, this would signal to members of a locomotive crew how they were to proceed at a particular station. Larger communities, county seats, those at railroad junctions or those that contained railroad servicing facilities, like shops and roundhouses, had larger depots with more facilities, including lunchrooms and newsstands. In some cases, separate passenger and freight depots were erected. As communities evolved, railroad companies made changes to their depots. Early on, it meant adding electricity and indoor plumbing. An increase in business might result in additions to either the passenger or freight ends or perhaps a totally new depot. Sometimes, the original combination depot would be reused as a freight depot, and a separate new passenger depot would be built. In other cases, the old depot might be sold, moved from the right-of-way, and repurposed. Unfortunately, early frame depots were susceptible to fires from faulty potbelly stoves and passing sparks from locomotives. Also, here in the plateau, annual flooding led to depot damage.

I estimate there were some 325 depots that once served the east-central area of Ohio. This includes originals and many replacements. This book includes only a sampling of the many depots that once played an important role in the development of this region.

One

Baltimore and Ohio Lines

The Cleveland, Lorain & Wheeling Railway originated in 1870 with the incorporation of the Lake Shore & Tuscarawas Valley Railway, which completed a line from Elyria through Massillon and New Philadelphia to Uhrichsville in August 1873. By May 1893, after a number of reorganizations and mergers, the 192-mile line operated from Cleveland to Bridgeport with branches from Bridgeport to Bellaire and Martins Ferry. The line was intended to provide a direct connection between the developing lake ports of Cleveland and Lorain and the coalfields of Belmont and Harrison Counties. It became part of the Baltimore & Ohio system in 1909. In 2017, the line has been abandoned south of Uhrichsville and operated by R.J. Corman Railroad Group from Clinton to Uhrichsville.

Another B&O line was incorporated in August 1871 as the Valley Railway Company to build a line from Cleveland southward passing through Akron and Canton to the coal lands of Tuscarawas County. Passenger service began between Cleveland and Zoarville (later Valley Junction) in fall 1882. Trackage rights over the Wheeling & Lake Erie (W&LE) allowed the line to reach Bowerston in 1884. In 1895, the line was reorganized as the Cleveland, Terminal & Valley Railway. A short branch was laid to Magnolia in November 1898. Another branch led east into coal lands southeast of Mineral City. The B&O took over in 1909. In 2017, the Cuyahoga Valley Scenic Railroad, the new Wheeling & Lake Erie Railway, and CSX operate portions of the old Valley Railway.

Beginning at Lodi on the main line of the B&O and running south through Wooster and Holmesville, to Millersburg was the Cleveland, Wooster & Muskingum Valley Railroad. This line opened in 1895 as a subsidiary of the B&O. The stretch between Wooster and Millersburg was abandoned in 1928; that between Lodi and Wooster is no longer used by CSX as of 2017.

Other than brick passenger depots constructed at Canton, Massillon, Midvale, and New Philadelphia, the B&O lines were served by frame combination depots. Earlier designs attributed to the Cleveland, Lorain & Wheeling; Lake Shore & Tuscarawas Valley; Valley; and other predecessor lines were replaced in some communities by structures built to c. 1905 B&O depot plans.

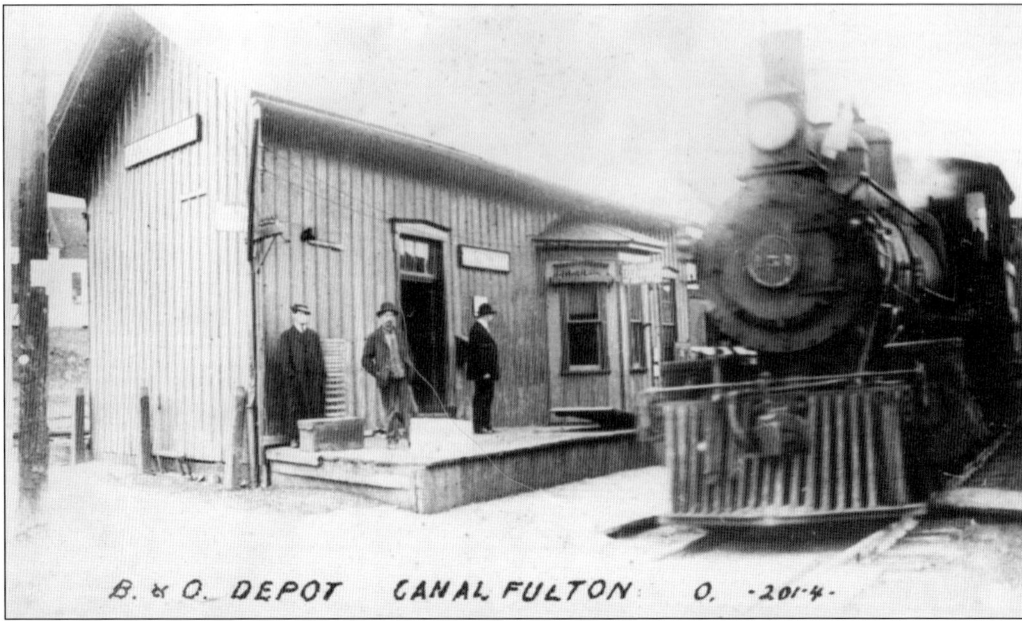

The Lake Shore & Tuscarawas Valley Railway opened its line from Elyria to Uhrichsville, passing through Canal Fulton, in 1873. By the time of this c. 1910 view, the B&O had taken control of its successor: the Cleveland, Lorain & Wheeling Railway (CL&W). Here, the agent and helpers wait to load baggage onto the arriving passenger train. This depot once sat along Market Street, but has been gone at least 50 years. The Pennsylvania Railroad (PRR), originally the Massillon & Cleveland Railway, arrived in 1870 and once maintained a frame combination depot just northeast of B&O's facility. (Author's collection.)

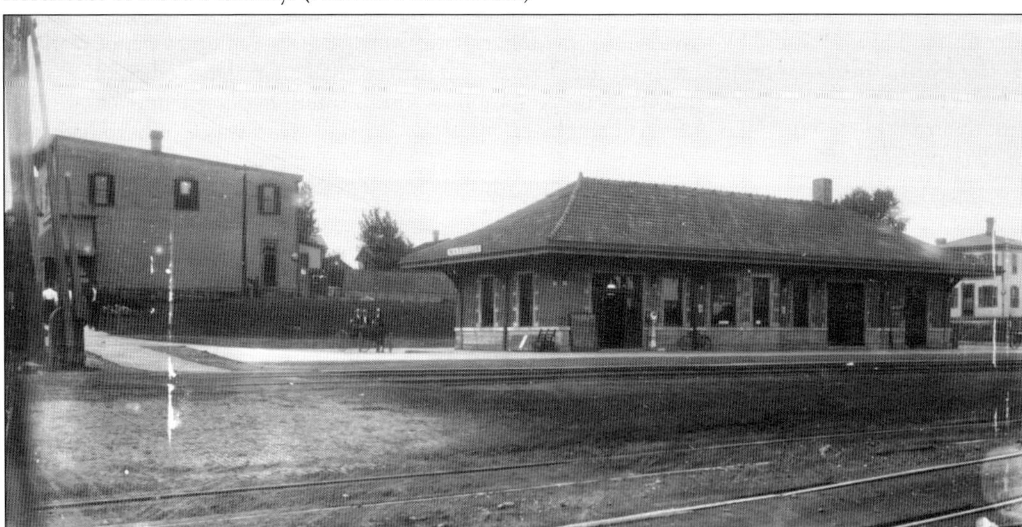

This is the second B&O passenger depot to serve Massillon; it was built in late 1905 at an expenditure of $15,000 to replace an earlier frame Lake Shore & Tuscarawas Valley structure. This depot and the Canal Fulton structure was susceptible to periodic flooding since they were built on the floodplain of the Tuscarawas River. A separate frame freight house of B&O design was located nearby. It continued to serve the railroad long after the passenger depot was removed, but it too has since disappeared. (Stan Baltzly photograph, Massillon Museum collection.)

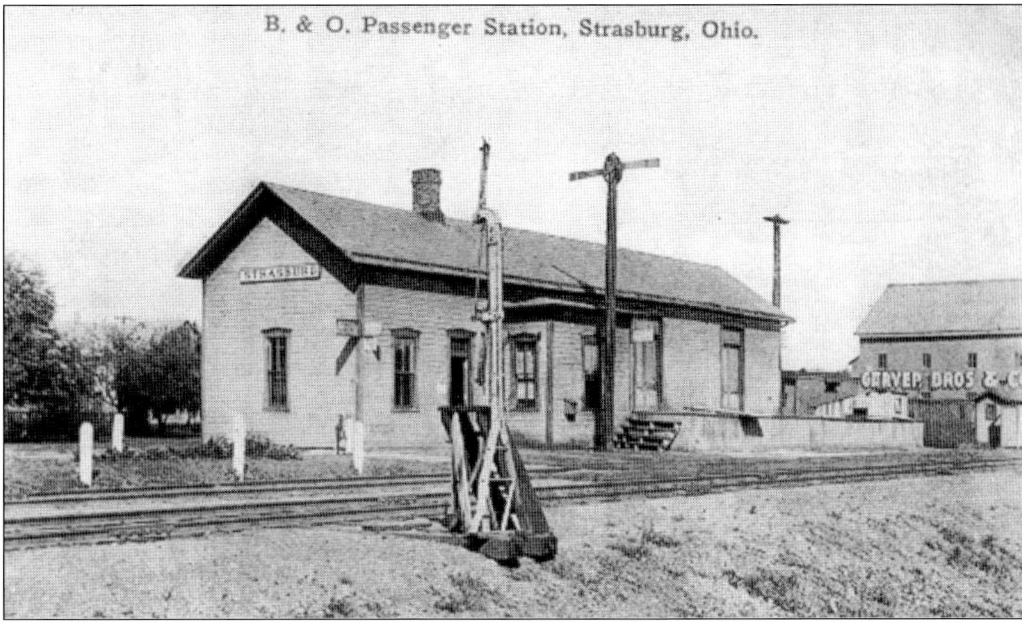

The Strasburg combination depot dates to the early days of the Lake Shore & Tuscarawas Valley (LS&TV) Railway. Compare the architecture to the Canal Fulton depot. The LS&TV depots had an angled vestibule with a separate roof, a raised wooden platform on the freight end, and ornate window frames. A standard wooden orderboard was mounted on an upright rectangular pole. The semaphore blade could be raised or lowered by the agent from within the depot in order to provide a message to the train crew of the next train due at the station. Across the track from the depot in the c. 1910 view above is a mail crane. The depot staff would attach an outgoing linen mailbag to this to be grabbed by personnel in the mail/baggage car of certain passenger trains. Incoming mailbags would be tossed onto the depot platform to be gathered up by depot workers. By the 1940s, the depot had been modified. The freight portion had been removed, another door had been added on the former passenger waiting room, window frames replaced, and a new taller orderboard added. The depot was still trackside in 1971. (Both, Tuscarawas County Historical Society collection.)

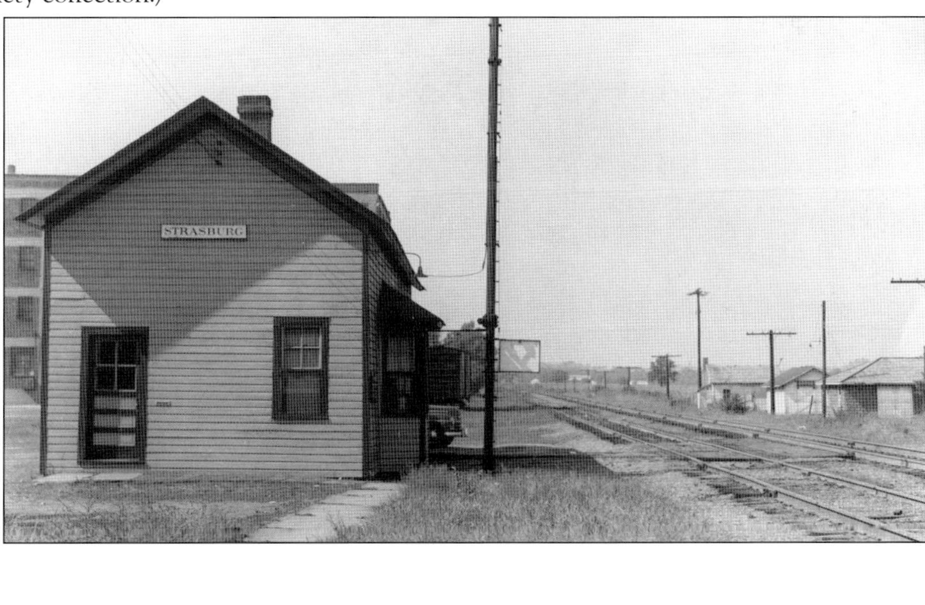

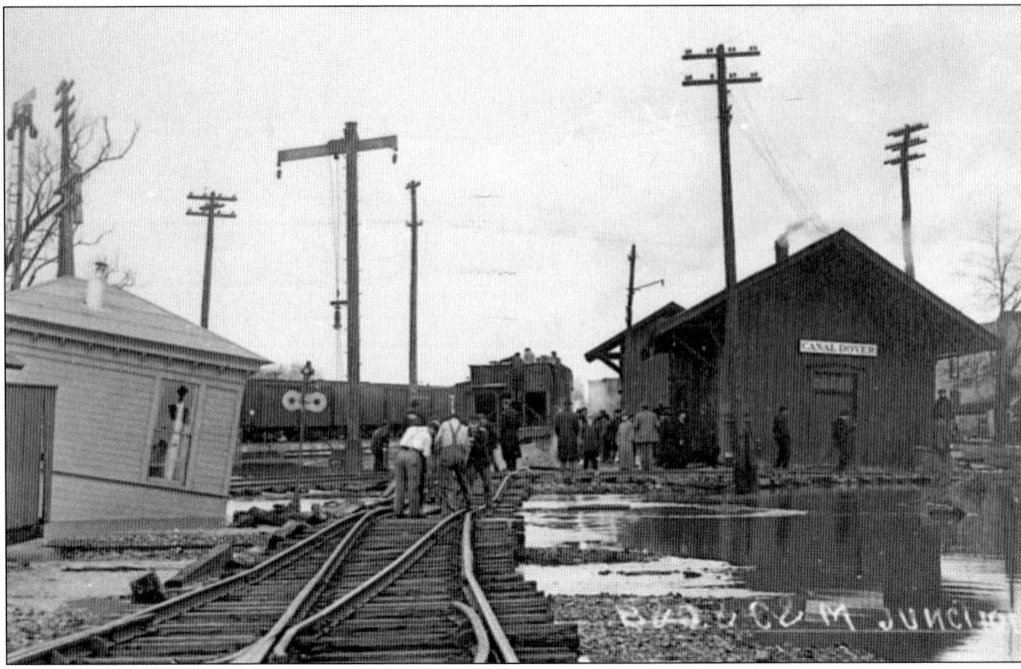

Farther south at Canal Dover (later just Dover), the flooding Tuscarawas River continued to plague the B&O and its predecessors. This is where the LS&TV crossed the PRR's Tuscarawas branch. During the 1913 flood, the Pennsylvania Railroad's single-story signal tower (in the above photograph to the left) nearly floated away, the B&O's depot was damaged by debris-laden floodwaters, and ballast was washed from under the tracks. Note this depot is also of early design, probably from around 1874, and comparable to Canal Fulton and Strasburg. This important junction was quickly repaired. The 1967 view below shows the PRR tower and a modified B&O depot. It is not known whether this is the original depot rebuilt in later years by the B&O or a new depot built to replace the flood-damaged one seen above. The depot pictured below was torn down in April 2013. (Above, Dan West; below, Charles Garvin photograph.)

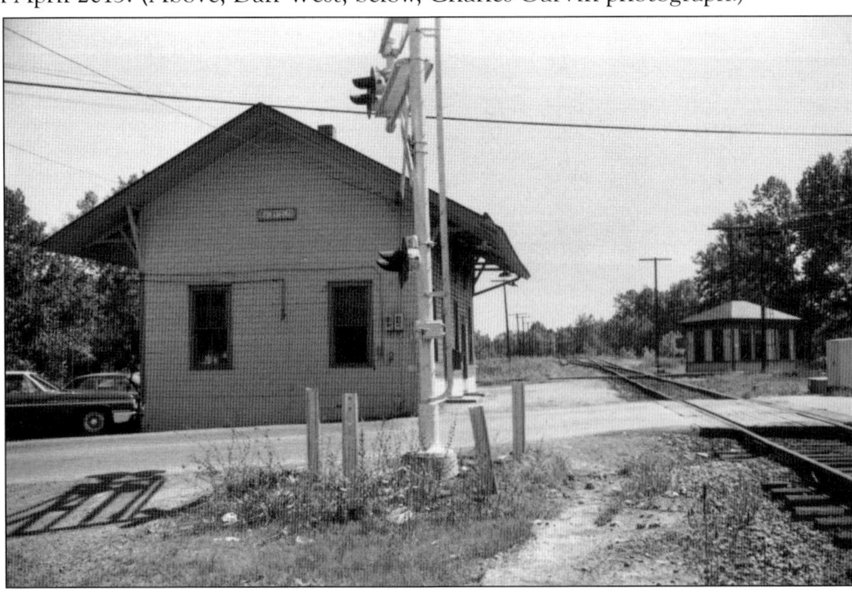

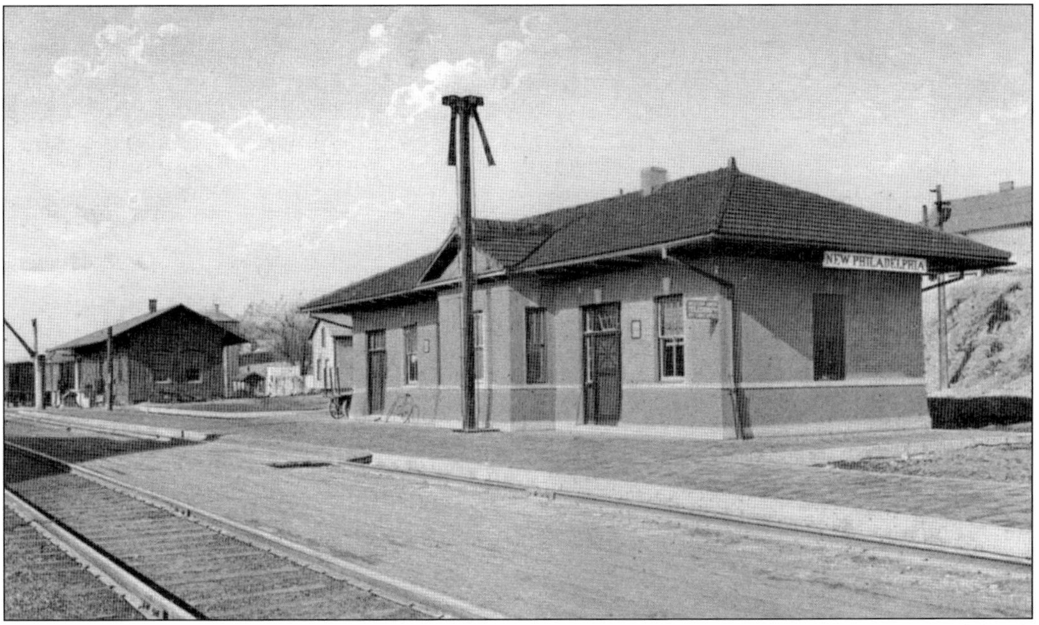

New Philadelphia, the county seat of Tuscarawas County, welcomed a new gray pressed-brick B&O passenger depot in 1905. A baggage room and gentleman's waiting room were located on the east end, separated from the ladies' waiting room on the west end by the office area. Toilet rooms were located off the two waiting rooms. The building was heated from a basement furnace. The depot replaced an earlier frame depot, seen in the background, that was then converted into a freight house. The freight house disappeared before 1970, while the passenger depot was still there in 1971. (Tuscarawas County Historical Society collection.)

The most recent combination depot at Midvale was constructed of brick, supporting the local brick and hollowware plants. The second floor was uncommon for B&O depots in eastern Ohio, but was necessary for extra office space to handle the large amounts of brick and tile shipped from this station. This 1959 photograph shows a well-kept structure. The depot has since been demolished. (Bob Lorenz photograph.)

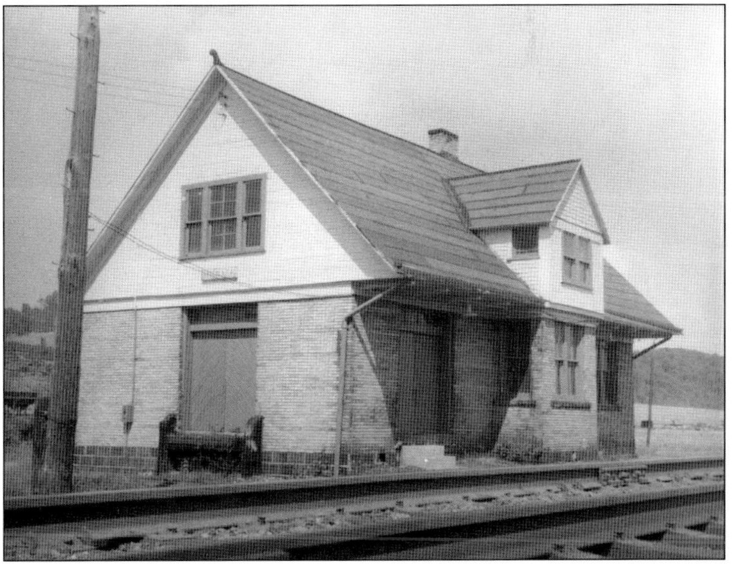

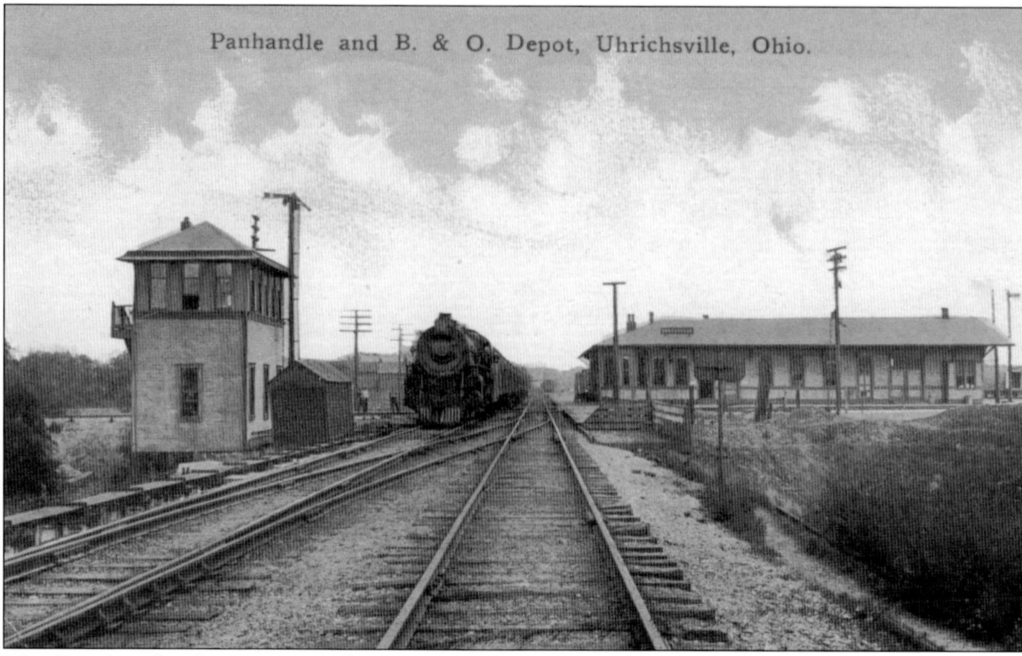

The Pittsburgh, Cincinnati, Chicago & St. Louis (PCC&StL) and B&O shared this union station at the crossing of their lines in Uhrichsville. This depot replaced earlier separate frame combination depots, which were then converted to freight use. A B&O roundhouse once existed east of the depot. The above c. 1910 view is looking east down the Panhandle with an arriving passenger train and shows the interlocking tower that protected this busy junction. The respective waiting rooms are next to the corner office; double doors mark the baggage room on the B&O side of the depot. The view below shows the back side or street-side of the depot during a somber occasion. Note the shorter PCC&StL section. The depot and tower were gone by the 1970s. (Both, author's collection.)

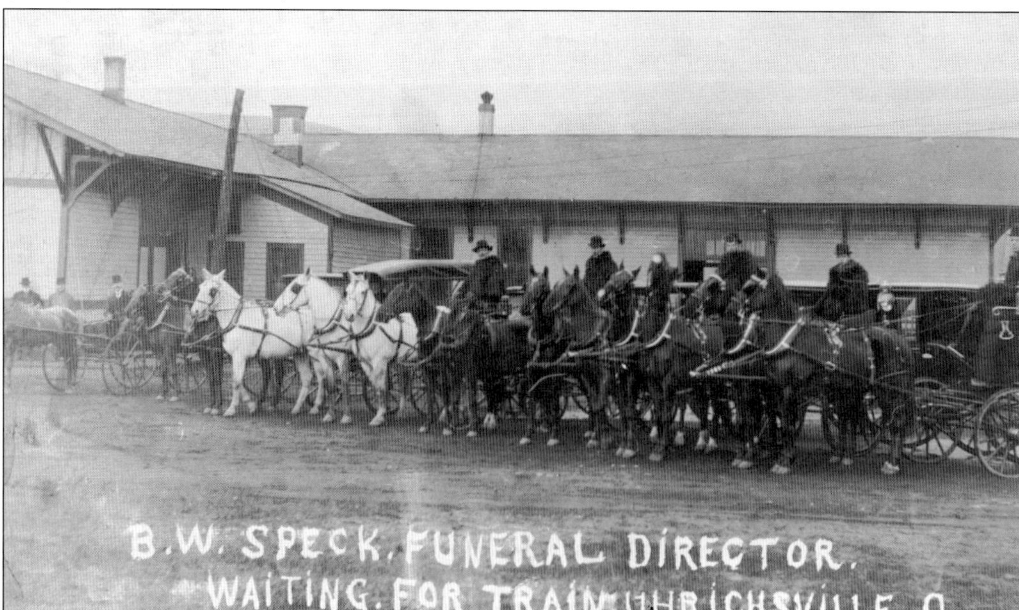

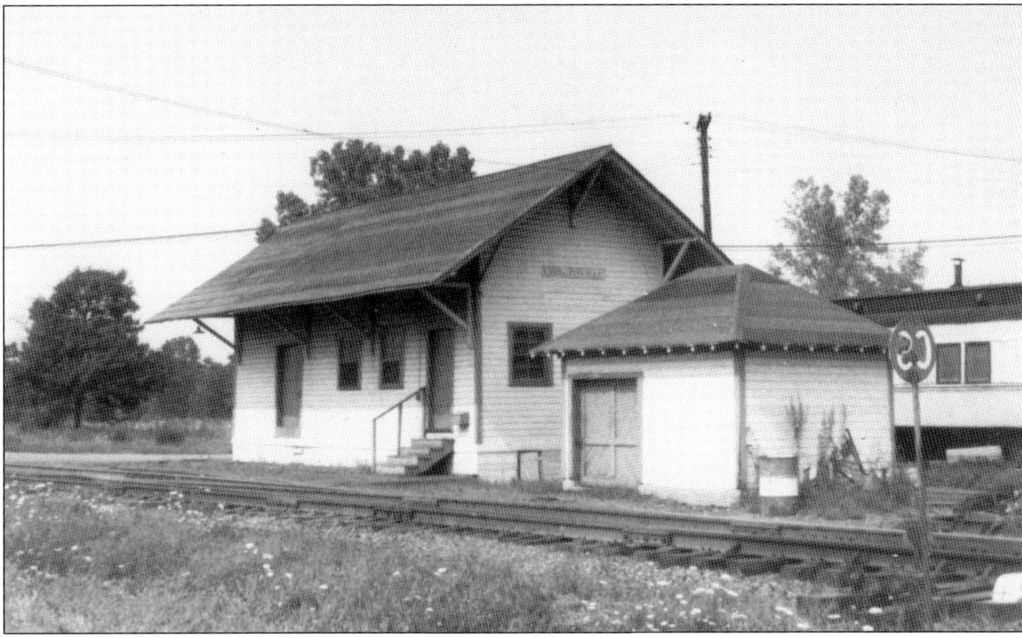

Still there in 2017 is this B&O freight house near the crossing of the RJ Corman line (former B&O) and Ohio Central (former PRR) in Uhrichsville. This view shows it in 1970. The shingled roof has been replaced by tar paper. The outbuilding is a toolshed used by maintenance-of-way crews. (Author photograph.)

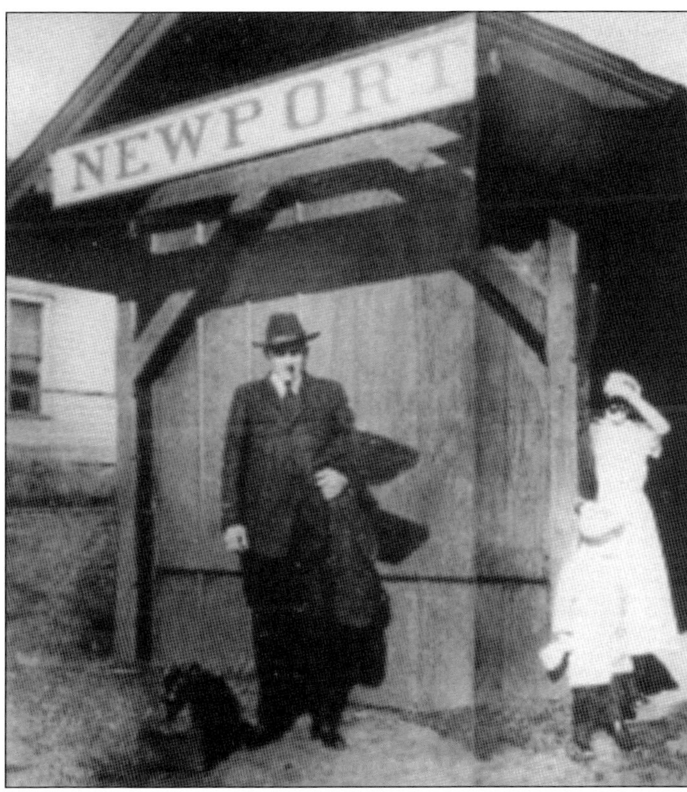

The Lake Shore & Tuscarawas Valley filed to extend its line from Uhrichsville to around Tippecanoe in March 1873; however, by July 1874, the company had foreclosed and was sold in January 1875, becoming the Cleveland, Tuscarawas Valley & Wheeling Railway. So, from Uhrichsville to Tippecanoe, the original builder of the depots is uncertain. Folks await a train to take them into the city at the small flag stop of Newport, south of Uhrichsville. The enclosed three-sided shelter was typical of the facilities provided at smaller communities not generating enough business to need a staffed depot. (Tuscarawas County Historical Society collection.)

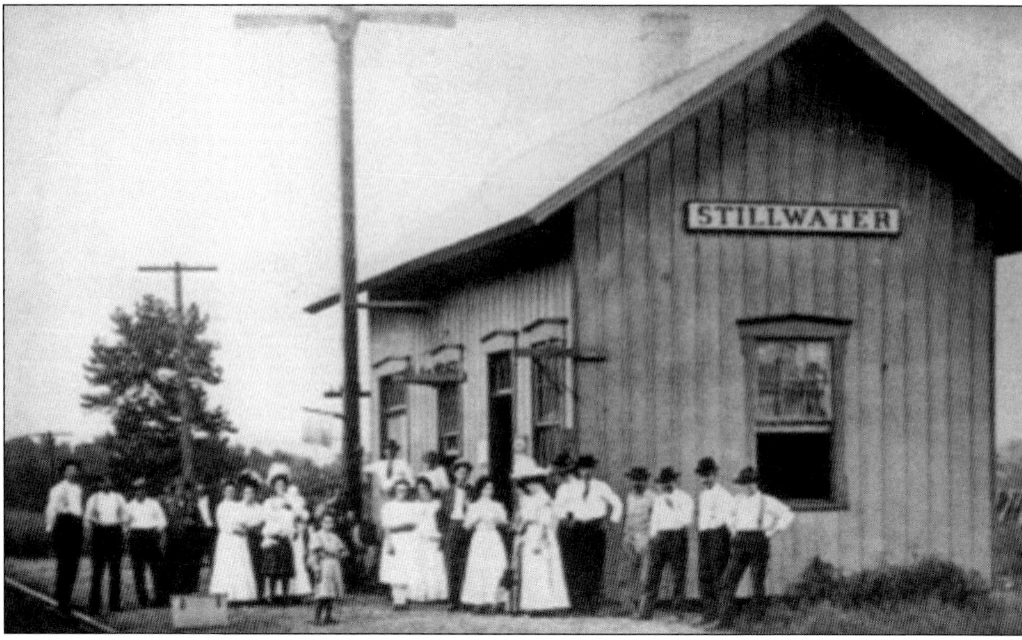

Stillwater lies south of Uhrichsville on the former Lake Shore & Tuscarawas Valley line as the railroad passes into rich coal lands. This combination depot was probably built in 1873–1874. The occasion is unknown, but something important drew this crowd out on a nice warm day in the early 1900s. A local photographer duly recorded the crowd. Note the orderboard is set for a train to stop, and a white flag suggests a special or extra train is due. Also note the wooden brackets holding insulators for the depot's telegraph system. (Tuscarawas County Historical Society collection.)

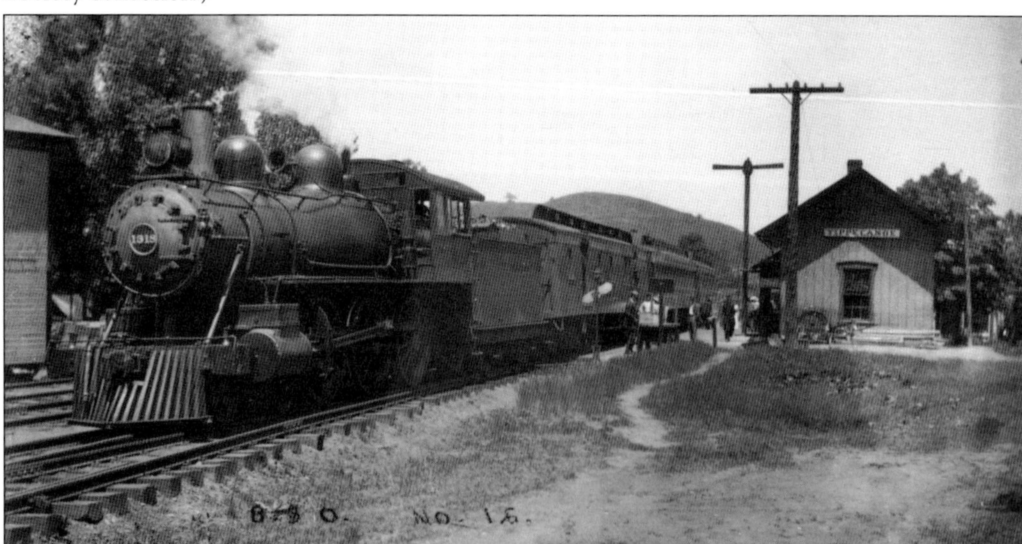

Around 1910, daily passenger runs of the B&O were busy in coal country. Here, a train loads at Tippecanoe at a standard-design combination depot. Since this was as far as the Lake Shore & Tuscarawas Valley extended before it was sold, it could be to plans of the Cleveland, Tuscarawas Valley & Wheeling. A baggage cart is loaded with parcels as people mill about the platform. This depot was torn down in the 1940s. (Tuscarawas County Historical Society collection.)

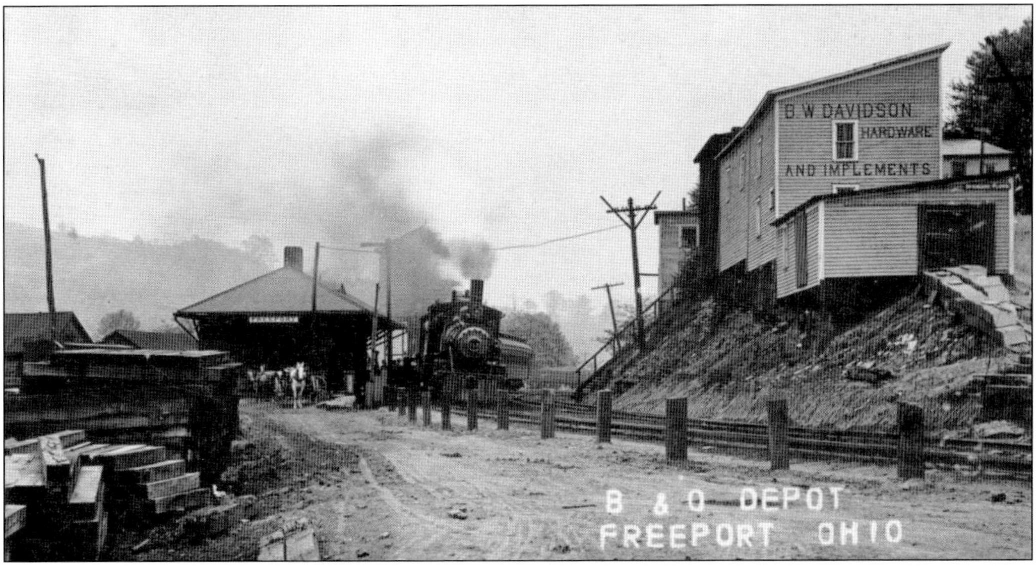

By the time of this c. 1910 view, Freeport has received a new depot of B&O design. The previous depot was probably built by the Cleveland, Tuscarawas Valley & Wheeling (CTV&W) around 1875–1876. A hack waits at the depot to take arrivals into town. Piles of new ties lie stacked in the foreground. A water tank adjacent to the depot is available to replenish thirsty locomotives. Its railroad days done, the depot was relocated to the town park. (Author's collection.)

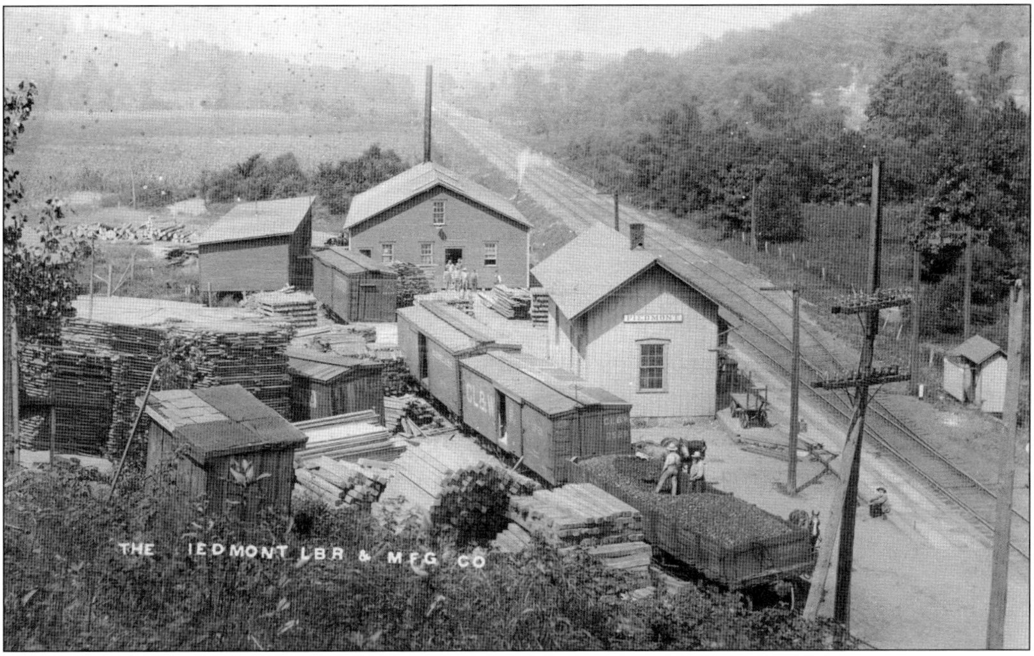

Besides providing coal, the forested plateaus of eastern Ohio were major sources of timber. In the backyard of the CTV&W design combination depot in Piedmont is the Piedmont Lumber & Manufacturing Company. The closest boxcar in the siding is marked for the CL&W, the most recent predecessor of the B&O. The men are unloading gravel or coal from the B&O gondola. At the door to the sawmill in the background, the lumberyard workers pose for the postcard photographer exposing this overview. (Author's collection.)

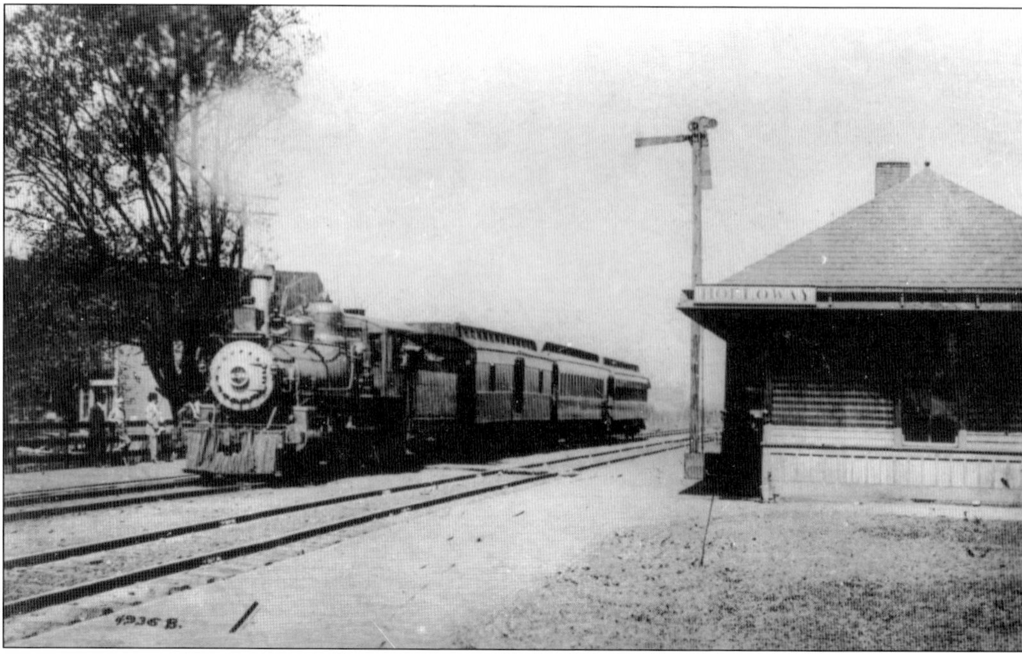

Holloway was once the site of a large yard for the B&O and its predecessor, Cleveland, Lorain & Wheeling. A 22-stall roundhouse, coal and water facilities, and other structures needed for servicing steam locomotives opened here in 1905. As was typical of locomotive terminals, it was in an isolated location to keep noise and dirt away from residential areas. The depot seen here is a standard-design B&O combination depot built to 1905 plans. It replaced an earlier CL&W-design depot built around 1883 that was wrecked after two locomotives plowed into the building in December 1902. (Both, author's collection.)

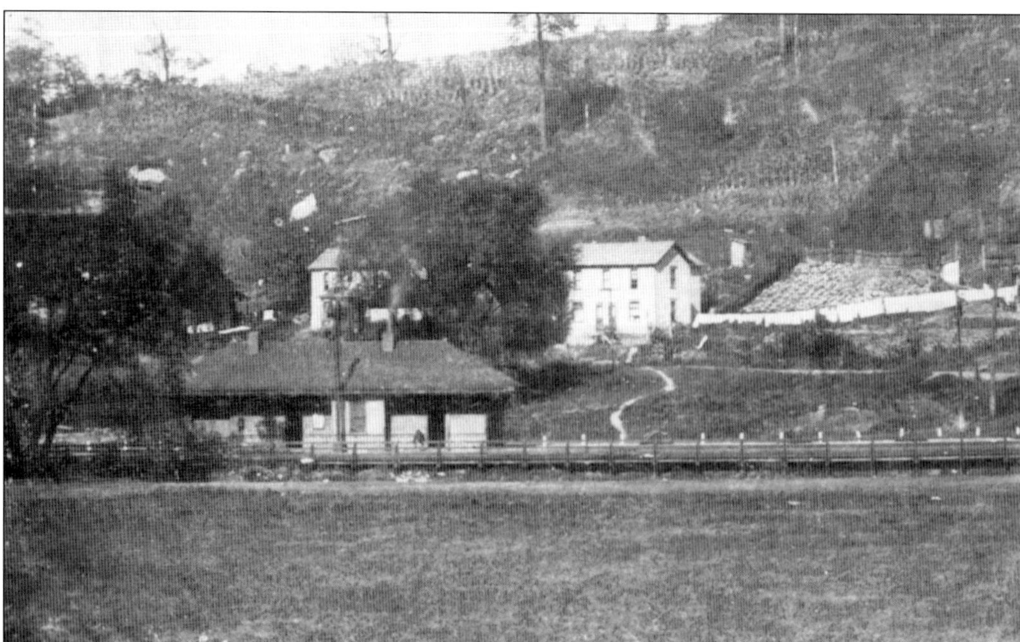

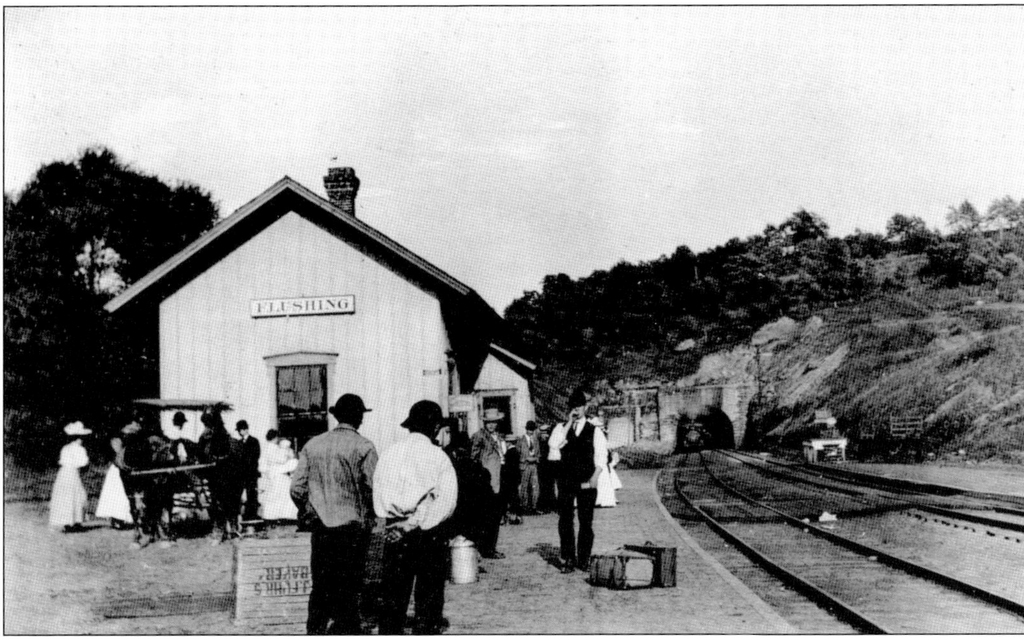

The track from around Tippecanoe to Bridgeport was laid down during the realm of the Cleveland, Tuscarawas Valley and Wheeling Railway and Cleveland, Lorain & Wheeling Railway. It is not clear how far toward Wheeling the CTV&W was able to lay track. Compare the depots at Flushing. Above is the original combination depot probably built to CTV&W plans and erected around 1877. Flushing was in the heart of coal country; the CL&W had numerous mine spurs in this area. In the background is the old sealed single-track tunnel and to the right, the 1904 double-track tunnel. Below is the replacement depot built to 1905 B&O plans. Only the abandoned tunnels remain. (Both, author's collection.)

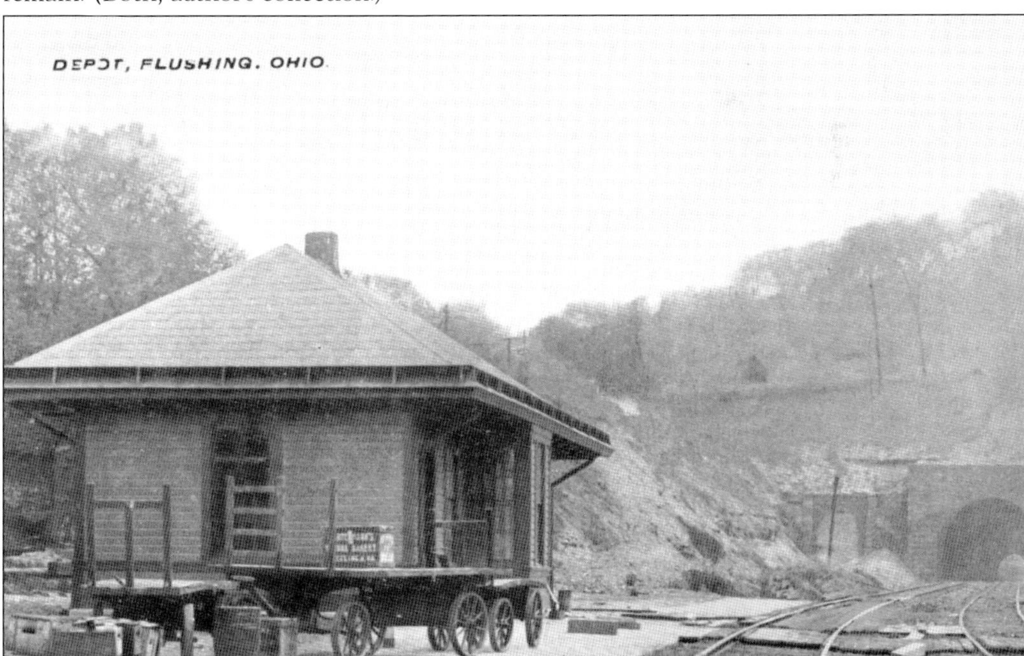

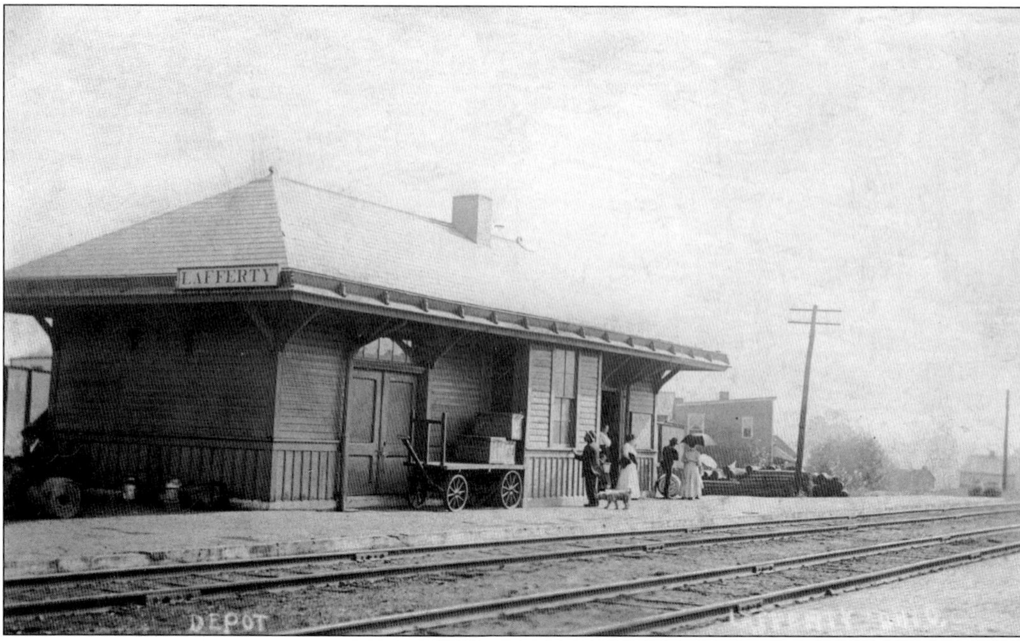

Lafferty's second depot was this standard B&O combination depot. These were built to plans developed around 1905. Hundreds of these were built as replacement structures all across the B&O system. Note the lack of an orderboard. The original depot was probably similar to the older depot at Flushing. (Author's collection.)

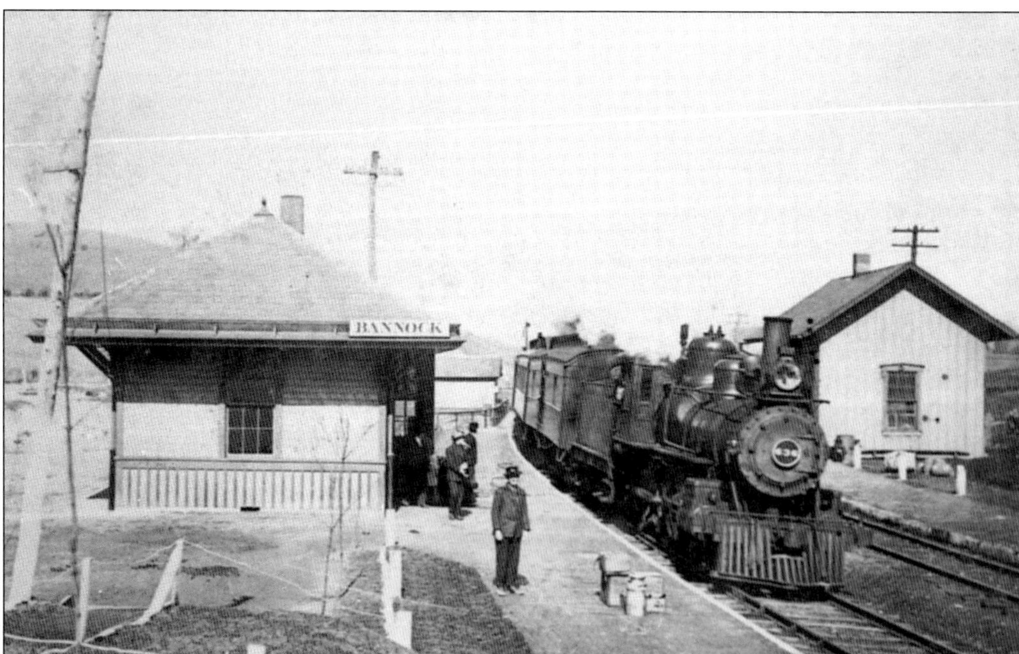

Extra busy Bannock led the B&O to keep the original CL&W combination depot and reconfigure it for freight storage. Across the tracks in the foreground is the 1905 vintage B&O passenger depot. (Author's collection.)

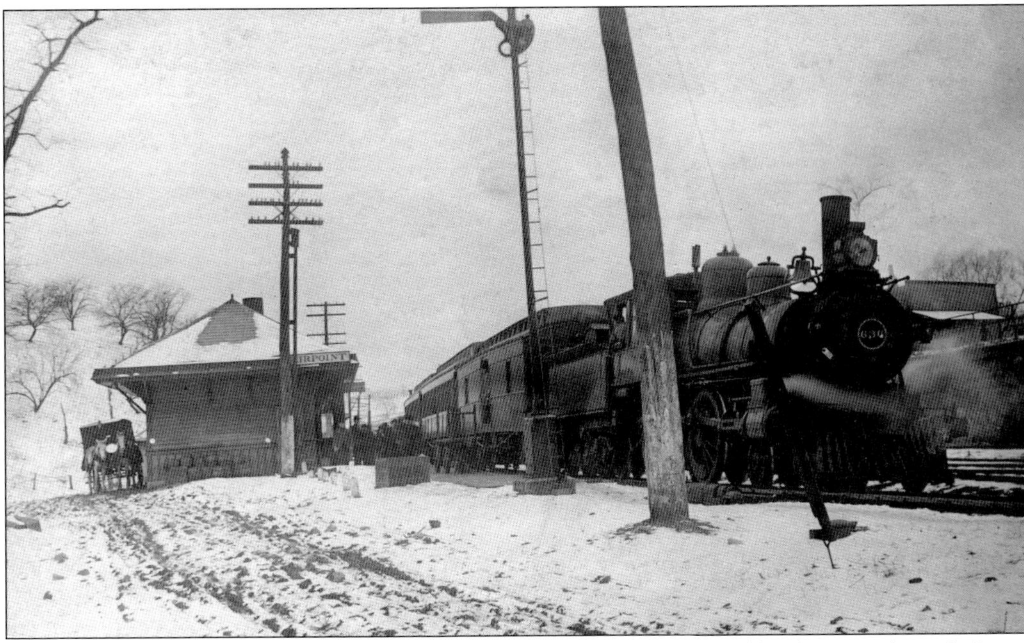

It is a cold winter's day at train time in Fairpoint, complete with a hotel hack. Note the orderboard is entirely separate from the 1905 vintage B&O combination depot. Fairpoint developed as the CL&W laid track through the area. The earlier depot burned down in the early 1900s. A similar design depot once served nearby Maynard. (Author's collection.)

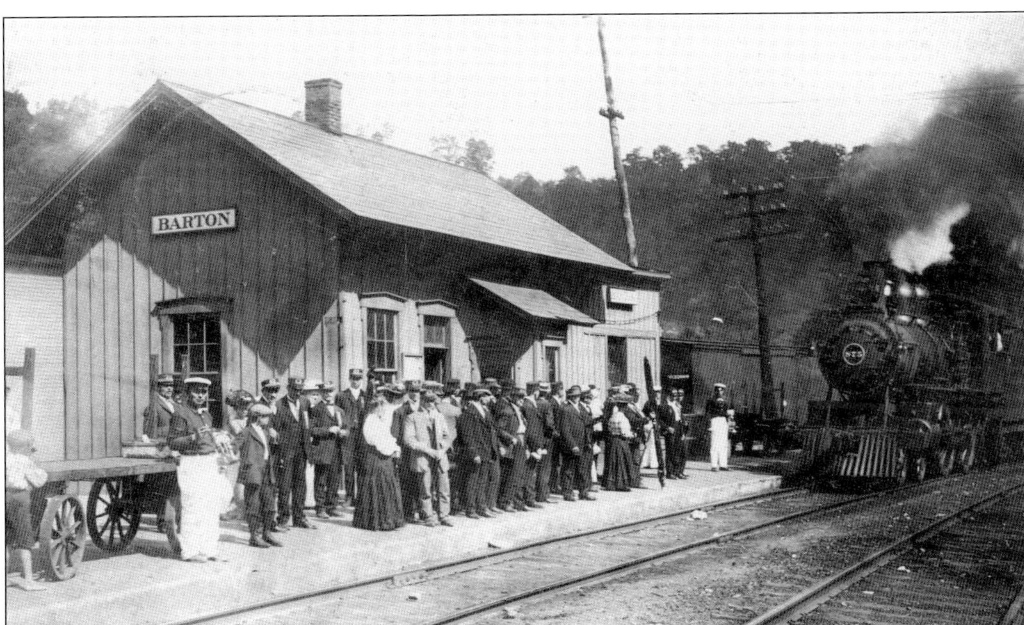

The depot at Barton was built by the CL&W around 1880. The St. Clairsville & Northern Railway, incorporated in 1882, headed west from Barton to the county seat of St. Clairsville. It eventually was taken over by the B&O to provide a connection between the old CL&W main line and the B&O Southwestern at McClainville. (Author's collection.)

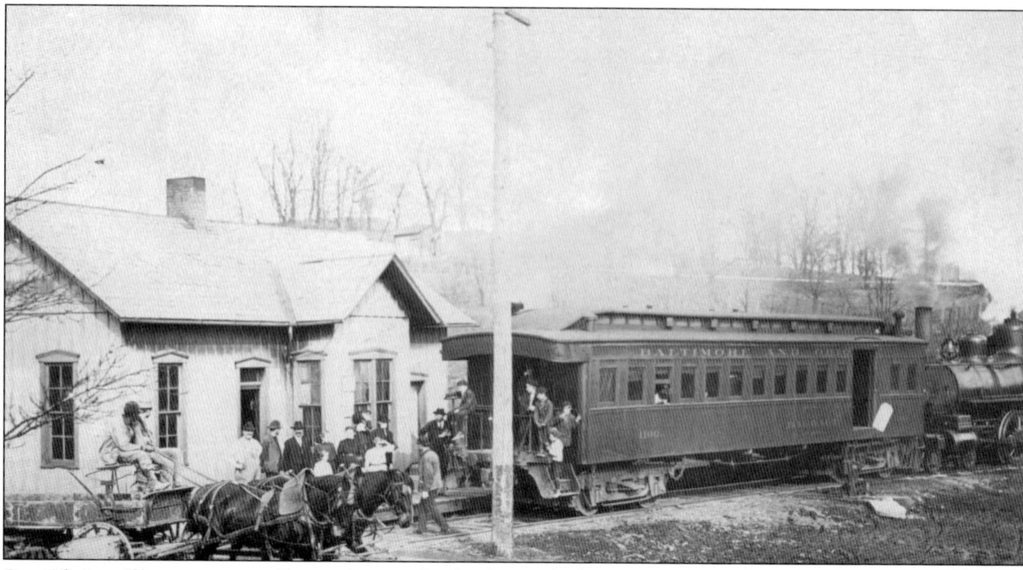

St. Clairsville was initially at the end of a branch beginning at McClainville on the B&O Southwestern. A typical CL&W combination depot was erected, and apparently, business never justified building a larger depot usually typical of a county seat. A one coach accommodation train is pushed into town in this c. 1910 postcard view. This depot continues as a storage building. The track is long gone. The Wheeling & Lake Erie and St. Clairsville & Northern also had depots in St. Clairsville. (Author's collection.)

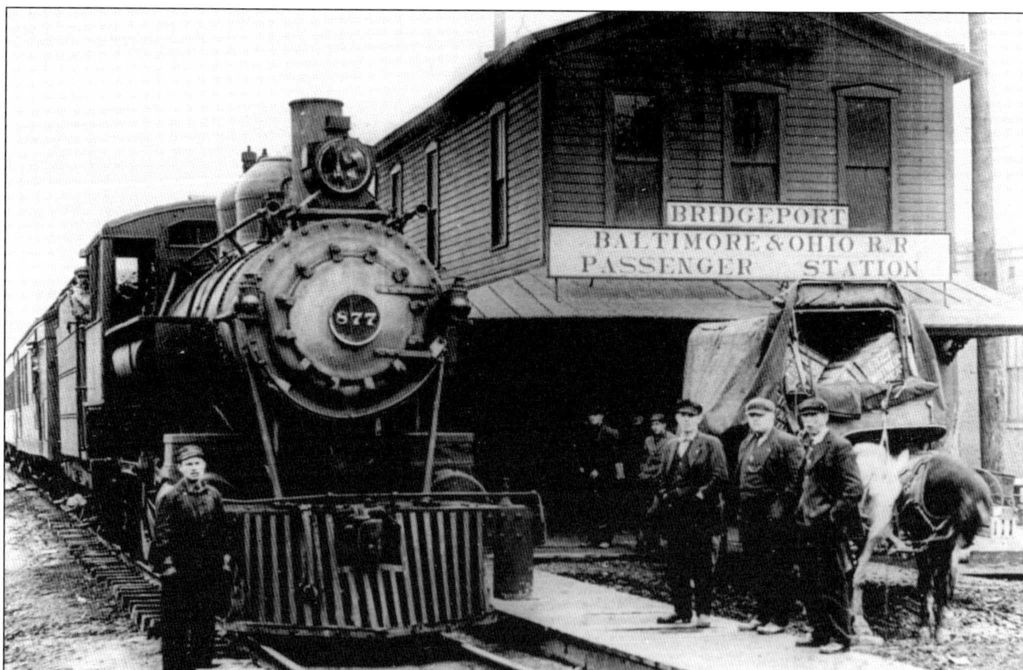

This two-story passenger depot in Bridgeport dates to CL&W days, probably around 1889. The B&O erected a large frame freight house there around 1905. Nearby were the passenger and freight depots of the Cleveland & Pittsburgh Railroad (later PRR). Little evidence of their existence remains in 2017. (Author's collection.)

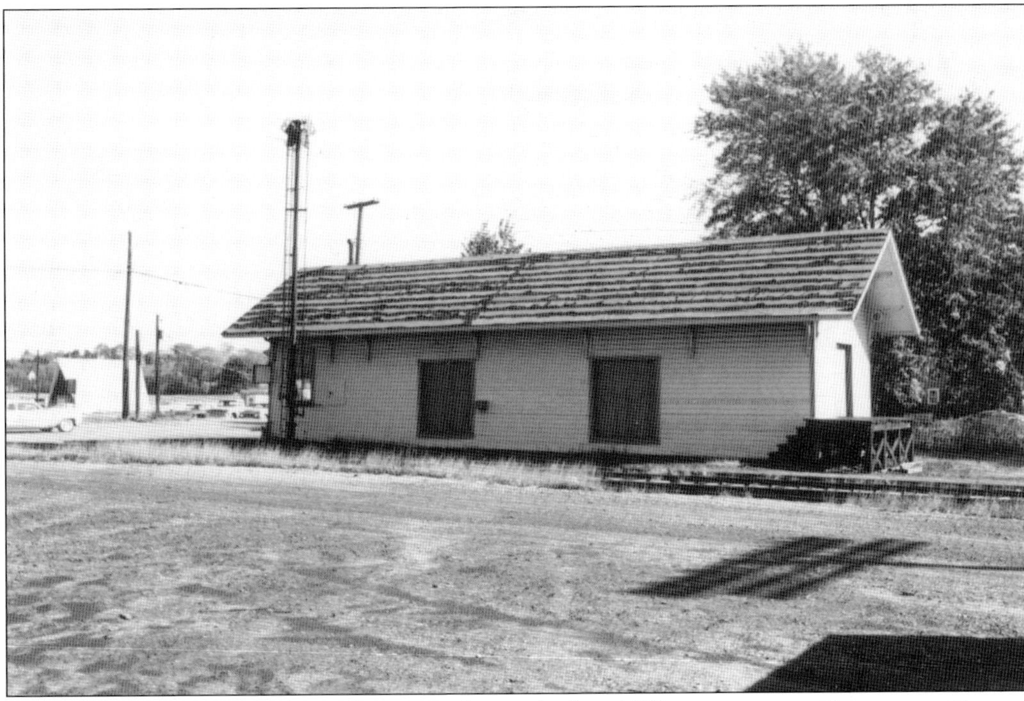

The Valley Railway built through New Berlin in the late 1870s on its way to Tuscarawas County. Since then, the town was renamed North Canton and this depot constructed. Through the years, the B&O remodeled the depot, removing any unnecessary architectural embellishments. In 2017, it remains on-site in business use. (Author photograph.)

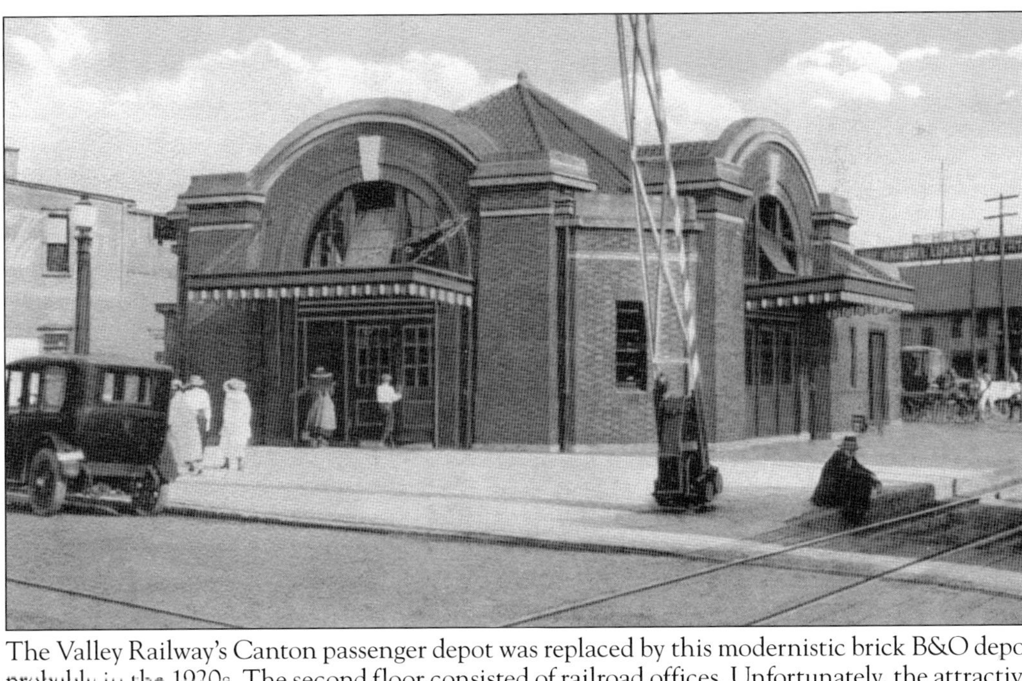

The Valley Railway's Canton passenger depot was replaced by this modernistic brick B&O depot probably in the 1920s. The second floor consisted of railroad offices. Unfortunately, the attractive building has been gone for decades. (Author's collection.)

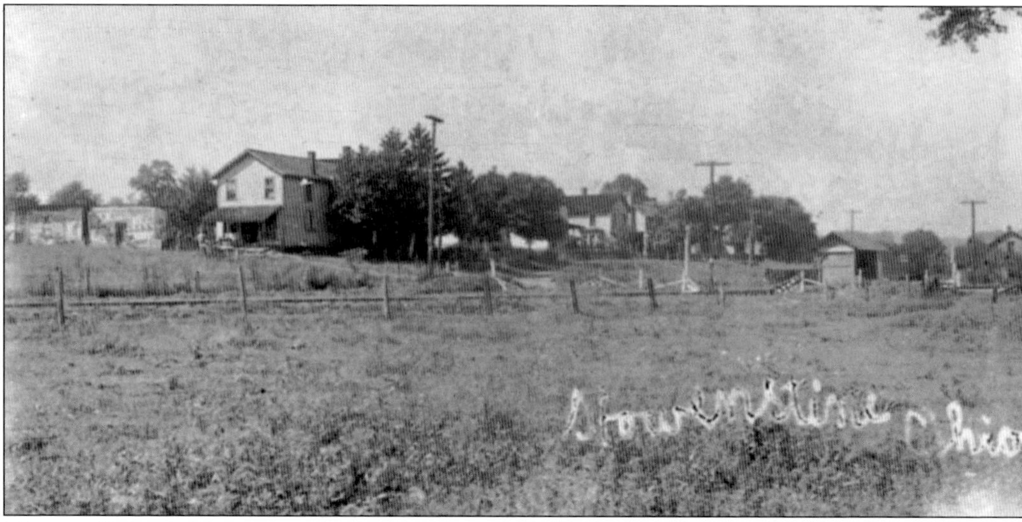

The small Stark County crossroads community of Howenstine, just south of North Industry, was served by this three-sided shelter of Valley Railway design. Next depot to the south was a frame combination depot at East Sparta. Sandyville was the first Valley Railway depot south in Tuscarawas County. It had a frame combination depot and was a water stop for trains between Canton and Valley Junction. Little trace remains in 2017. (Dan West.)

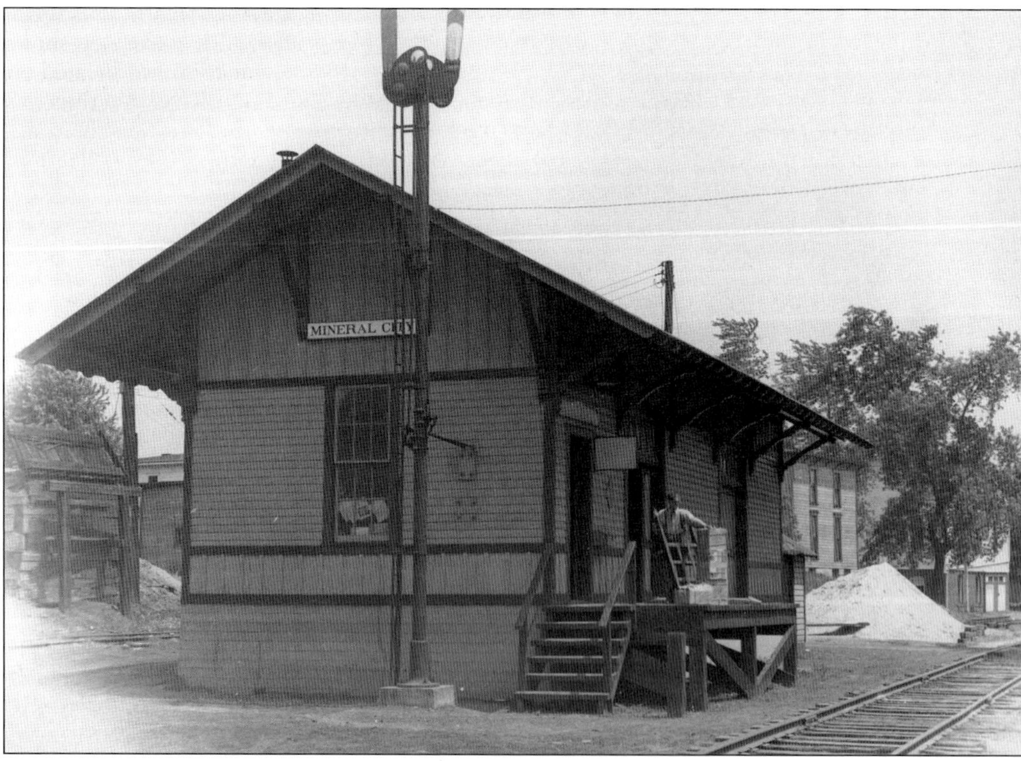

The B&O passenger depot in Mineral City was gone from trackside by 1949, but this freight house, directly across the tracks, survived into the 1970s. In an atypical manner, the orderboard was attached to the freight house. In this c. 1940 view, the freight agent works with a parcel shipment. Nearby was a PRR combination depot. (Tuscarawas County Historical Society collection.)

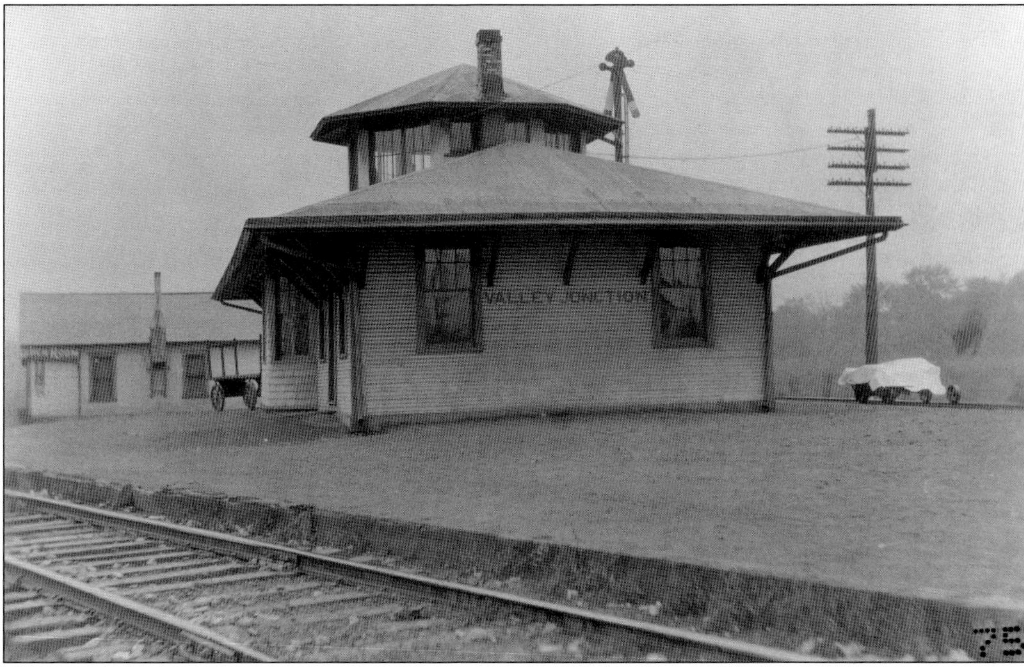

The B&O track ended at Valley Junction and trains continued with trackage rights. This is the second of three joint depots to be located at this somewhat remote location. The above view shows the B&O side of the Wheeling & Lake Erie built depot in 1927. Valley Junction was located on the floodplain of Connotton Creek near its confluence with the Tuscarawas River and thus was subject to periodic flooding. Below, a W&LE freight tackles the floodwaters in 1936. Shortly, a dam project and a new rail alignment led to the replacement of this depot. (Both, W&LE collection, Special Collections, Michael Schwartz Library, Cleveland State University.)

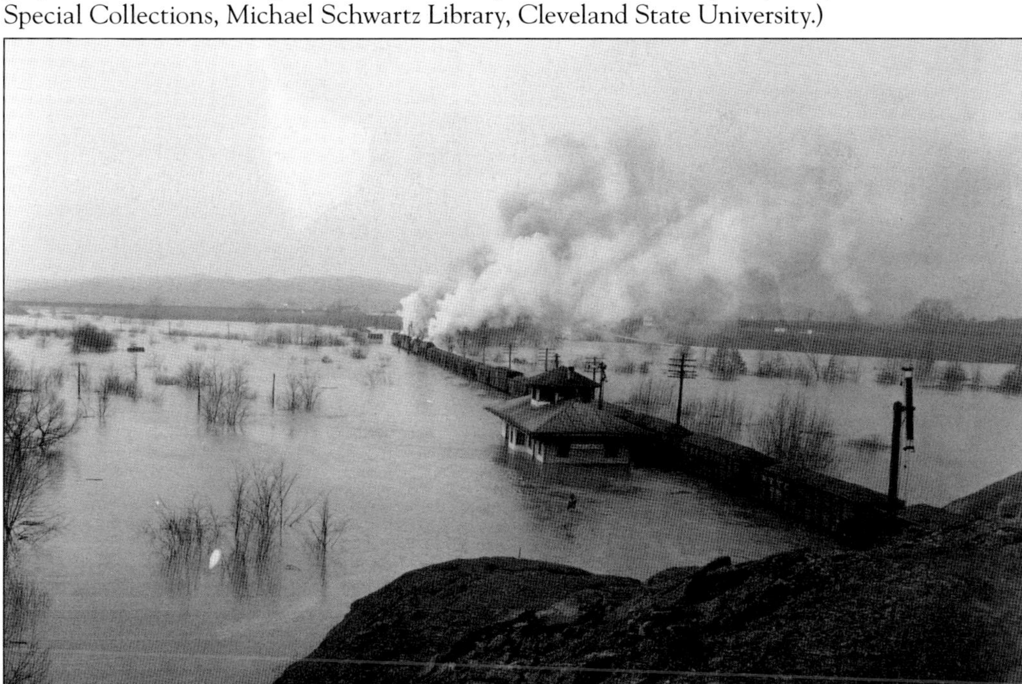

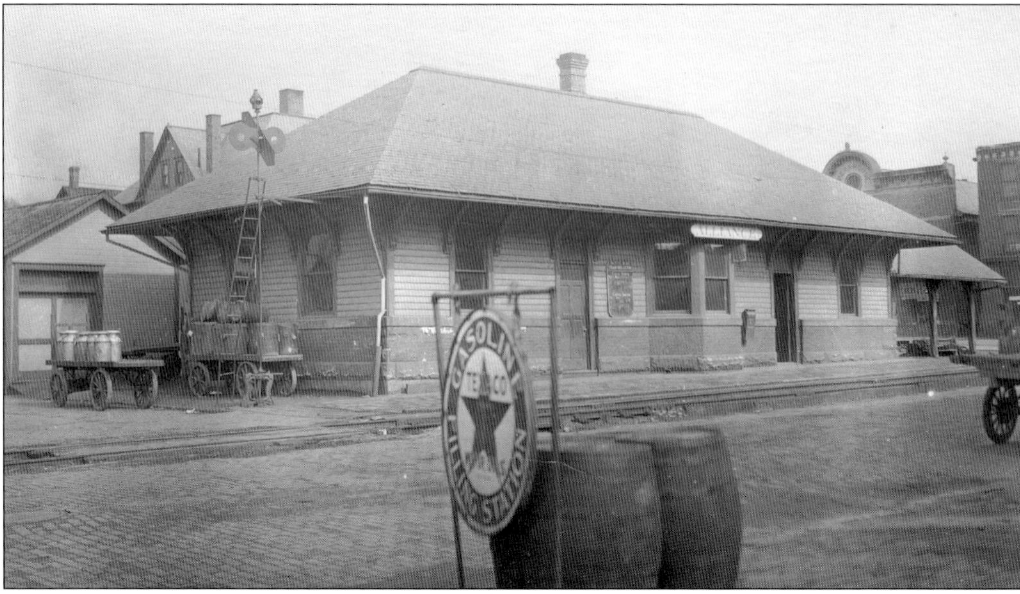

The Lake Erie Alliance & Wheeling Railroad (LEA&W) maintained a downtown passenger depot along South Mechanic Avenue in Alliance. A freight house was located nearby. Tracks of the LEA&W extended northward from here to junctions with the B&O at Newton Falls and the Erie at Braceville and Phalanx and southward to Dillonvale. This was the largest depot built by the LEA&W. After passenger service ended, the depot was converted to business use and was eventually torn down in the late 1960s. This photograph was taken in May 1919. (Allen County Historical Society collection.)

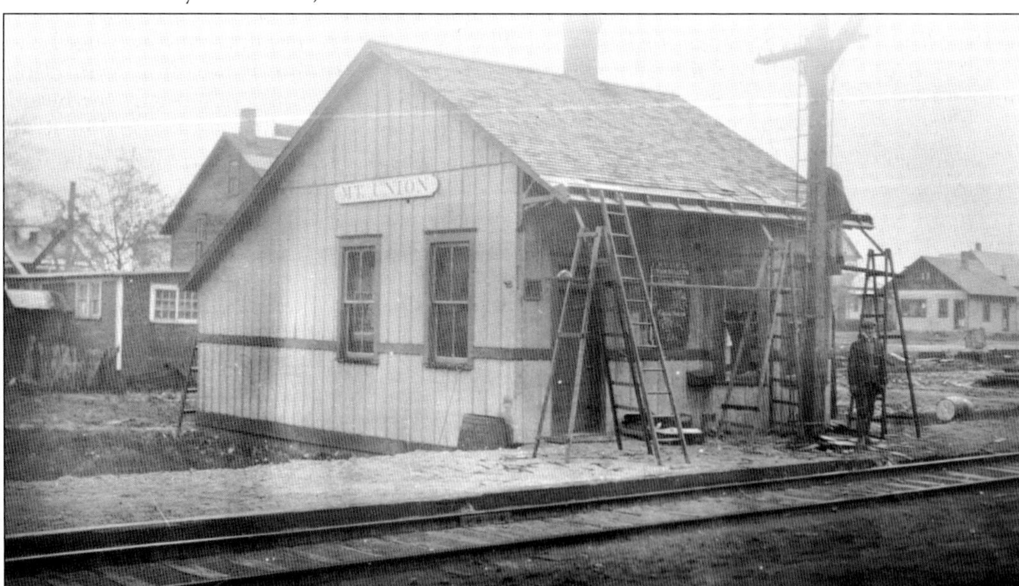

This LEA&W passenger depot was used by many Mount Union College students and faculty through the years. The village of Mount Union was annexed to Alliance in 1889. Workmen were finishing work on the roof when photographed on May 9, 1919, by the New York Central for valuation purposes. This depot probably disappeared from trackside by the 1930s. (Allen County Historical Society collection.)

Two

New York Central Lines

Another railroad chartered to haul coal from the hills of Harrison and Jefferson Counties was the Lake Erie, Alliance & Wheeling Railroad (LEA&W). This line began as narrow-gauge Lake Erie, Alliance & Wheeling Railroad incorporated in February 1874 to build a line connecting Fairport Harbor on Lake Erie to Bridgeport on the Ohio River. Construction began northward from Alliance in 1875, but monetary issues halted construction and the road was sold in 1878. After another unsuccessful attempt to connect the line to Lake Erie, it was decided by the new owners, Cleveland, Youngstown & Pittsburgh Railway, to convert the line to standard gauge and build southward from Alliance. By November 1883, the line reached Bergholz in Jefferson County. After other corporate changes, the line once again became the Lake Erie, Alliance & Wheeling in 1901. Within the next year, the line was extended to Dillonvale about 15 miles short of its namesake, Wheeling, West Virginia. In 1903, the line became part of the Lake Shore & Michigan Southern, which in turn became New York Central property in 1914.

The LEA&W shops were established at Minerva, the halfway point between Phalanx on the Erie Railroad and Dillonvale on the Wheeling & Lake Erie Railroad. Frame combination depots were designed by the LEA&W engineering department. Separate freight depots were in use at Alliance and Dillonvale.

The LEA&W route remains in use in 2017 from Minerva to Hopedale by Ohi-Rail Corporation. Instead of mainly the coal industry, the line is now serving the oil and gas industry. Most of the depots are gone, but the Watheys depot has been relocated to the Algonquin Mill Complex in Petersburg and is maintained by the Carroll County Historical Society. The nicely restored structure is a good example of LEA&W architecture. The Dillonvale depot remains as a storage facility.

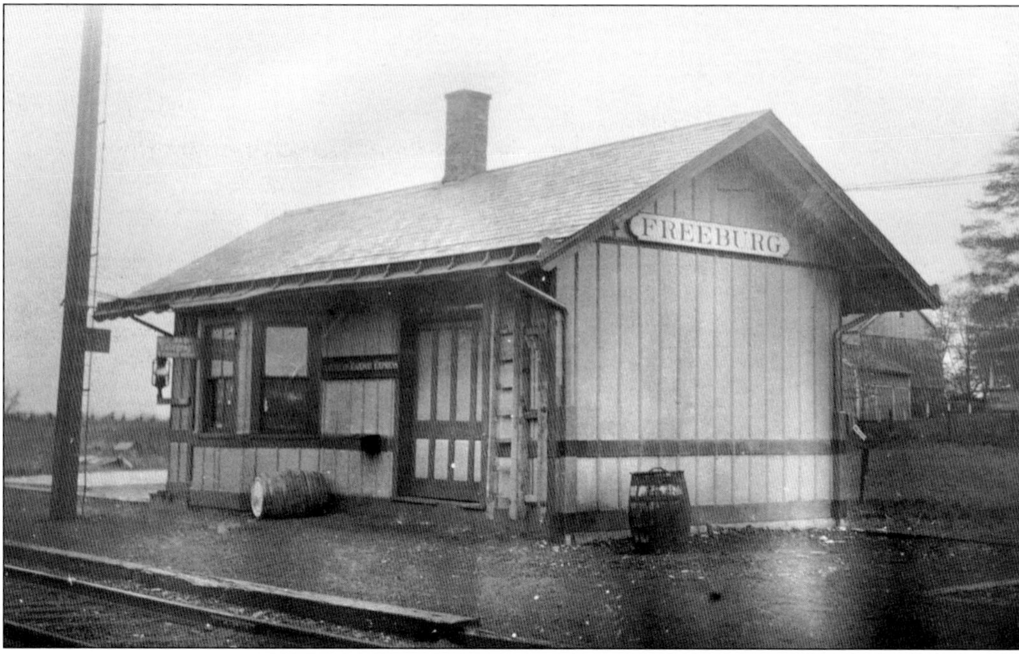

Freeburg depot is an example of one of the standard plans of the LEA&W. All LEA&W combination depots were of frame construction. Freeburg had a small undivided passenger waiting room separated from a slightly larger freight room by a vestibule office area. Note the kerosene platform lantern, ladder, tall orderboard, and water barrel. This photograph was taken in May 1919. (Allen County Historical Society collection.)

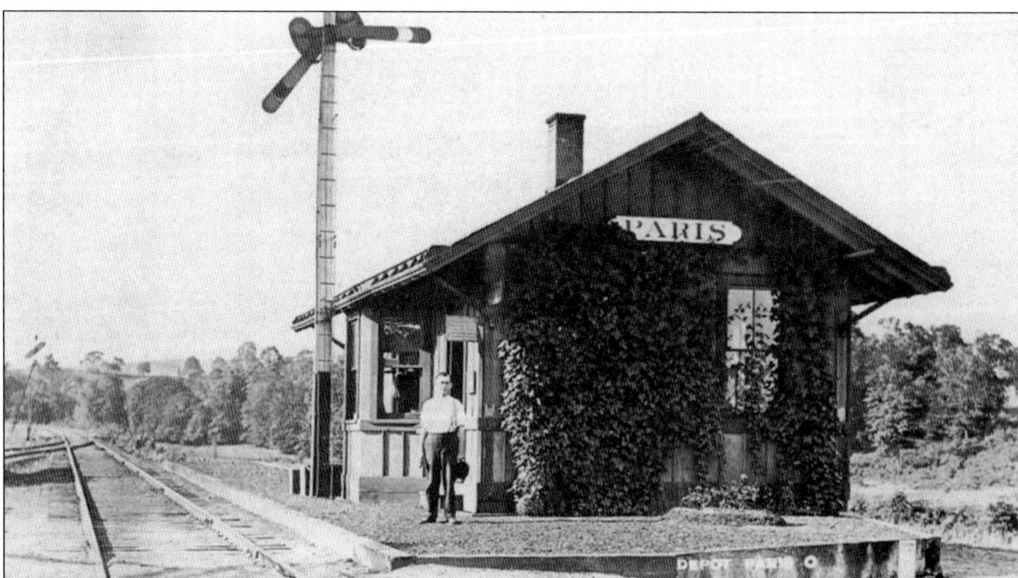

Evident in this c. 1910 image of the LEA&W's combination depot at Paris is the gravel platform, another trademark of the LEA&W. The agent at this depot obviously had a "green thumb." (Bob Chilcote collection.)

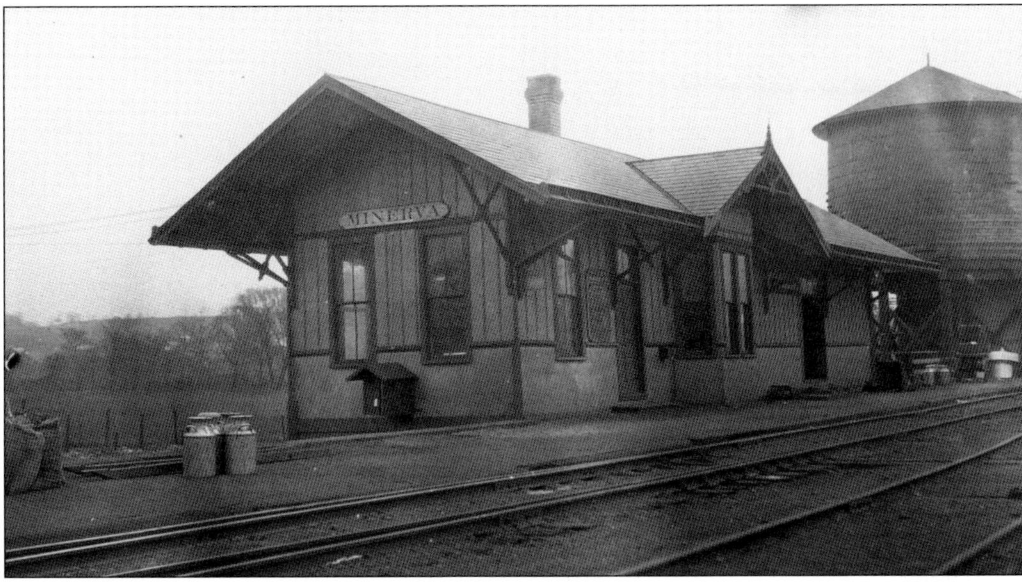

Minerva, laid out in 1835, was the site of the LEA&W shops, an important stop on the line, and thus had a larger depot. Pictured in May 1919, this combination depot plan was used in larger communities and at busier stations. Note the small box on the near wall of the depot—it is a phone box for use by railroaders when the depot is not open. Beyond the water tank were a roundhouse, coaling station, and other shop buildings. This LEA&W depot was torn down in 1958. The PRR and W&LE also had depots in Minerva. (Allen County Historical Society collection.)

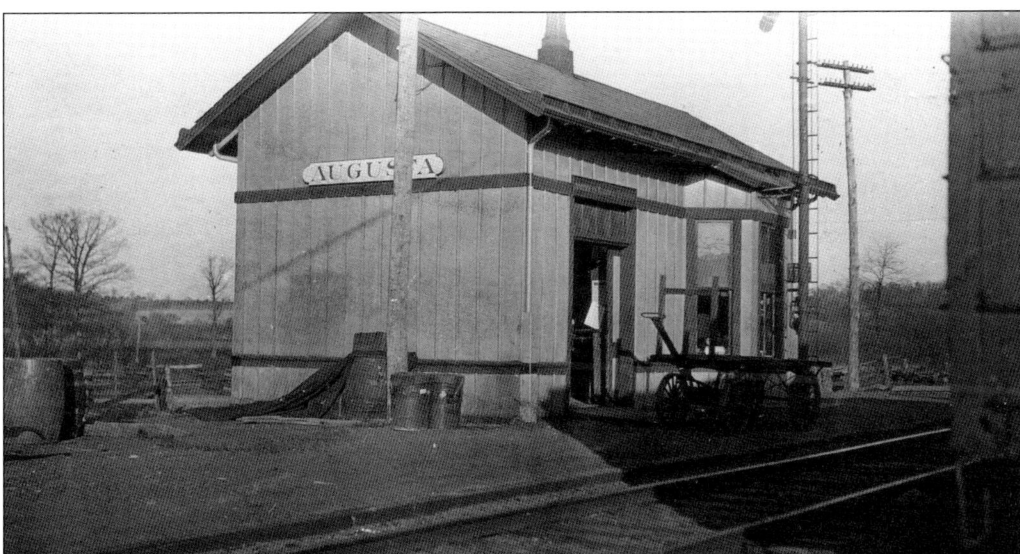

The LEA&W built through Augusta (Pattersonville) in 1883 and erected another standard-plan combination depot. The second depot built in 1902 is shown here in May 1919. Compare it to Freeburg. The roof overhang is more extended and the waiting room and freight room are switched. Just by slight changes like these and rearrangement of windows and doors, two depots built to the same floor plan could be made to look different. Even though the depot was a small version, a baggage cart was a necessary accessory. (Allen County Historical Society collection.)

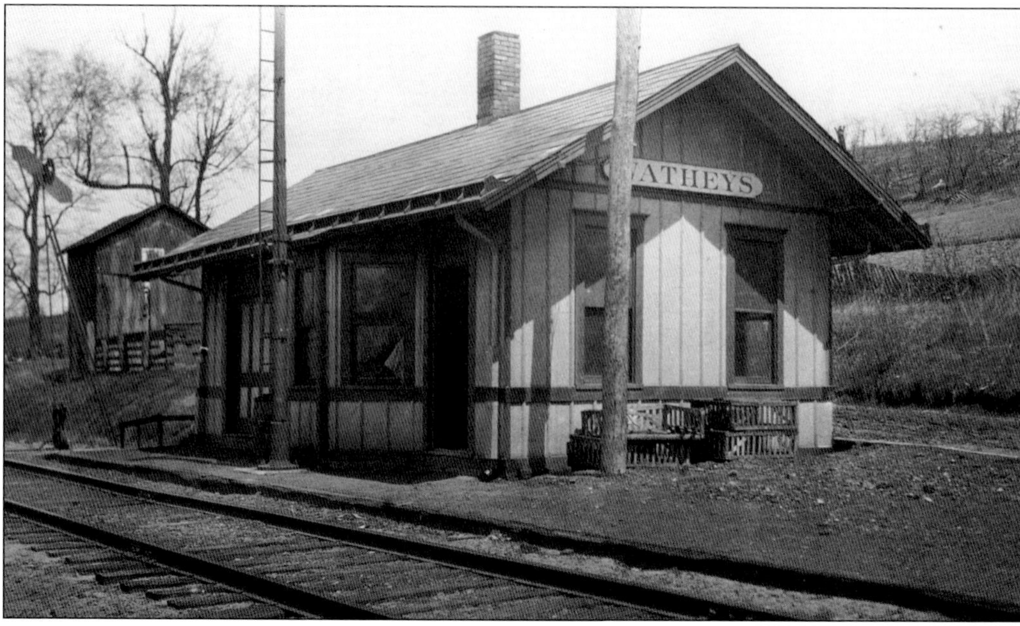

Watheys's LEA&W combination depot, also photographed in May 1919, is the only known LEA&W depot to be restored. It reportedly was built in November 1912. It was moved from trackside in 1935 and repurposed. In 1976, it was moved to the Algonquin Mill Complex of the Carroll County Historical Society in Petersburg, just outside Carrollton. The restored depot now contains a popular model railroad. (Allen County Historical Society collection.)

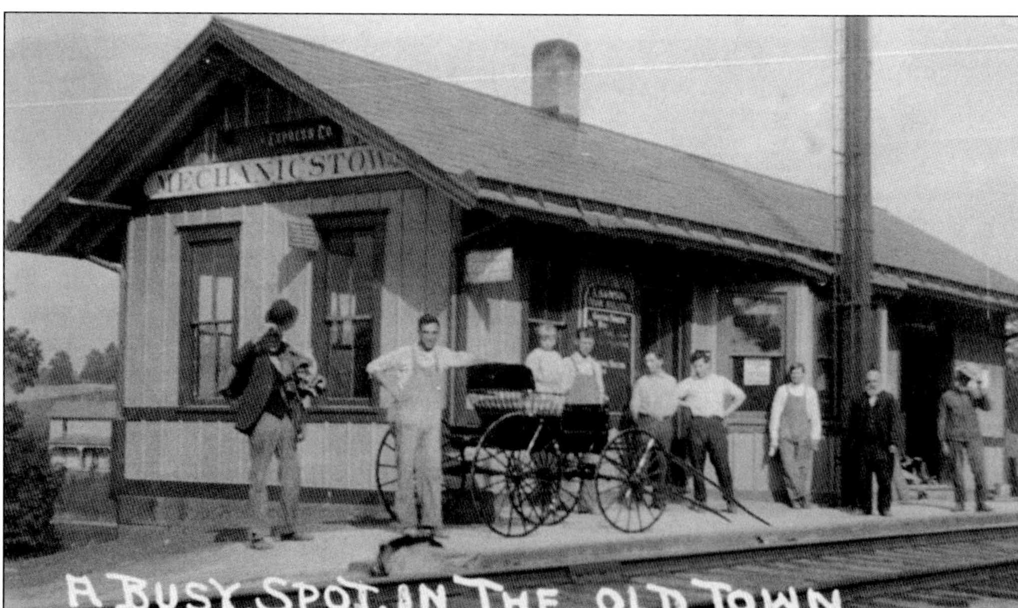

The LEA&W depot in Mechanicstown is depicted here around 1910 while under Lake Shore & Michigan Southern ownership. Locals have pulled a carriage onto the platform for a local postcard photographer. (Author's collection.)

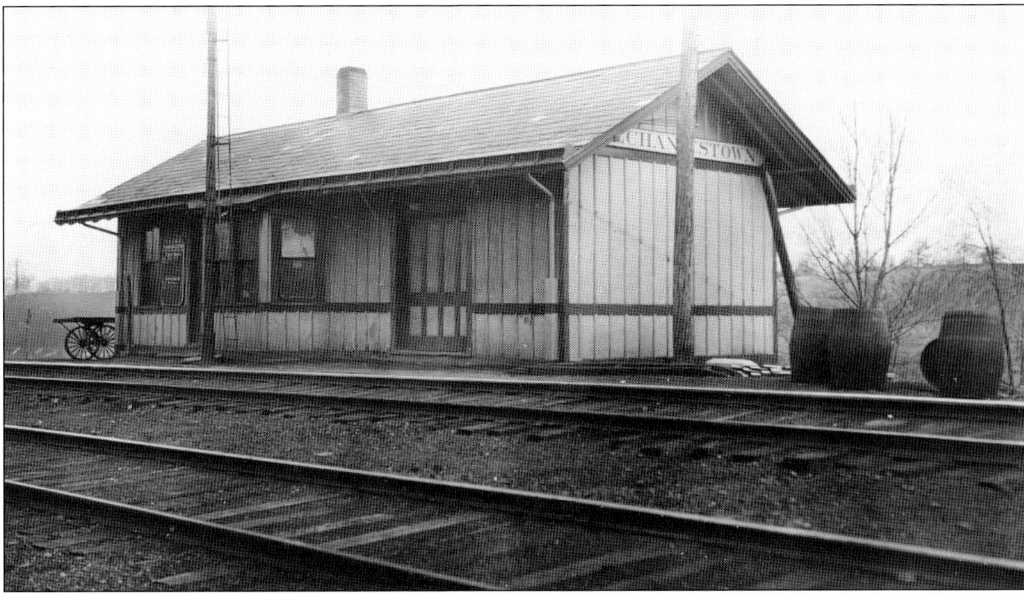

By May 1919, the Mechanicstown depot is within 10 years of losing passenger service. Although still possessing Lake Shore & Michigan Southern town boards, the depot is now officially part of the New York Central System. (Allen County Historical Society collection.)

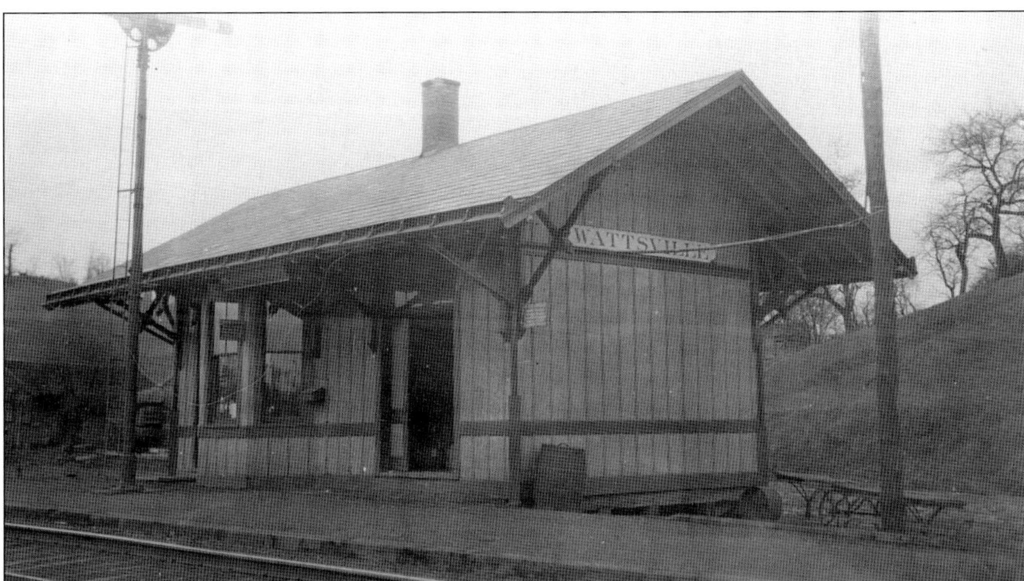

Wattsville was served by this LEA&W combination depot, photographed in May 1919. It has a wider overhang and more evident roof brackets than other LEA&W depot styles. (Allen County Historical Society collection.)

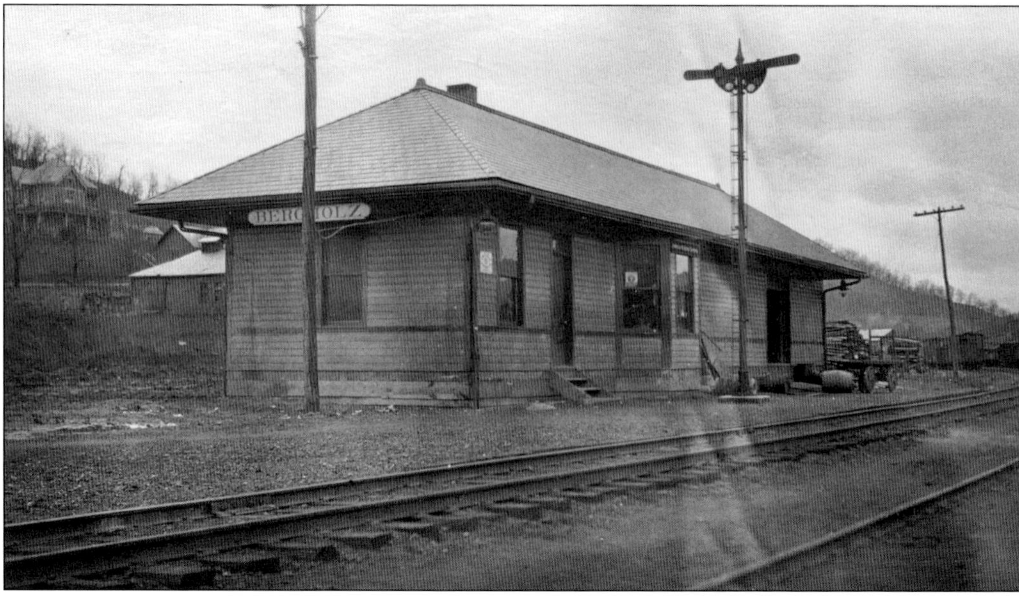

This depot is similar in design to many New York Central (NYC) depots and was in active use when this view was recorded in April 1919 by an NYC photographer. Bergholz was a busy station in the early 1900s due to several nearby coal mines. The depot was closed in 1958 and then used as a storehouse for a couple of decades before being abandoned. Bergholz depot was torn down around 2000; the site is now occupied by a food mart. (Allen County Historical Society collection.)

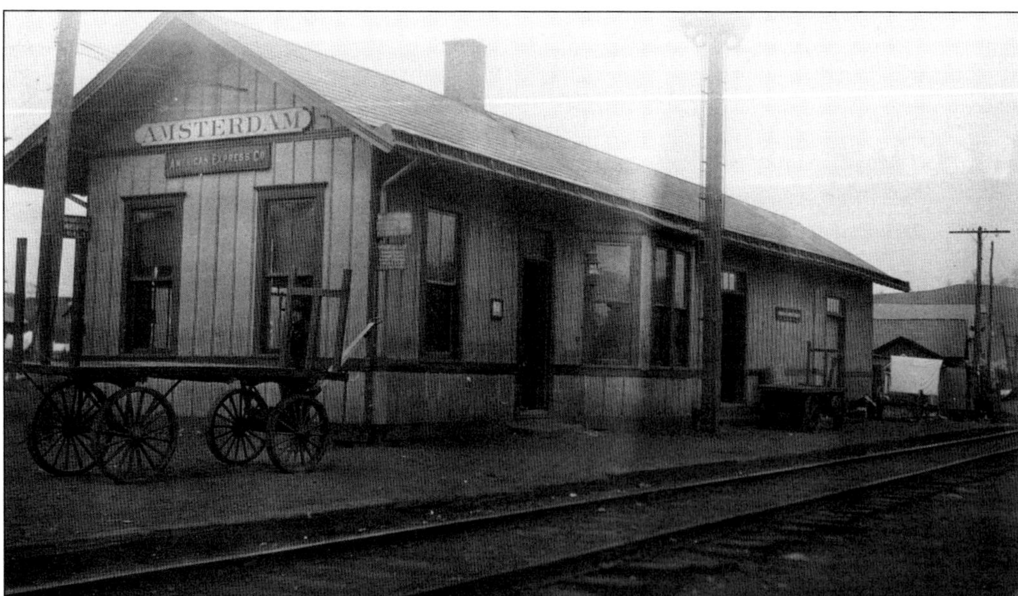

This April 1919 view of Amsterdam's LEA&W depot shows all the components of a small-town combination depot—platform lantern, water barrel, baggage carts, orderboard, and express and telegraph company signs. The depot was closed as a freight agency in 1958 and passed into nonrailroad uses. (Allen County Historical Society collection.)

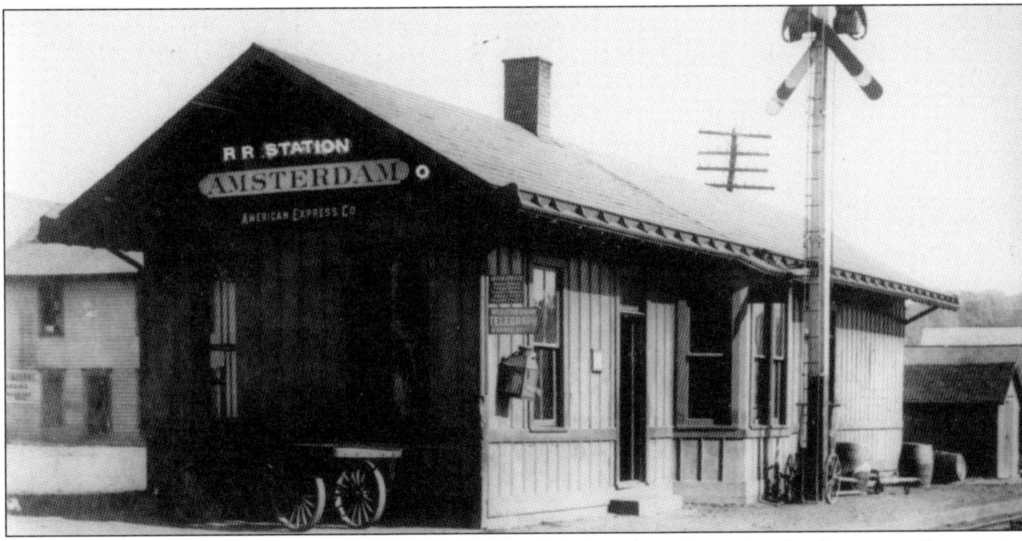

"RR Station" was inked on the negative above the town board to clarify this view. Beginning in 1958, after the Amsterdam agency closed, the depot was bought and used in various ways but primarily became a storage building. Eventually, lack of general maintenance led to roof problems in November 2002. It was soon torn down. (Author's collection.)

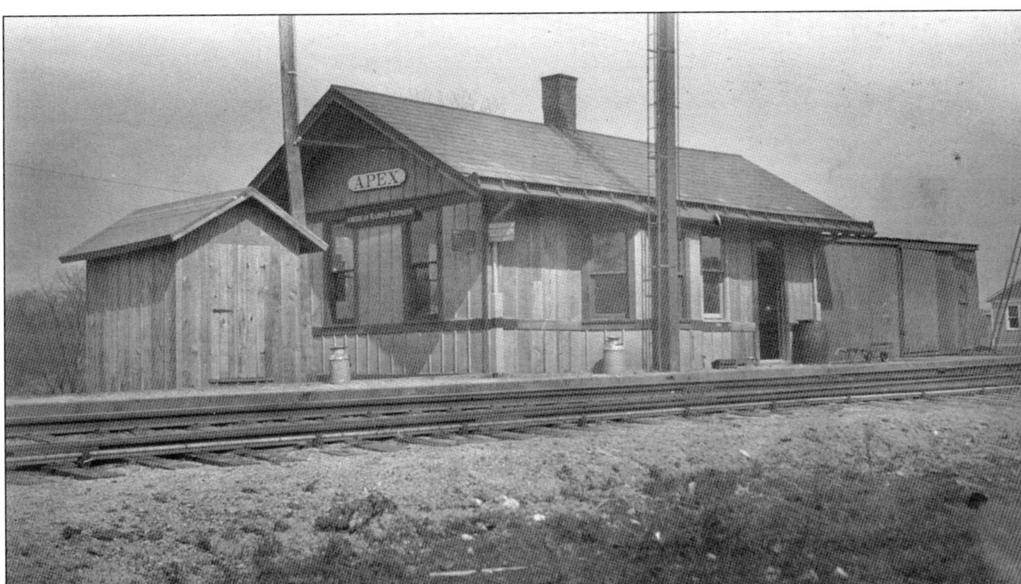

The LEA&W depot named Apex served as the station for Germano, a small village just to the west in Harrison County. Few passengers used this station, and it became mainly a telegraph office by the time of this photograph dating to April 1919. In 2017, most of the nearby landscape has been strip-mined and except for the track, one would never know of the depot's existence. (Allen County Historical Society collection.)

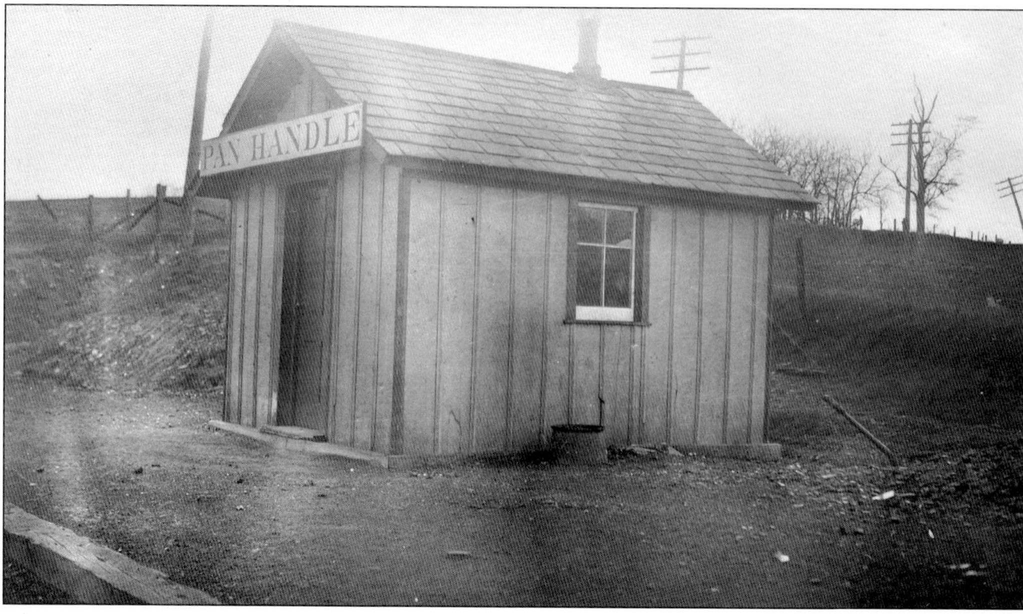

The LEA&W passenger facilities at Panhandle—where the line crossed the Pittsburgh, Cincinnati, Chicago & St. Louis Railroad (also known as the Panhandle) in east central Harrison County—consisted of this small shed in 1919. On cold days, a fire would be started in the potbelly stove. This is illustrative of a true flag stop. To stop a local passenger train, a patron would have to stand on the platform and signal the engineer that passengers were waiting to board. (Allen County Historical Society collection.)

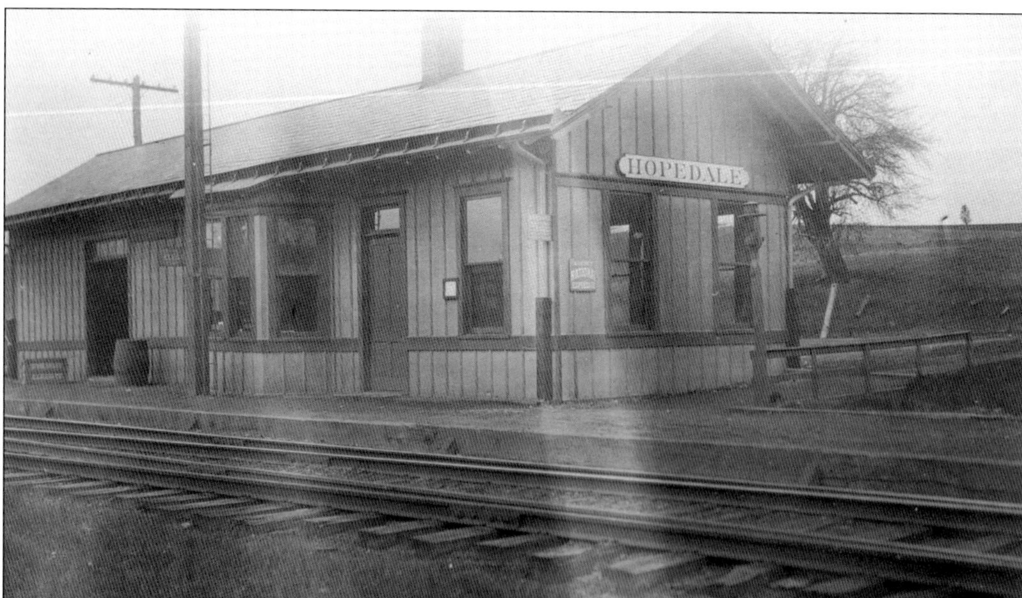

Hopedale passengers were served by this larger LEA&W combination depot. Compare it to Amsterdam. The depot was recorded in April 1919 by a New York Central photographer for valuation purposes. Hopedale also had a depot along the Pittsburgh & West Virginia Railway. (Allen County Historical Society collection.)

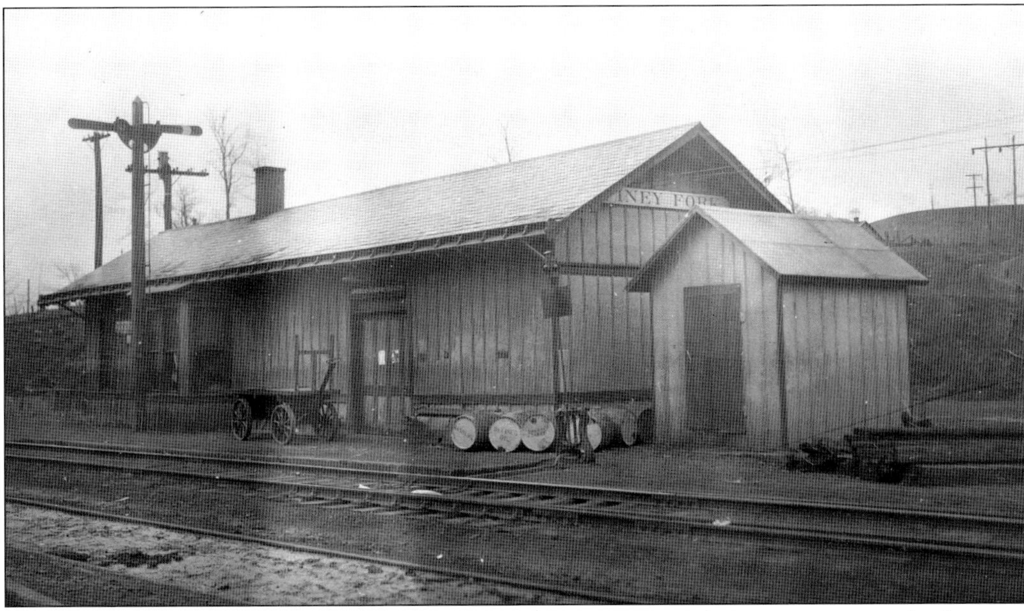

The extended freight room of the LEA&W depot at Piney Fork is testimony to the business generated by nearby coal mines. The railroad brought temporary prosperity to this mining village, and a post office was opened in 1902. This valuation photograph dates to April 1919. (Allen County Historical Society collection.)

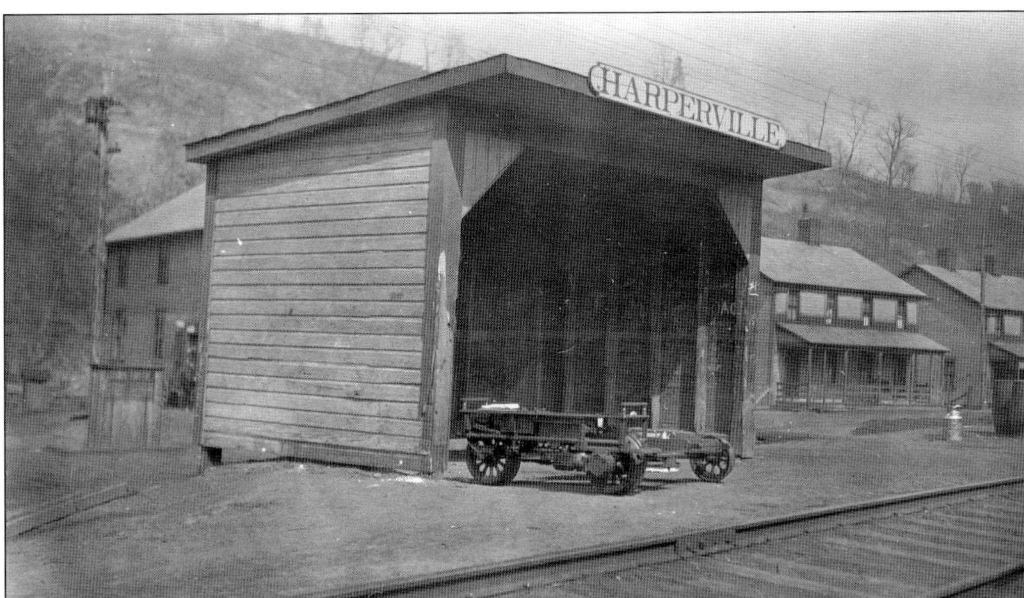

A large Jefferson Coal Company mine was served by the LEA&W at Harperville. This small shelter was built to provide the mining community with shelter while waiting for the local passenger train. This image is from April 1919. (Allen County Historical Society collection.)

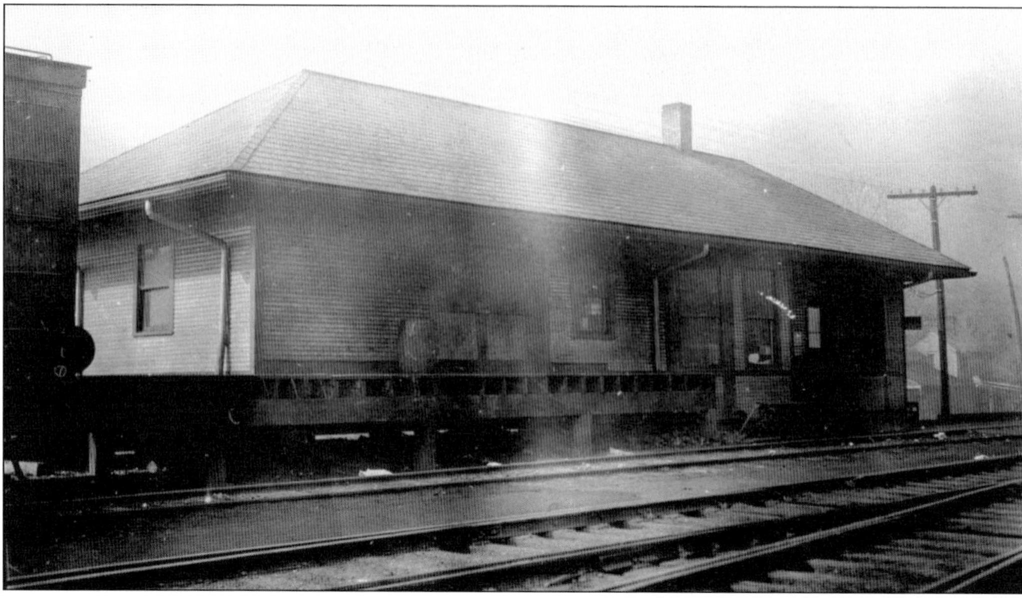

Dillonvale is the southern terminus of the LEA&W and a connection with the Wheeling & Lake Erie Railroad. This larger combination depot served this coal mining center well for many years. It was closed by the New York Central around 1958. It remains in 2017 as a storage building. These valuation photographs date to April 1919. Note the raised freight platform. (Both, Allen County Historical Society collection.)

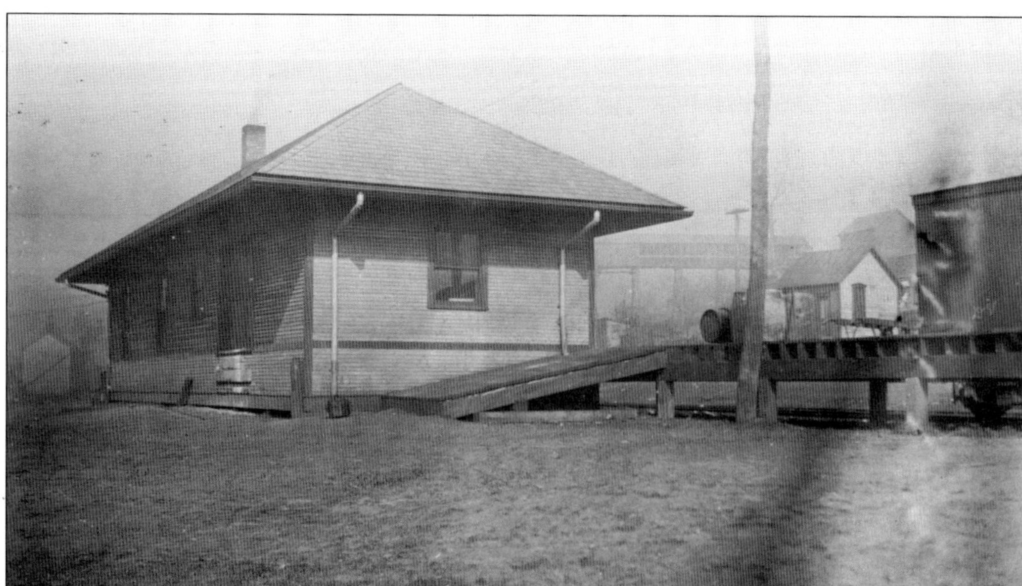

Three

Pennsylvania Railroad Lines

The first railroad to traverse east-central Ohio was the Ohio & Pennsylvania Railroad, chartered to connect the Pittsburgh area with a point on the Indiana-Ohio border. The line opened to Mansfield in April 1853 by way of Salem, Alliance, Canton, Massillon, and Wooster. After mergers, it became the Pittsburgh, Fort Wayne & Chicago (PFtW&C) Rail Road in July 1856. The Pennsylvania Railroad leased this line in July 1869.

The Cleveland & Pittsburgh (C&P) Railroad was promoted as an early attempt to link Lake Erie to the Ohio River valley. The C&P opened from Cleveland to Wellsville in 1852. Another line of the C&P ran through Akron and reached Orrville in 1854. This line was opened to Columbus in September 1873, becoming the Cleveland Akron & Columbus (CA&C) Railway in December 1885. The CA&C opened a branch to Trinway in 1888. The Tuscarawas branch of the C&P, beginning at Bayard and running through Minerva, Dover, and on to New Philadelphia, opened in December 1854. The PRR leased the C&P in December 1871 and controlled the CA&C by 1912.

Another PRR line was originally incorporated as the Steubenville & Indiana Railroad in February 1848 and given the task of completing a line from Steubenville to a point on the Indiana-Ohio border. The financially strapped road opened between Steubenville and Newark in April 1855 by way of Dennison, Uhrichsville, Newcomerstown, and Coshocton. A branch also extended south to Cadiz. In December 1868, this line was merged with other PRR-controlled lines to become the Pittsburgh, Cincinnati, & St. Louis (PC&StL) Railway or Panhandle. In 1890, further consolidation created the Pittsburgh, Cincinnati, Chicago & St. Louis (PCC&StL).

The PRR was also behind the development of the Walhonding Valley Railway (soon to be renamed the Toledo, Walhonding Valley & Ohio [TWV&O] Railway) in 1889. The line provided a connection from the PFtW&C at Loudonville with the PC&StL at Coshocton. The line was abandoned when the Mohawk Dam construction inundated a portion of the right-of-way in 1936. One other PRR line, the Cincinnati & Muskingum Valley Railroad, which originally was built between Zanesville and Morrow, was extended from Zanesville to Trinway on the PC&StL and CA&C by the PRR in 1870.

Since the PRR absorbed many predecessor lines, architectural styles of depots varied. Replacement PRR depots were built to a series of standard plans; some larger passenger depots were designed by selected architectural firms.

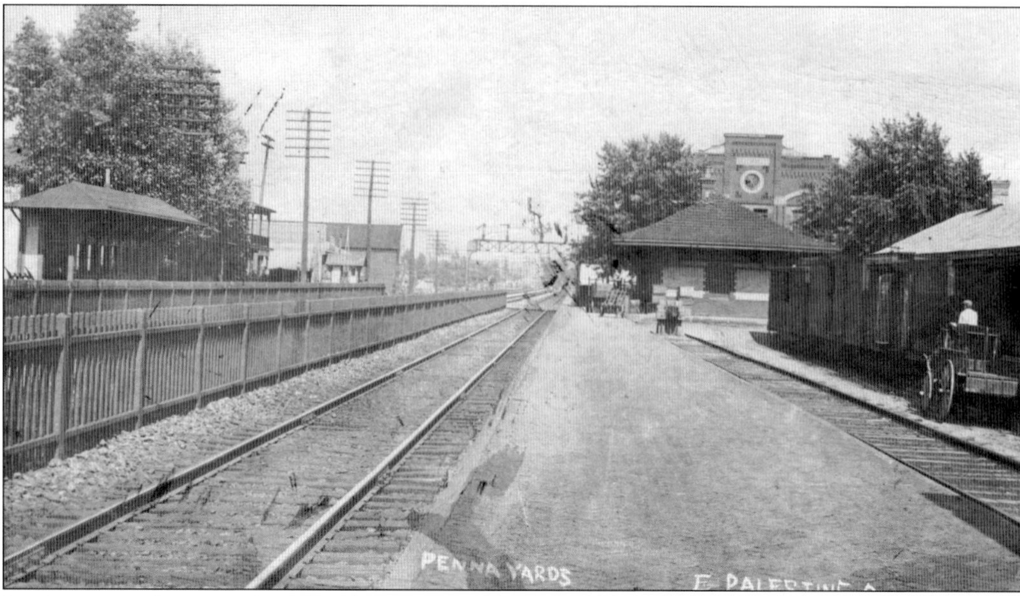

Looking east down the Pittsburgh Fort Wayne & Chicago's (PFtW&C) double-track main line, this 1910 vintage postcard shows the brick East Palestine passenger depot and opposite umbrella waiting shelter. This is at least a third-generation depot since the railroad opened through here in January 1851. Just beyond the shelter is a guard shack for the Market Street grade crossing. Just east of the depot is the Meek House, a local railroad hotel and beyond that a PRR signal bridge spans the tracks. In the foreground is the PRR freight house, which still stands in 2017. (Author's collection.)

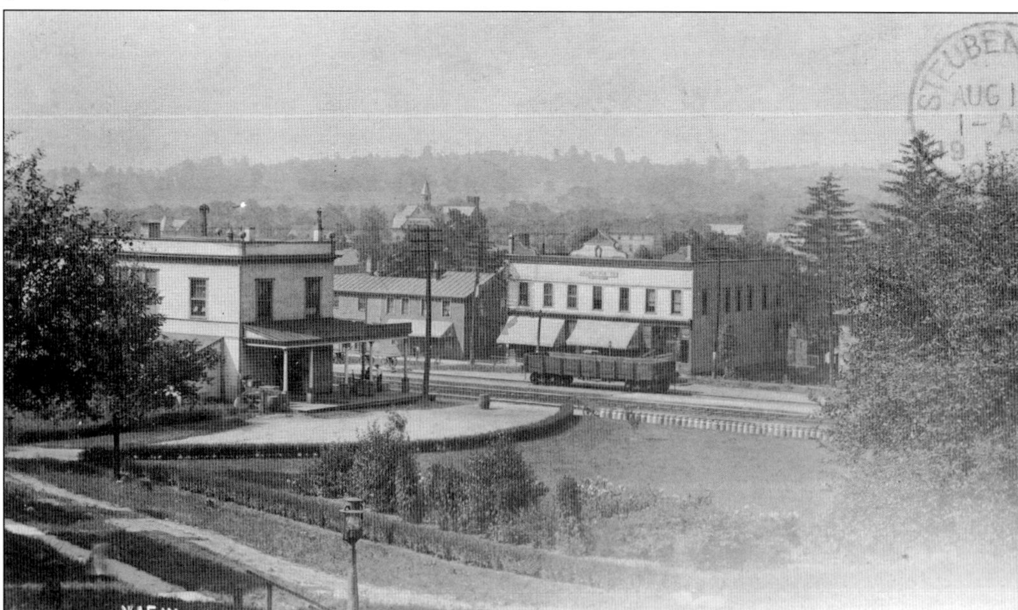

New Waterford is the next station on the PFtW&C west of East Palestine. The rail reached town in 1851. This two-story passenger depot was built in 1883 by the Pennsylvania Railroad, replacing an earlier frame depot. Note the well-tended landscaping and garden surrounding the depot and kerosene railroad lantern on the carriage path down to the depot. (Author's collection.)

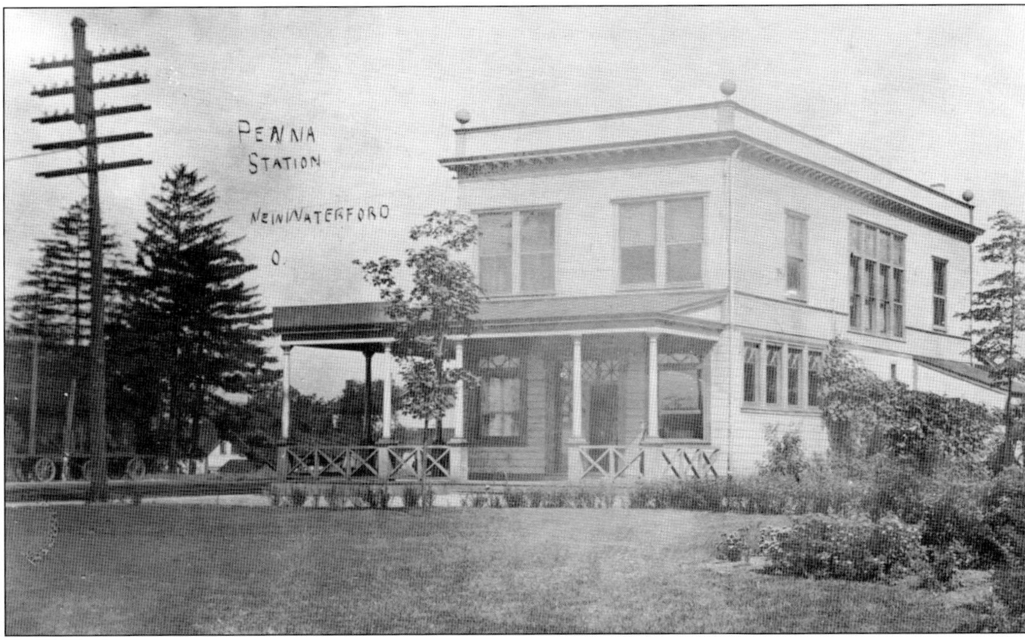

At several stations along its system, the PRR maintained greenhouses where flowers and shrubs were grown for use on depot grounds. New Waterford's depot was surrounded by a pleasant garden tended by PRR horticulturists. The design of the New Waterford passenger depot was an early one and was used at only a few stations along the line. Nearby was a frame freight house. Seen in the view below is a standard-plan PRR signal tower. These towers were located along the line at many stations, passing sidings, railroad junctions, and diamonds (locations where another railroad crossed at grade) to keep track of train movements and control important signals before the days of automated train control and interlocking. Each was manned by a telegrapher who would report all passing trains and, when necessary, relay important information to train crews. Later, towers located at junctions and diamonds included a series of levers that allowed the towerman to change the alignment of switches so that trains could pass or switch to other lines. (Both, author's collection.)

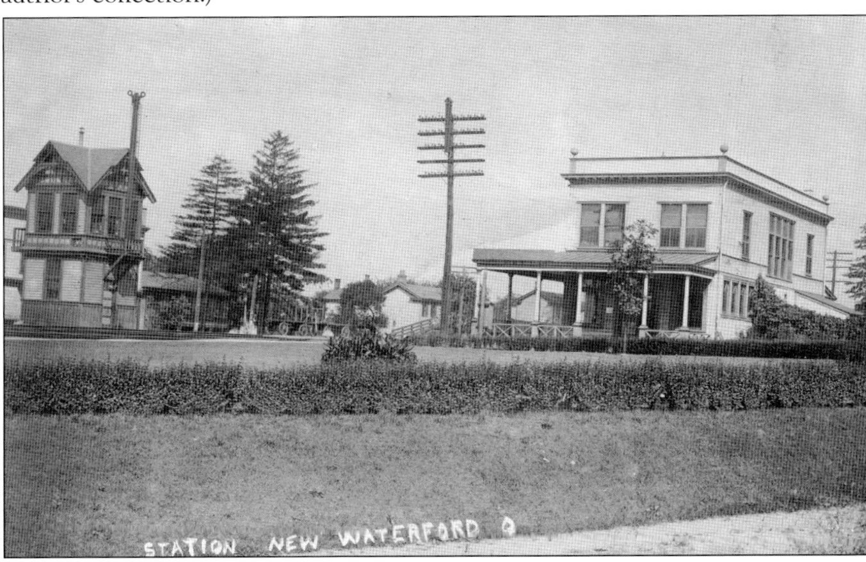

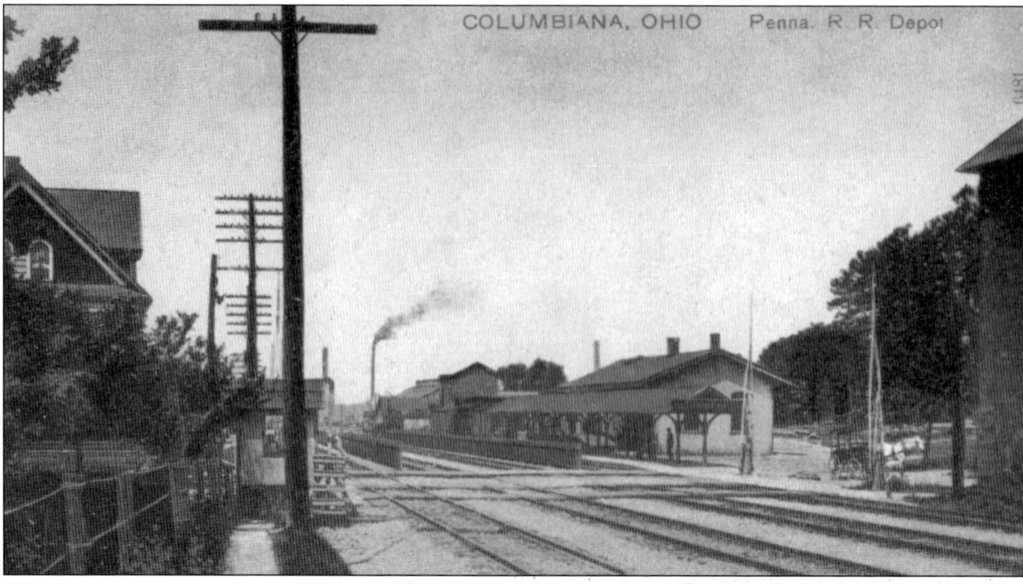

The first passenger train puffed into Columbiana in January 1852. The town was served by this brick passenger depot until the end of passenger service, when it was converted to freight use. Altogether, it stood for over a century. This c. 1910 postcard view shows the umbrella shelter; it was gone by the late 1960s. In the foreground is another PRR shack that provided shelter for the person controlling the crossing gates (they were not yet automated). Columbiana was also served by the Youngstown & Southern Railway, which connected Columbiana to Youngstown. (Author's collection.)

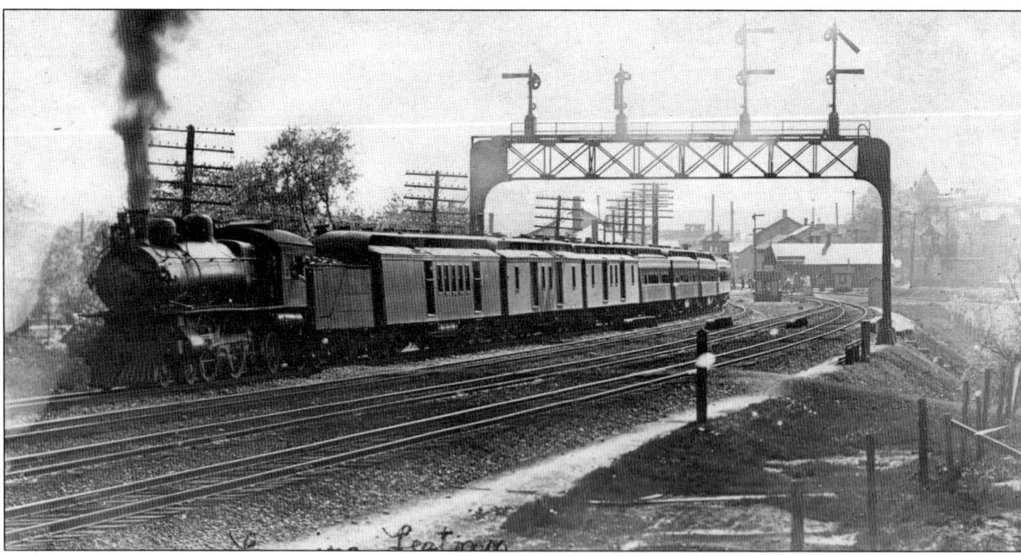

At Leetonia, the PFtW&C crossed the Erie Railroad's Lisbon branch and the Youngstown & Ohio River Railway (an interurban/steam line between Salem, Washingtonville and East Liverpool). A PRR passenger train is passing under the signal bridge as it leaves Leetonia's frame passenger depot (in the background) around 1910. The depot was T-shaped, with a separate frame freight house adjacent. This was a joint facility with the Erie. In the distance is the top of the interlocking tower, which has been restored and is the last remnant of this once busy junction. (Author's collection.)

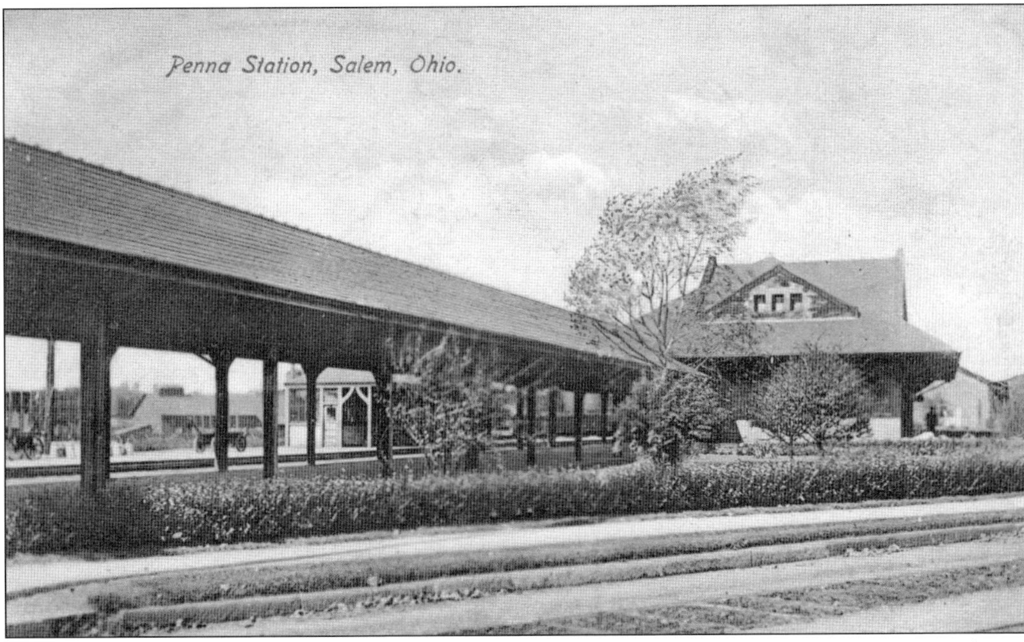

Salem's stone passenger depot on South Ellsworth Avenue was a third-generation depot replacing a PFtW&C depot (built in 1867) in 1892–1893. The sandstone came from a quarry farther east on the PFtW&C at Beaver Falls, Pennsylvania. Note the garden in the above 1912 view. Below is a view from the 1960s, after the platform shelters had been altered. This depot was certainly a candidate for historic preservation, but the derailment of 51 cars and 2 Conrail engines in front of the depot on July 31, 1997, resulted in collapse of half of the building. Beyond repair, it was subsequently demolished. Across from the PRR depot was the frame depot of the Salem Railroad, a seven-mile-long short line connecting Salem with Washingtonville. It was completed in 1892. This line was sold to the Pittsburgh, Lisbon & Western Railway in 1902 and ended up as part of the Youngstown & Ohio River Railway. After abandonment, the building was used for storage; it collapsed in 1966. (Above, author's collection; below, Charles Garvin photograph.)

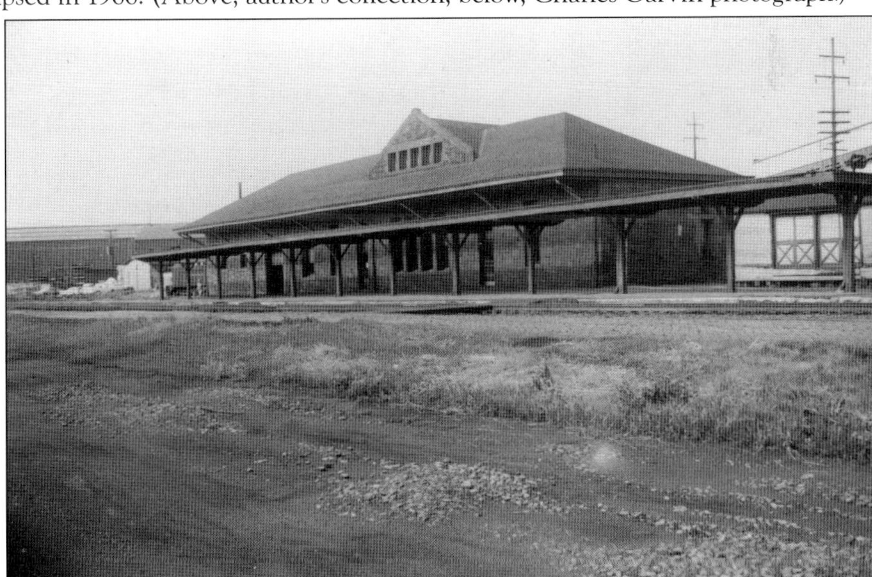

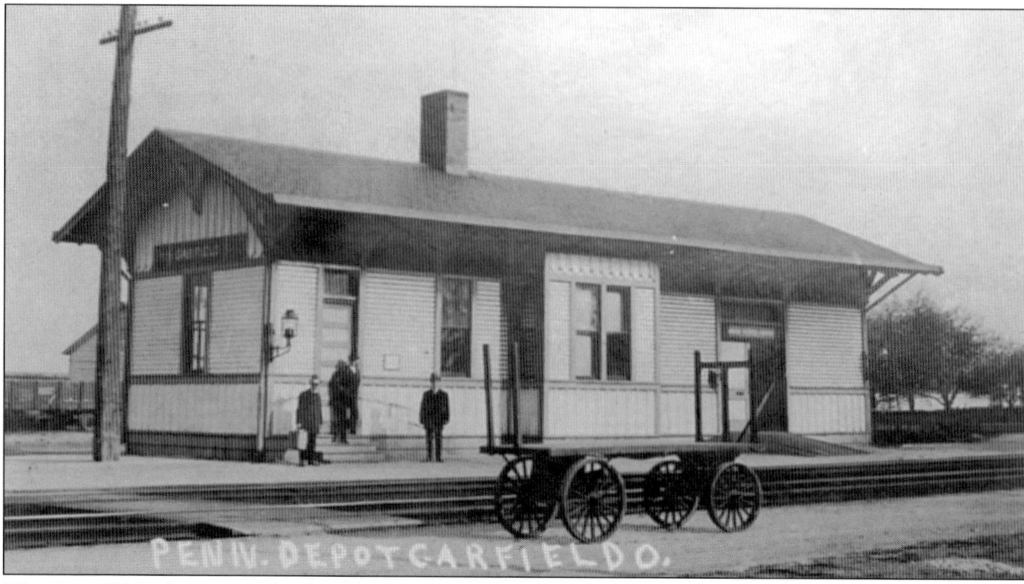

The first PRR depot on the line heading west into Mahoning County was at Garfield. This is a second-generation combination depot built to several floor plans of different lengths and widths, window and door placements, and arrangements and sizes of waiting rooms, offices, and freight rooms. Note that the town boards of PRR depots consisted of the station name bordered by the mileage to the cities at the end of the line, in this case Pittsburgh and Chicago. The plans called for scalloped ornamental siding in the eaves, complemented by narrow horizontal siding, and a vertical wainscot. (Dan West.)

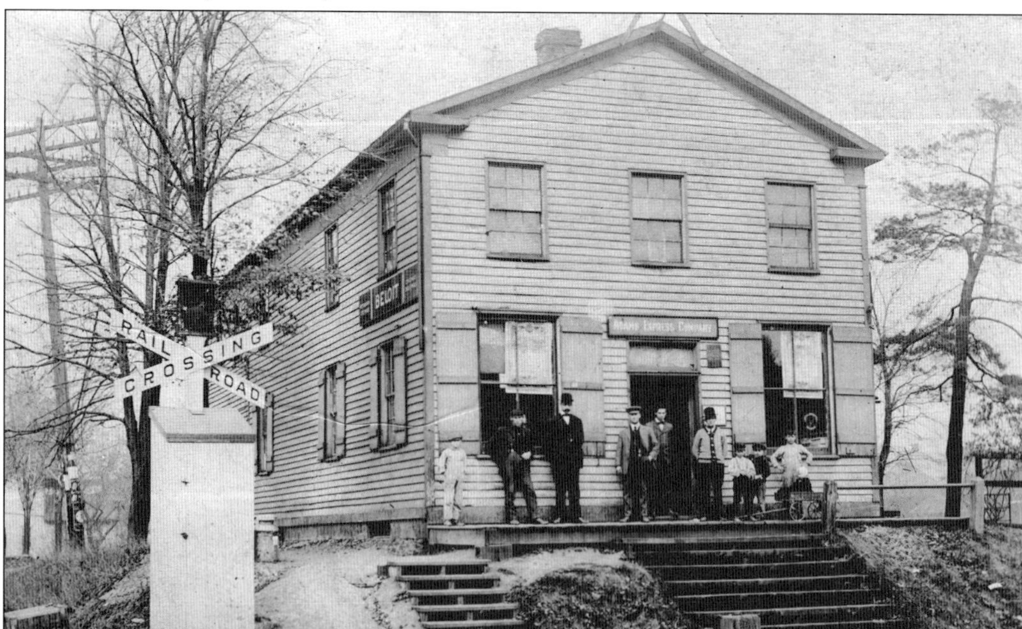

In some communities, the railroad might use an already existing structure and convert it to railroad use or perhaps just use a portion of it. Such was the case at Smithfield Station, renamed Beloit in 1863. A brick plant just east of town shipped its products through this depot along with nearby Garfield. (Author's collection.)

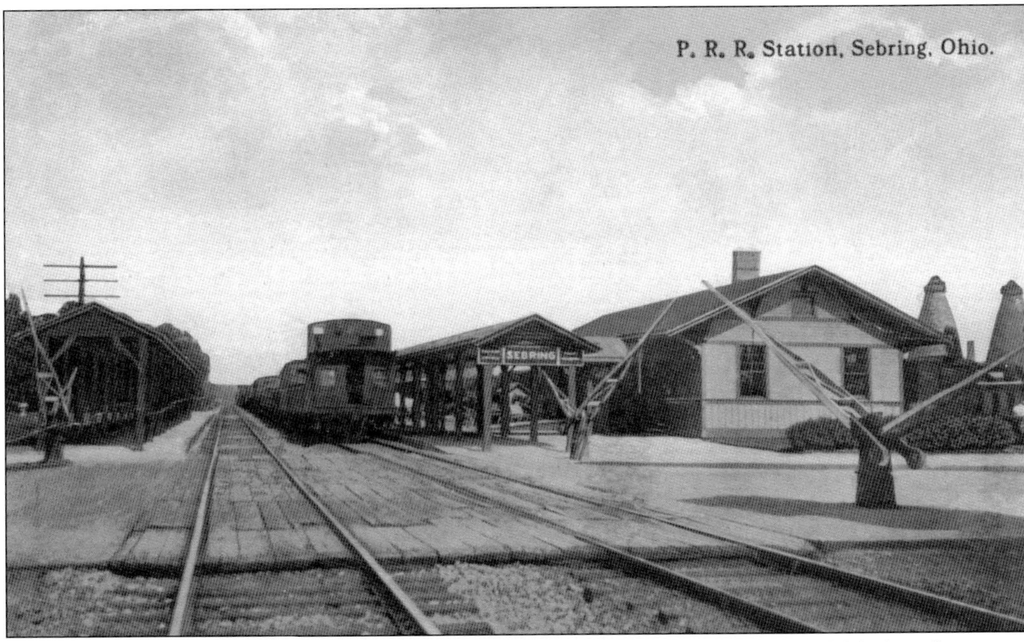

Sebring was laid out in 1898 as a pottery town; good-quality clay was available locally, as was coal to fire the kilns. The frame combination depot, pictured here around 1912 and in the 1960s, dates to 1898. Just to the west is Alliance Junction, where the PRR line from Niles connects with the main line of the former PFtW&C. The platform shelters are paired—one for westbound passengers and one for eastbound travelers. Instead of having an umbrella-type structure, they are supported by a double row of pillars. With the termination of passenger service, they were removed. In the background, beehive pottery kilns rise behind the depot. The depot has been restored and since 1974 has been the home of the Sebring Model Railroad Club. (Above, author's collection; below, author photograph.)

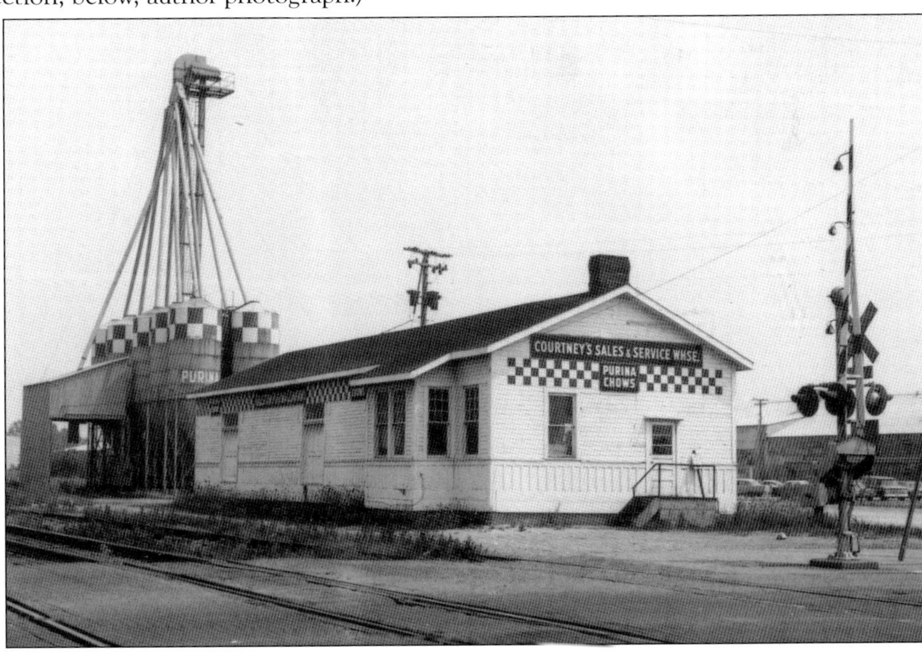

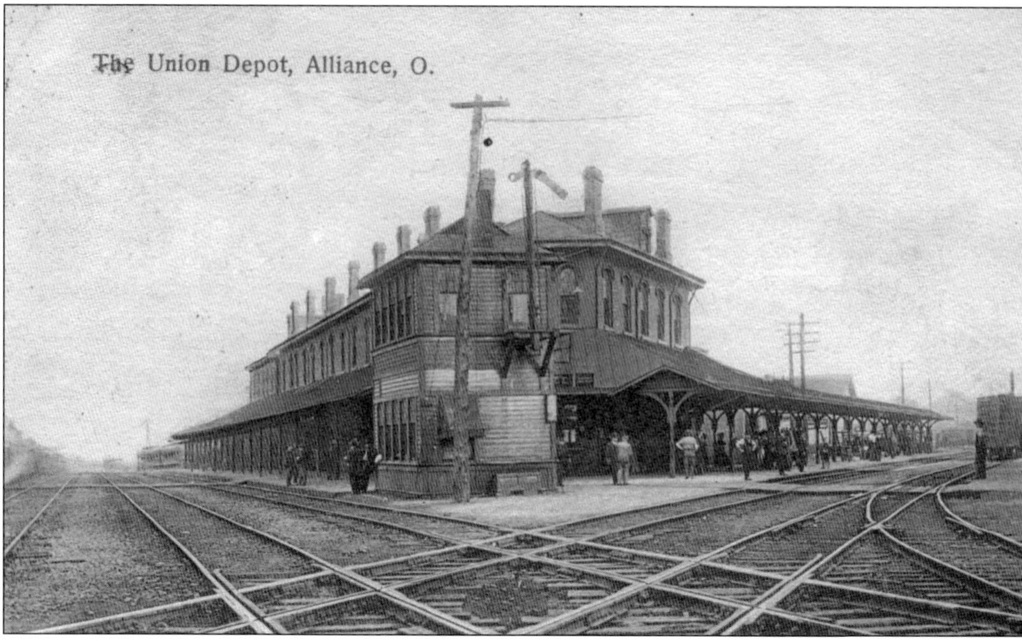

Before the railroads came—the Cleveland & Pittsburgh, in 1851, followed by the Ohio & Pennsylvania in 1852—this area was the site of three villages: Freedom, Liberty, and Williamsport. A joint depot was built at the junction in 1853, and the place became known as Alliance in 1854. The frame structure burned to the ground around 1863. This large brick passenger depot-hotel opened in September 1866. It was certainly one of the grandest railroad facilities in the region. It was a dining stop on the railroads before the days of dining cars and included the Hotel Alliance. The above c. 1910 postcard view shows the signal tower at the diamond. The C&P heads to the right; the PFtW&C is to the left. The view below shows a watchman's shanty for controlling gates at the nearby road crossing. To the far right is another railroad hotel. The former C&P tracks are on the upper right, while the main line of the PFtW&C is to the left in both views. Some 50 passenger trains were on the daily timetables in the mid-1940s. The depot was torn down in 1951–1952. (Both, author's collection.)

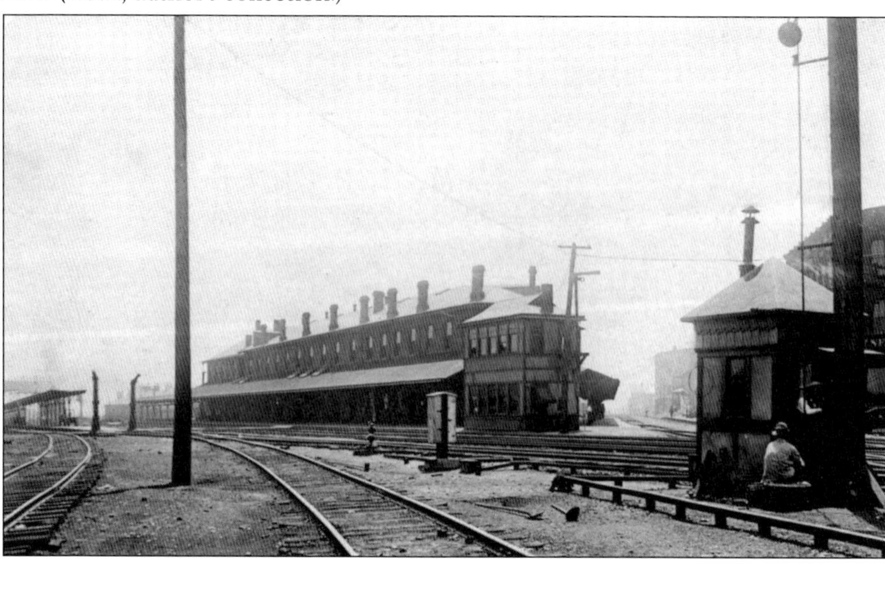

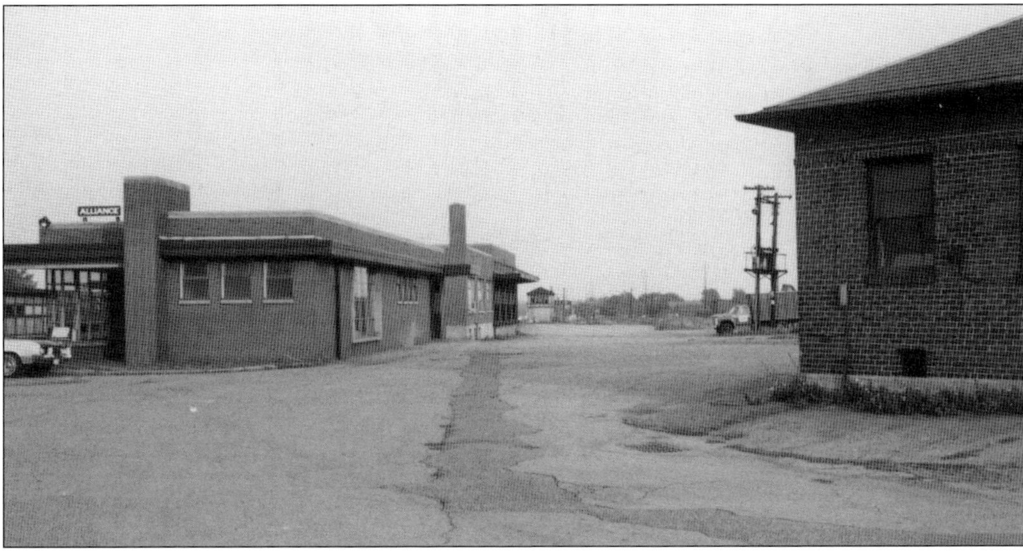

The new PRR passenger and baggage depot was built in 1952 and dedicated on February 23, 1953. As was the usual case, the local citizenry pushed for a new "modern" depot and a better welcome to visitors to their city. With declining passenger travel in the 1950s, the PRR also did not need such a large facility. This 1967 view also shows an interlocking tower at the crossing of the former LEA&W. In less than 20 years, this depot was unneeded. In 2017, it remains, but Amtrak passengers use a 2013-built shelter and lighted platform. (Author photograph.)

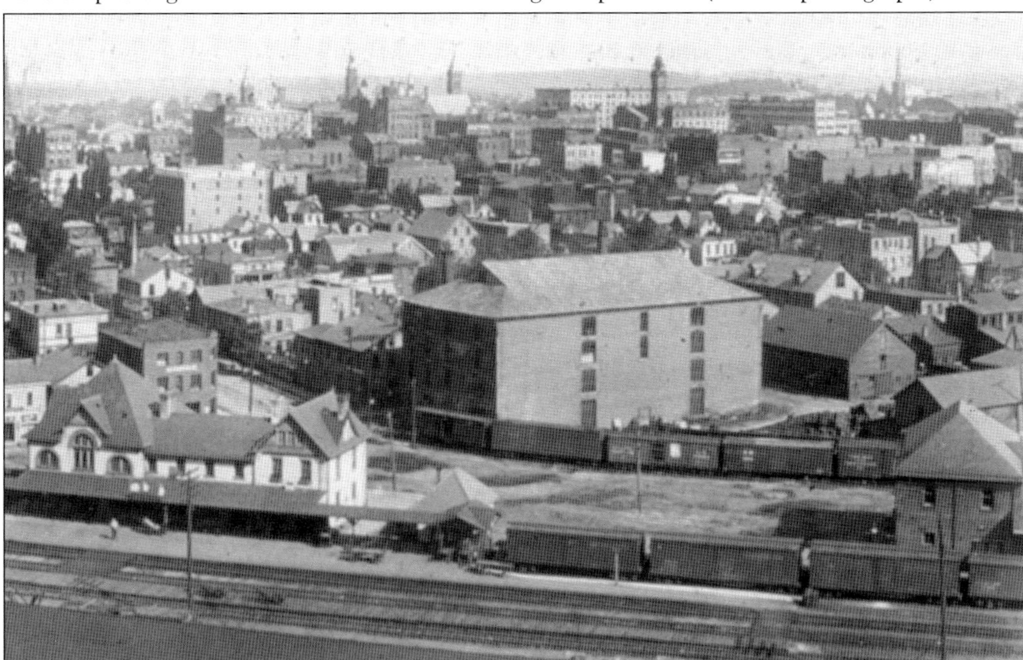

Between Alliance and Canton, the PRR had frame combination depots at Maximo and Louisville. Both were gone by the early 1970s. The Ohio & Pennsylvania rails reached Canton in late 1851; the line was officially opened between Pittsburgh and Massillon in March 1852. This two-and-a-half-story passenger depot was built by the PRR in 1887 to replace an earlier PFtW&C depot. The only thing that remains in 2017 is a brick PFtW&C freight house. (Dan West.)

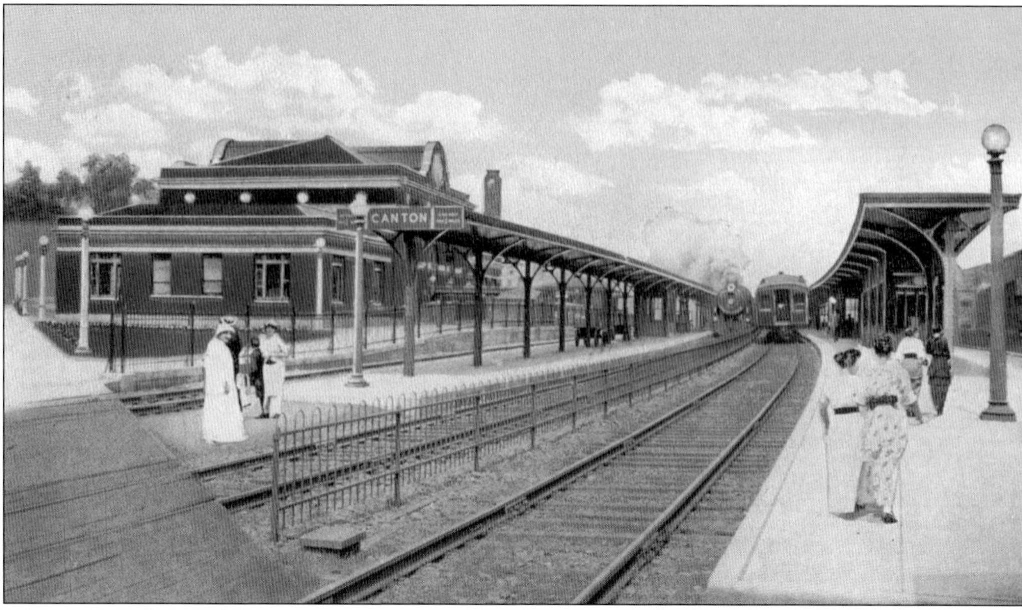

The PRR replaced the 1887 structure with this brick and stone passenger depot in 1915. It was a busy place in the mid-1900s. A tunnel under the tracks allowed passengers to safely reach the outer tracks. The station complex was once bordered by PRR interlocking towers and freight houses. Passenger service ended and the depot was closed May 1, 1971. The Canton depot was demolished in 1976. Amtrak brought passenger trains back to town and built a modern concrete block depot, but due to route change, the closest Amtrak depot in 2017 is located in Alliance. Only remnants of the passenger subway, the old PFtW&C freight house, and Amtrak depot stand in 2017. The PRR crossed the Wheeling & Lake Erie near the 1915 passenger depot. The PRR interlocking tower at this diamond was called Wandle (W and LE). PRR's McKinley tower guarded the crossing of the PRR and B&O (old Valley Line). The view below shows the depot in 1967. (Above, author's collection; below, author photograph.)

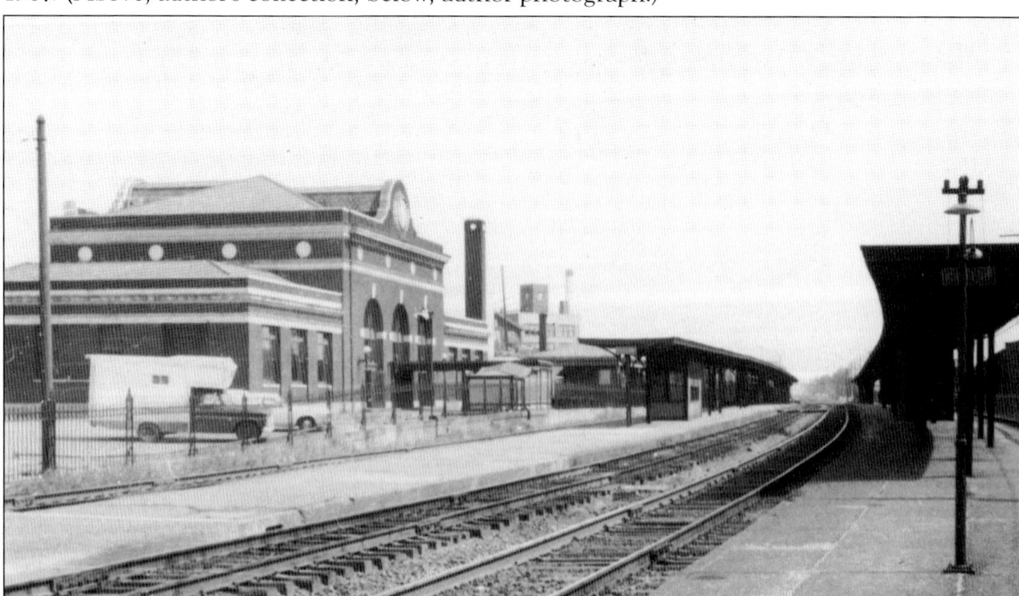

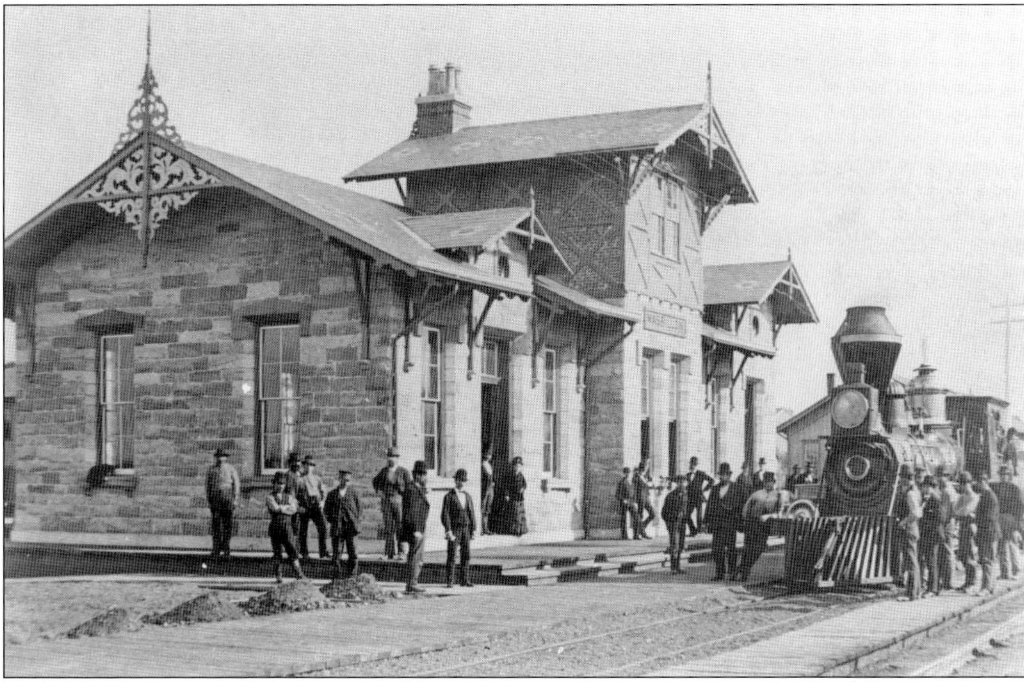

Massillon celebrated the arrival of the first official Ohio & Pennsylvania passenger train in March 1852. These views depict the cut stone depot as originally built with second-floor office area. As traffic increased, umbrella sheds were erected on the platforms. (Above, Massillon Museum collection; below, author's collection.)

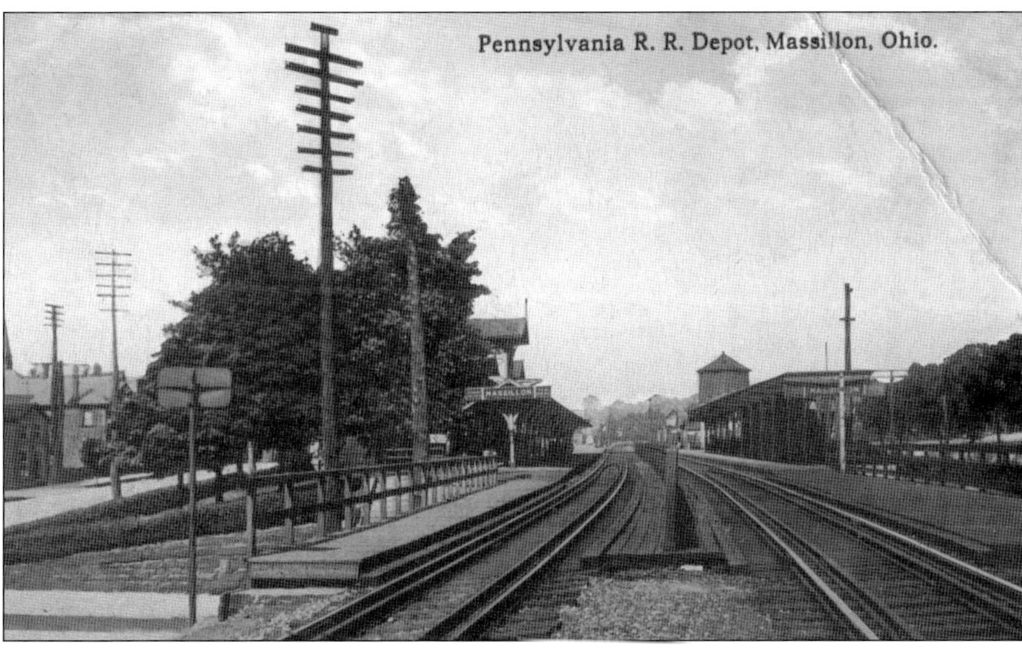

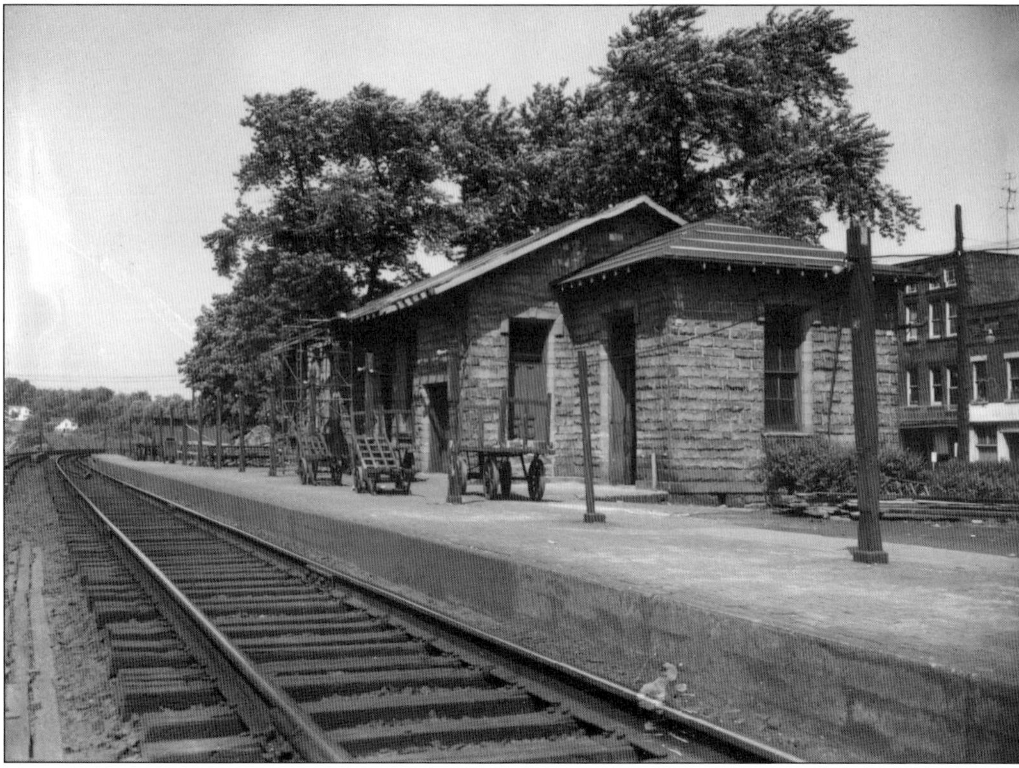

In 1953, the PRR remodeled the Massillon passenger depot by removing the frame second story and platform shelters. This was duly recorded by Jack Worthington of the *Evening Independent*. The depot would continue to serve passengers until the ending of service on May 1, 1971. The depot entered a period of non-railroad use. Its durable stone construction has held up well through the years. It remains a fixture on Penn Avenue in 2017. (Both, Massillon Museum collection.)

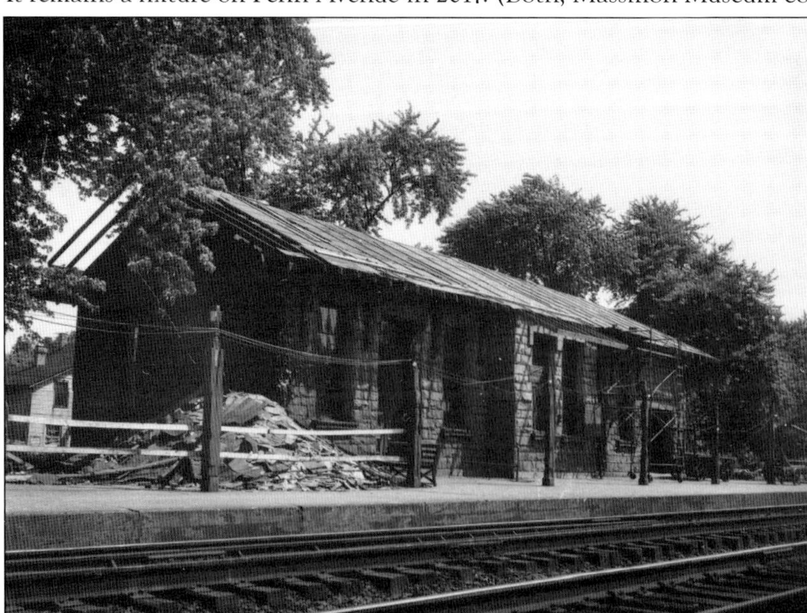

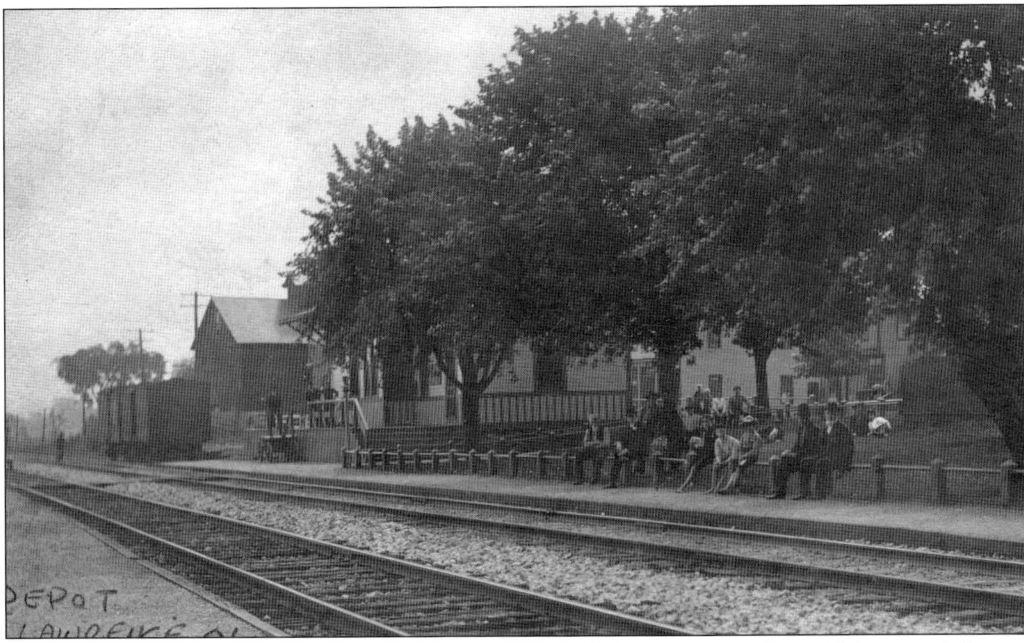

It is a pleasant summer day in the early 1900s in North Lawrence, and word has spread that an itinerant photographer would be exposing glass plates of the railroad depot. The depot park was a great place to have a picnic or just watch the comings and goings. Across and down the track was a PRR signal tower. The combination depot was built to one of the PRR's standard plans. The depot was still there in the late 1960s. (Author's collection.)

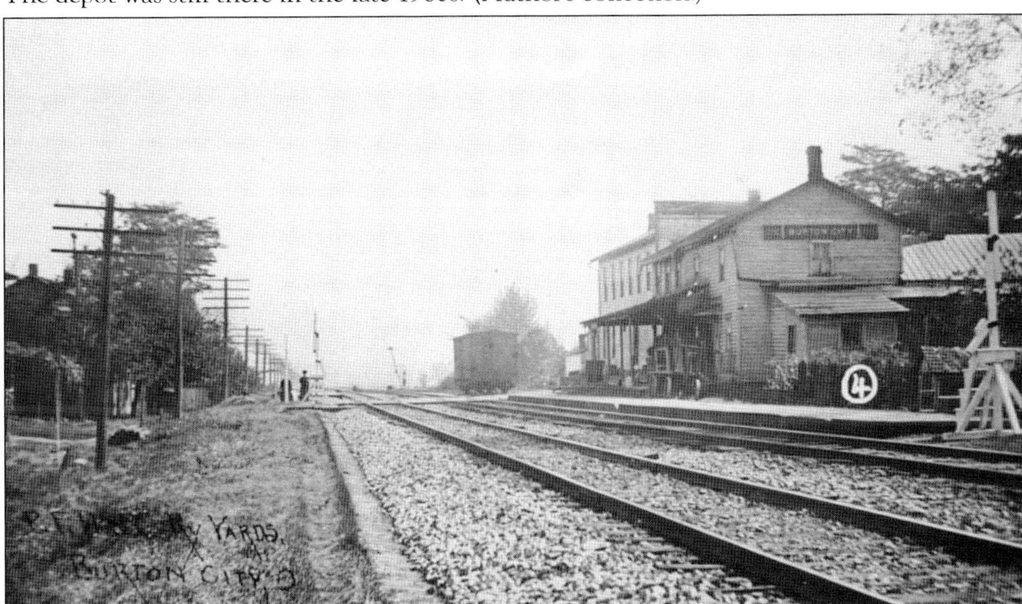

Burton City was originally known as Fairview when it was founded in 1850. It became Burton City in 1872. As at Beloit, farther east on the O&P, it appears the PRR converted an existing store into a ticket office and depot. From here west to Orrville, the original route of the Wheeling & Lake Erie paralleled the PRR tracks to the south. The W&LE depot was along Mount Eaton Road not far from the PRR structure. (Dan West.)

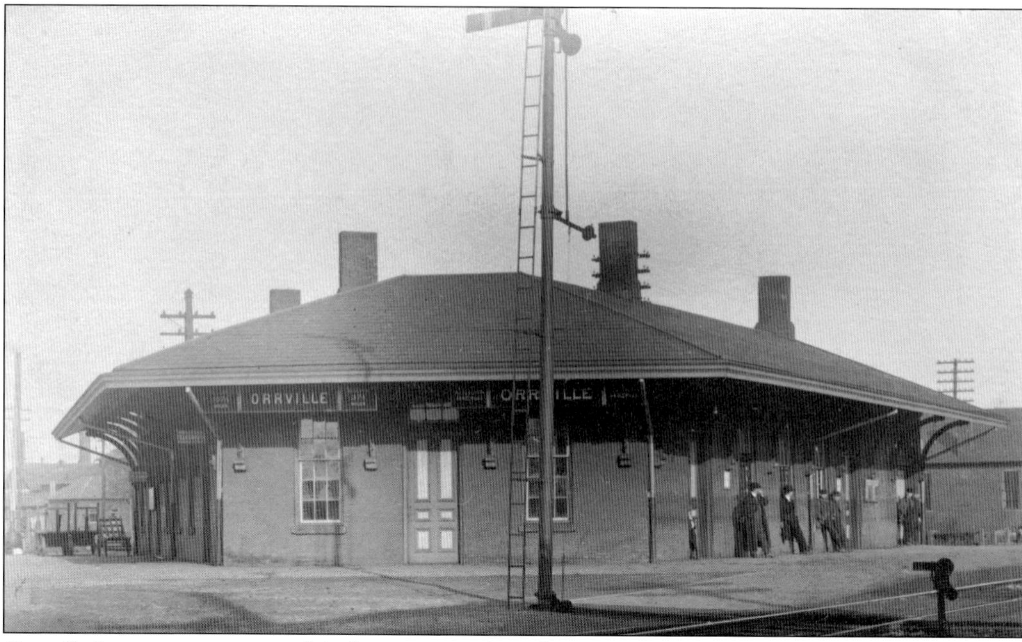

Orrville began as a water and fuel station on the Ohio & Pennsylvania Railroad in 1852. Next to enter the newly platted town was a branch of the Cleveland & Pittsburgh Railroad that reached town in 1854. This line became the Cleveland, Akron & Columbus Railroad when it eventually reached Columbus. The Wheeling & Lake Erie Railway added its tracks to the growing village in 1881. The first depot built at the crossing of the two PRR lines burned to the ground and was replaced by this brick passenger depot in 1868. The view below shows the interlocking tower at the crossing. A separate frame freight house was located down the tracks. Orrville served as a small terminal on the CA&C with a roundhouse and other locomotive service facilities. The double tracks mark the former O&P main line; the single track marks the CA&C. Passenger service ended in 1971 and the depot was used by railroad maintenance crews. The Orville Railroad Heritage Committee, now the Orrville Railroad Heritage Society, purchased the depot and tower in the early 1980s and began a long process of restoration. It is well worth a visit. (Both, author's collection.)

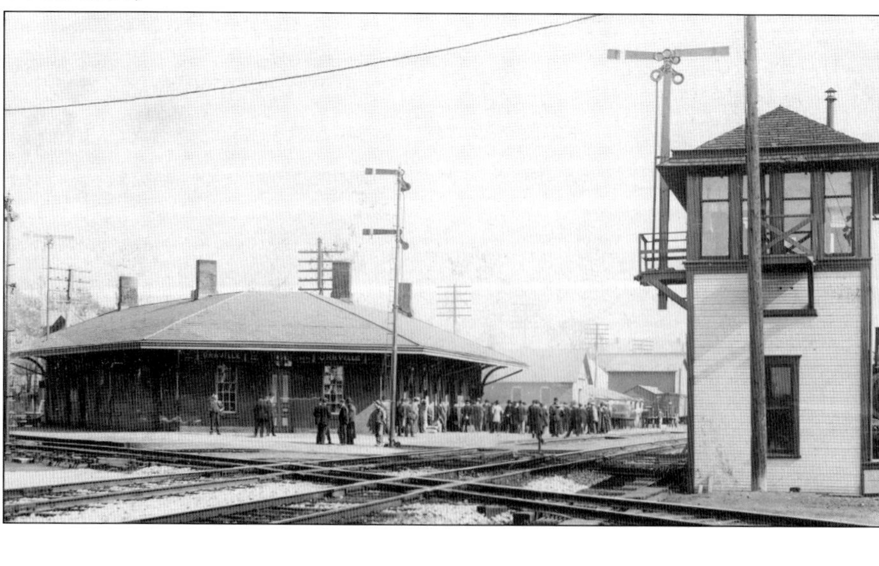

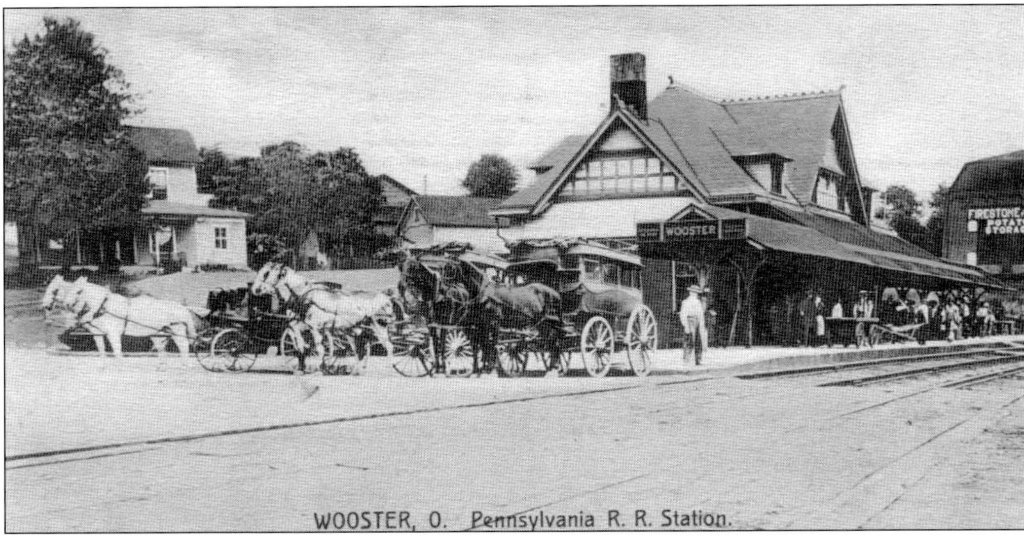

August 10, 1852, was a momentous day of celebration as the Ohio & Pennsylvania completed tracks from Orrville to Wooster. The year 1890 marked another celebration when the PRR completed this frame passenger depot, replacing an earlier frame structure. This particular design was repeated with slight modifications at a few other stations along the PRR's extensive system. The passenger depot came to an unceremonious end when a 31-car Conrail derailment sent loaded railroad cars crashing into the depot on August 8, 1977. The damage was beyond repair and another classic depot disappeared from trackside. This image was captured around 1910. (Author's collection.)

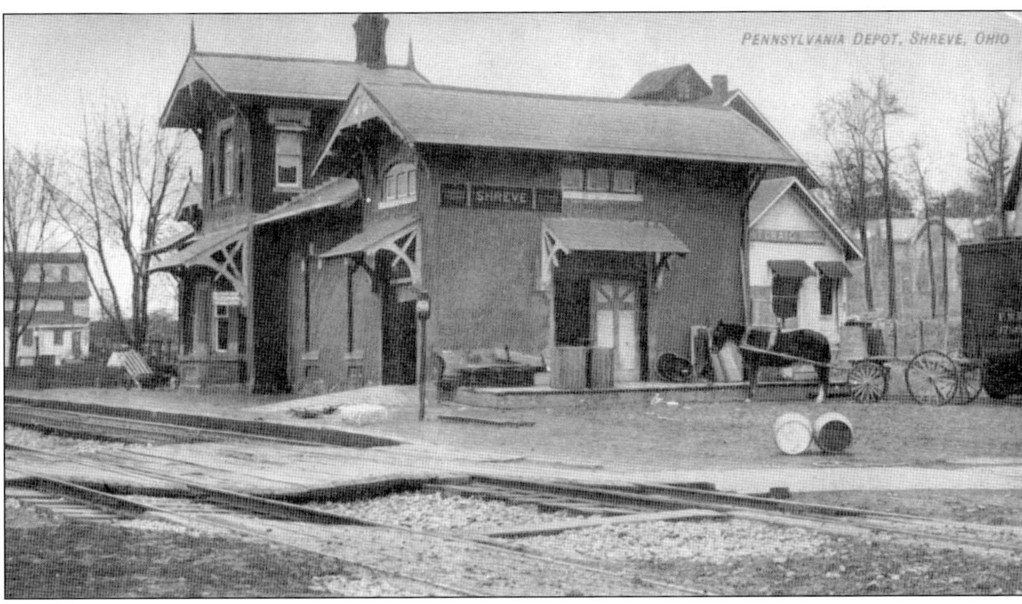

In 1853, the presence of a large spring led to the establishment of a water station on the Ohio & Pennsylvania Railroad at a place in southern Wayne County, which led to the platting of Shreve. A one-and-a-half-story brick combination depot (depicted on this c. 1910 postcard) was built here in 1878 by the PRR, replacing a smaller frame building. The second floor above the ticket and freight office provided a good overview up and down the tracks. The depot was torn down around 1963. (Author's collection.)

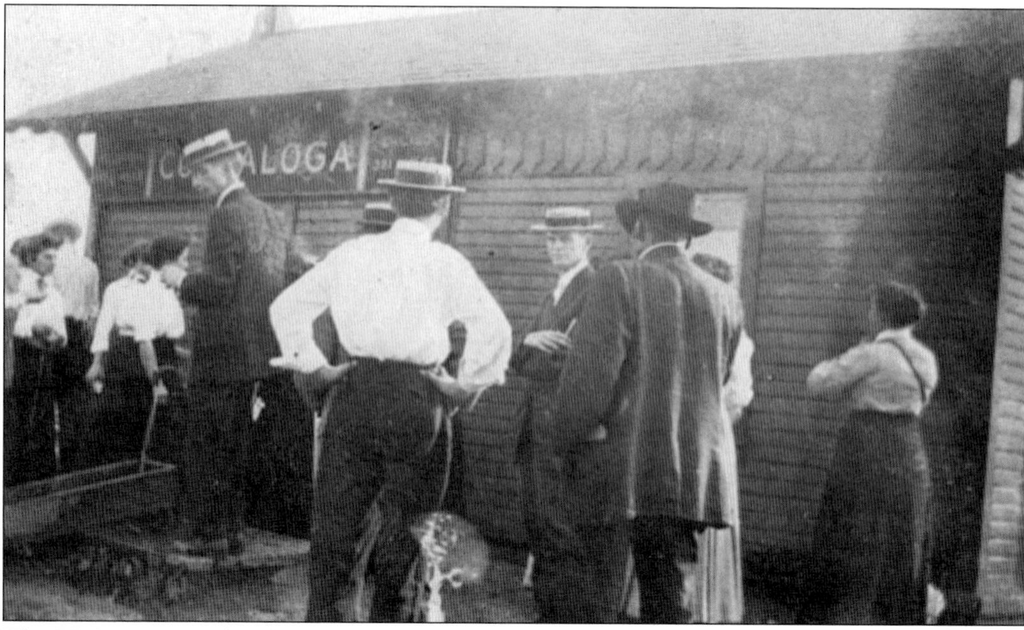

The PRR connected with the Ashland & Wooster Railway (A&W; later Lorain, Ashland & Southern Railroad) at Brown Junction, which was renamed Custaloga in 1900 when the PRR erected a small depot. The A&W maintained a small yard at this station to hold cars awaiting transfer to the PRR. This depot was struck by lightning and burned to the ground on June 26, 1914. An old passenger coach was used as the depot until 1925. Official abandonment of this station by the PRR came in 1926. Nothing remains in 2017. (Dan West.)

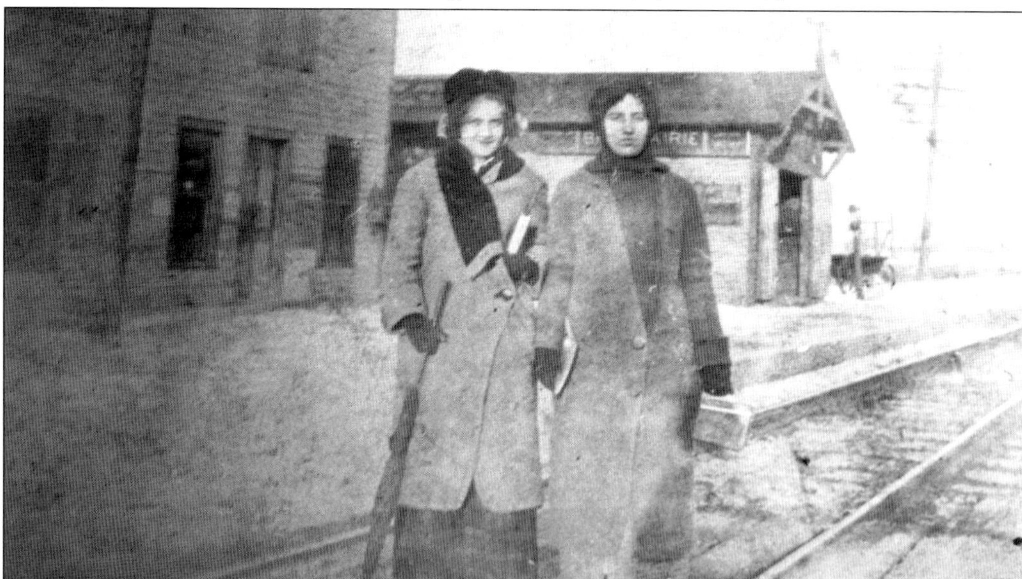

Big Prairie, situated right on the boundary between Wayne and Holmes Counties, was established in 1871. It was the home of the Monitor Sadiron Company, which was reason enough for the PRR to maintain a small depot there into the early 1900s. It also had a junction with the Lorain Ashland & Southern Railroad until 1925. The ladies in this c. 1910 photograph are dressed warmly for perhaps a shopping trip to Wooster or Loudonville. (Dan West.)

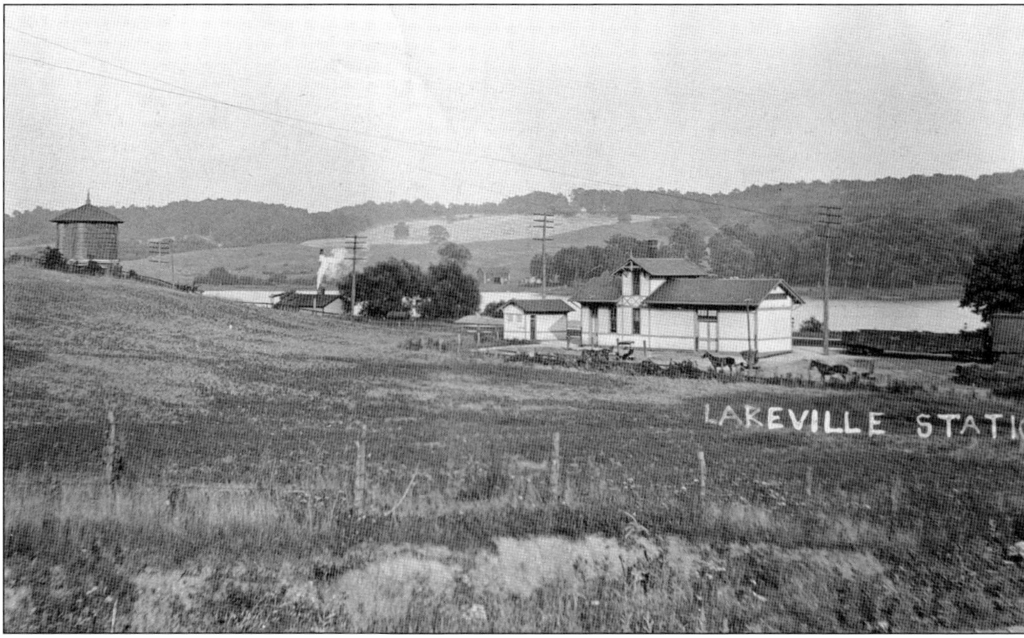

This c. 1910 postcard view shows the beautiful countryside around Lakeville. The town was platted in 1839 and gradually spread eastward to Odell Lake when the railroad passed through. Lakeville became a popular resort during the summer, with hotels and lakeside amusements. Pictured are a second-generation PRR combination depot and nearby water tank. During the winter, the railroad shipped blocks of ice cut from the frozen lake. (Author's collection.)

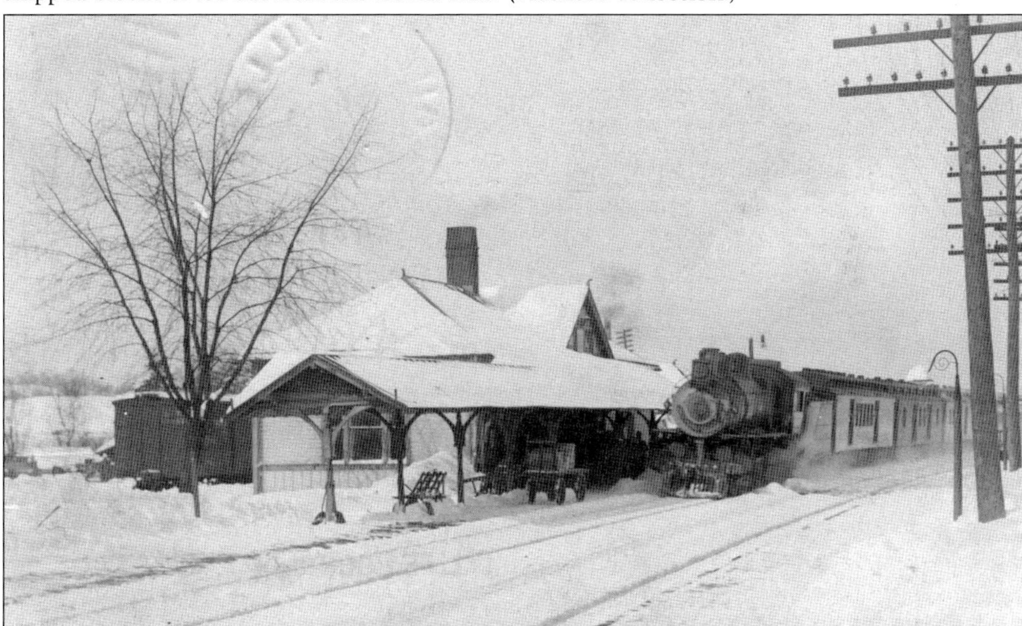

A PRR passenger train arrives at the depot in Loudonville on a snowy winter's day in the early 1900s. The snowfall was recent and heavy. The depot staff have not had time to clear the platform. Unfortunately, the depot has been torn down; it was still there in the 1970s. (Author's collection.)

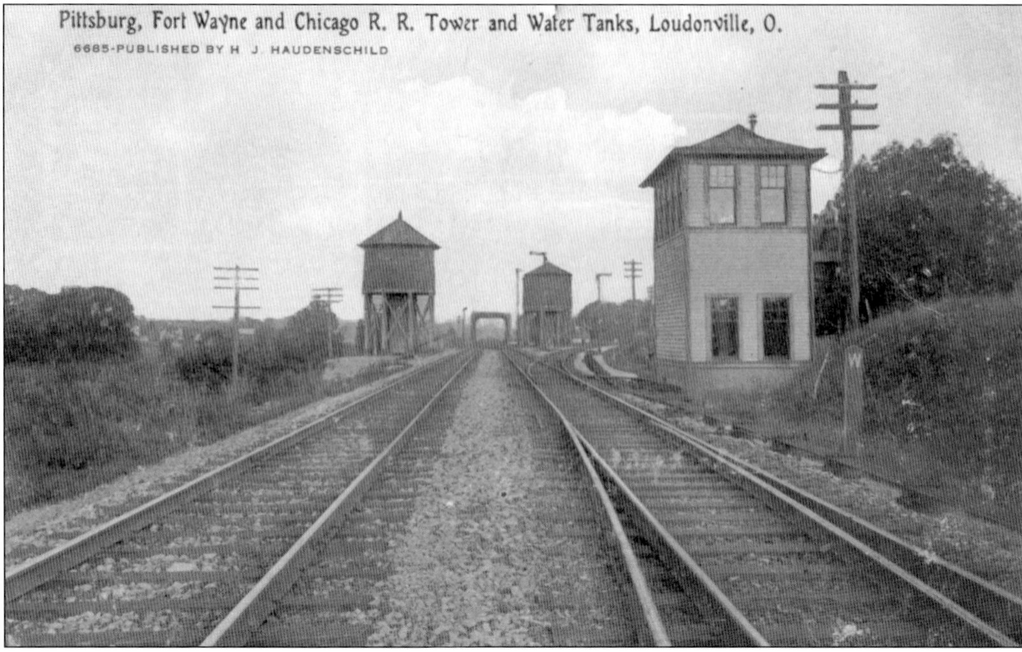

Just west of Loudonville, the Toledo, Walhonding Valley & Ohio Railroad (TWV&O) heads southward. This is Loudonville Junction. This c. 1910 view shows the PRR interlocking tower and two water tanks—one serving main line locomotives on the left and the other serving TWV&O engines. In the distance is a small PRR shelter, called West Loudonville, that served passengers on the main line. A short distance down the TWV&O was its Loudonville depot. (Author's collection.)

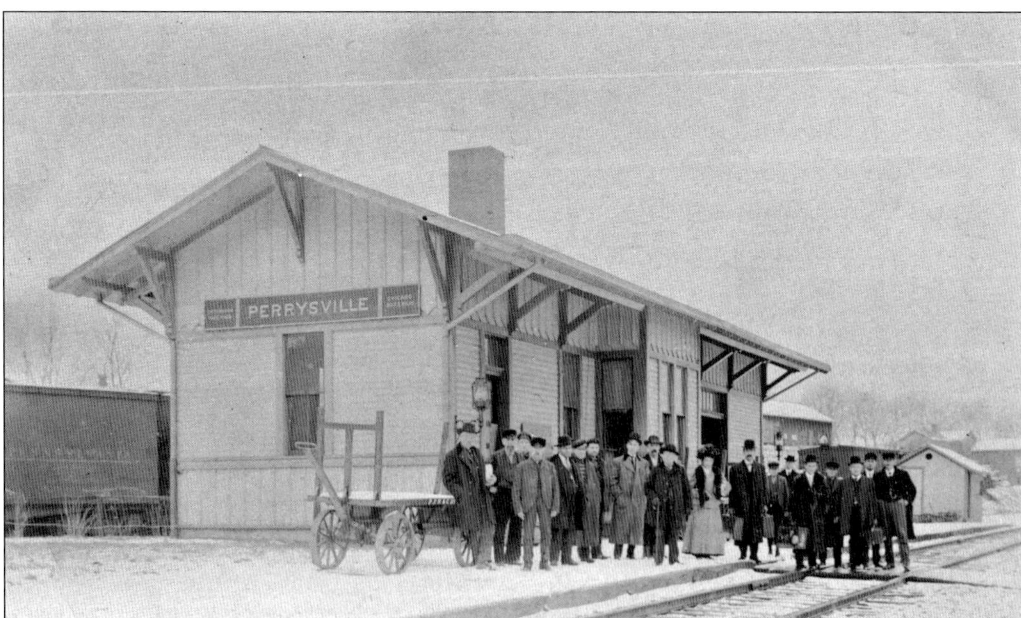

Another standard design PRR combination depot replaced an earlier frame depot at Perrysville. This structure was gone from trackside by the late 1960s. (Author's collection.)

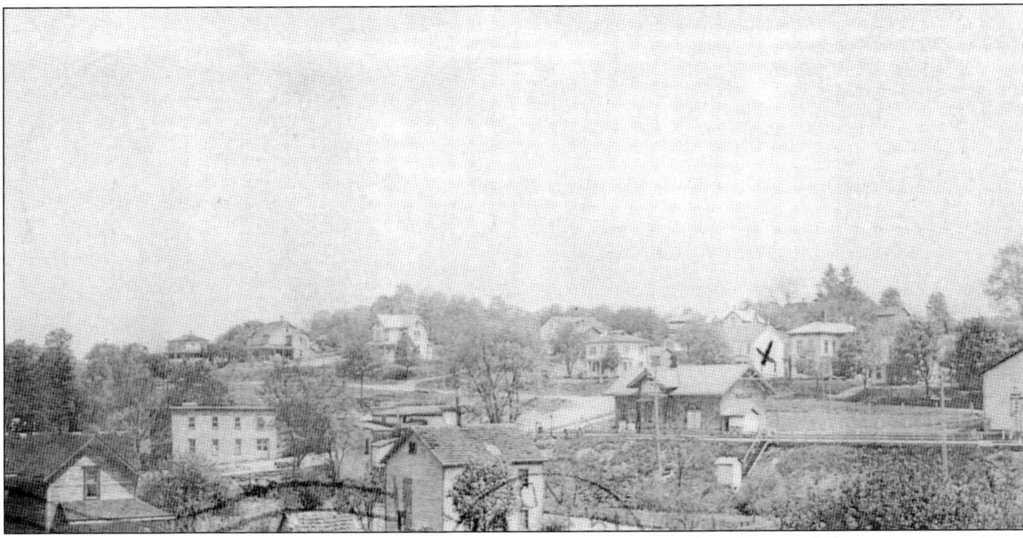

By the late 1960s, only a frame PRR interlocking tower remained in Lucas. This overview shows the brick PRR combination depot that was built by the PRR, probably in the 1870s, replacing an earlier frame building. (Mansfield Public Library collection.)

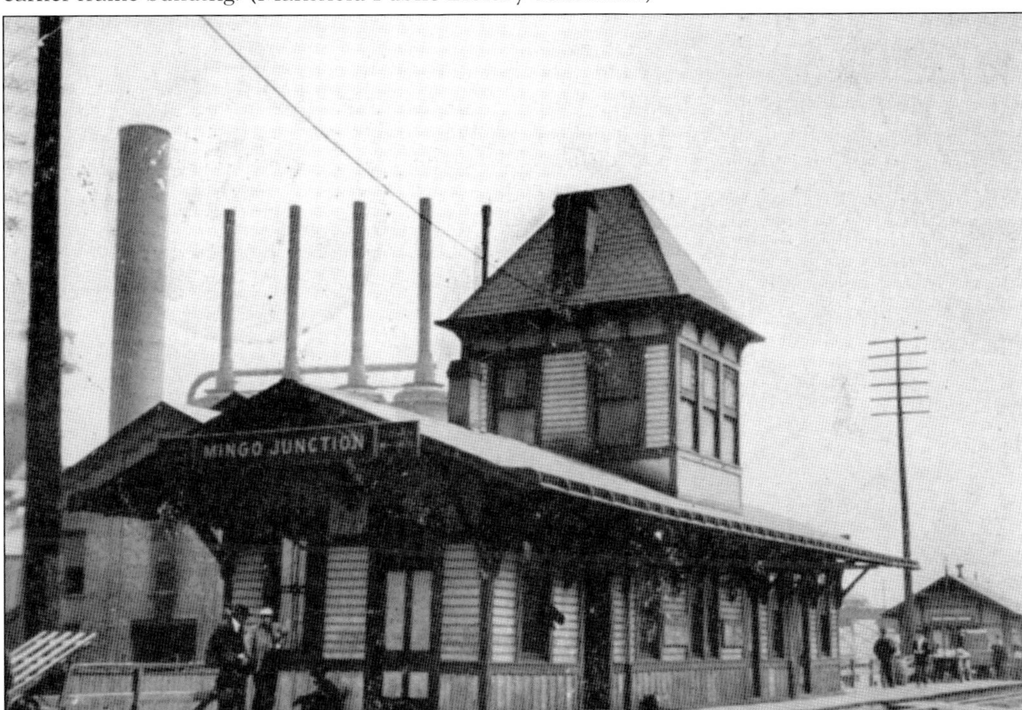

The Pittsburgh, Cincinnati & St. Louis Railway formed the more southern east–west route of the Pennsylvania Railroad. The Ohio portion began at Mingo Junction in Jefferson County, where the PC&StL and Cleveland & Pittsburgh Railroad ran on opposite sides of this passenger depot/ tower. It dates to 1888 and probably replaced two separate earlier depots. To the south is a freight house. One of Mingo Junction's blast furnaces rises behind the depot. The Wheeling & Lake Erie Railway also had a depot in this river town. (Dan West.)

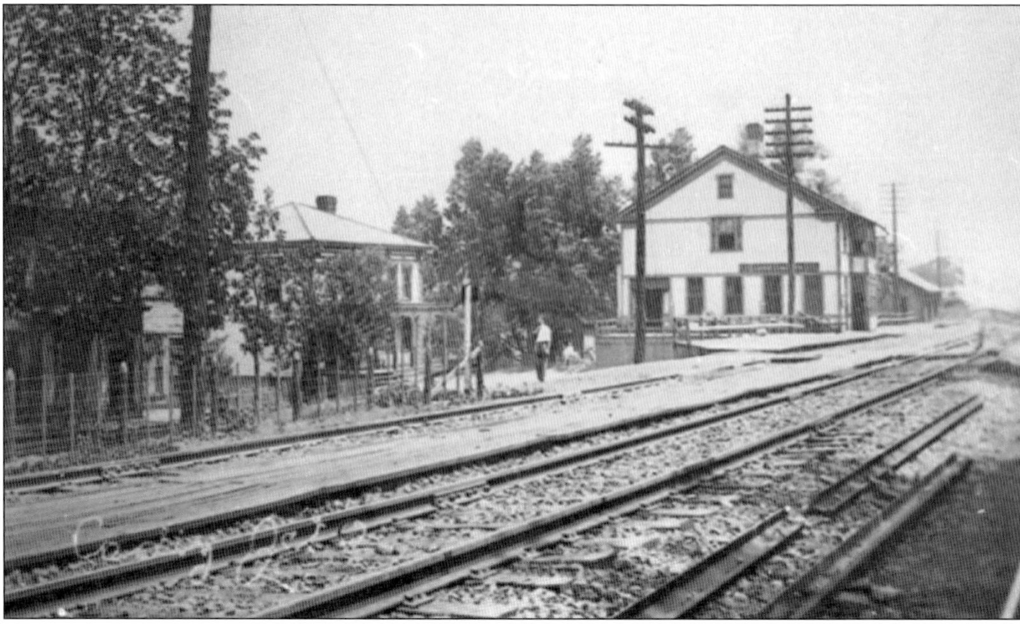

The PC&StL passed westward through Gould, New Alexandria, Fernwood, Reeds, Skelley, Fairplay, Unionport, and Miller before reaching Cadiz Junction. A large two-story frame passenger depot was located at this busy junction. Cadiz, to the south, is the Harrison County seat but was bypassed by the main line and had to settle for a branch line. Note the Cadiz Junction depot has a two-story vestibule with railroad offices on both floors. Nearby is the freight house. By the late 1960s, only a brick pump house remained at the junction. Heading south down the Cadiz branch, opened in June 1854 by the Steubenville & Indiana, the PCC&StL had flag stops at some eight mining towns. At the end of the line were the 1893 brick and frame Cadiz combination depot, an enginehouse, and a turntable. A one- or two-coach train would make the trip back and forth between Cadiz and Cadiz Junction daily, connecting with main line trains. A part of the depot still remained in the early 1970s. (Above, Dan West; below, author's collection.)

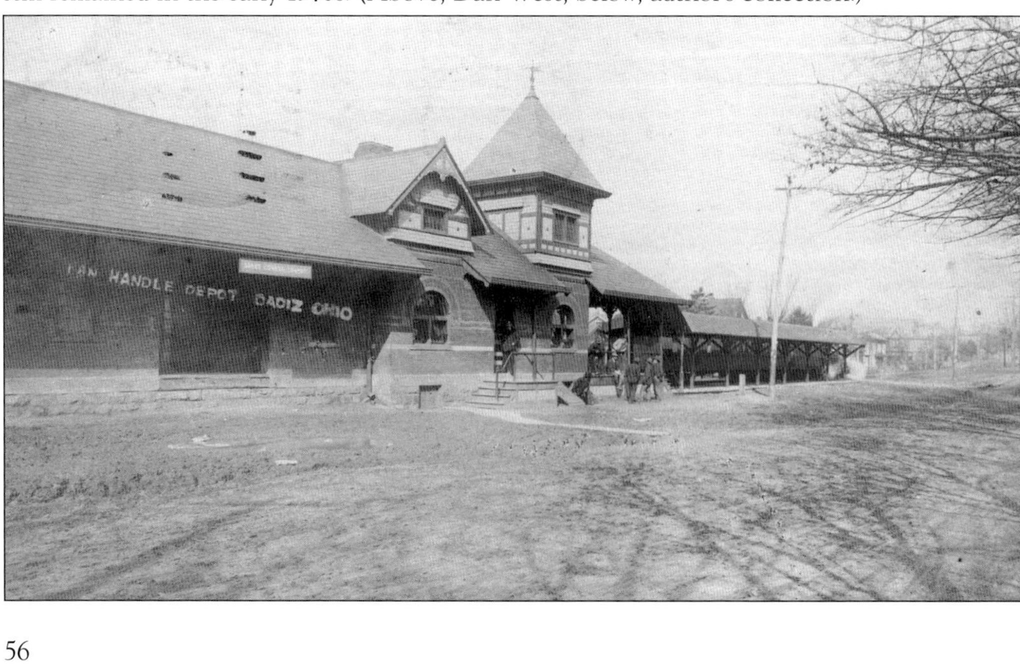

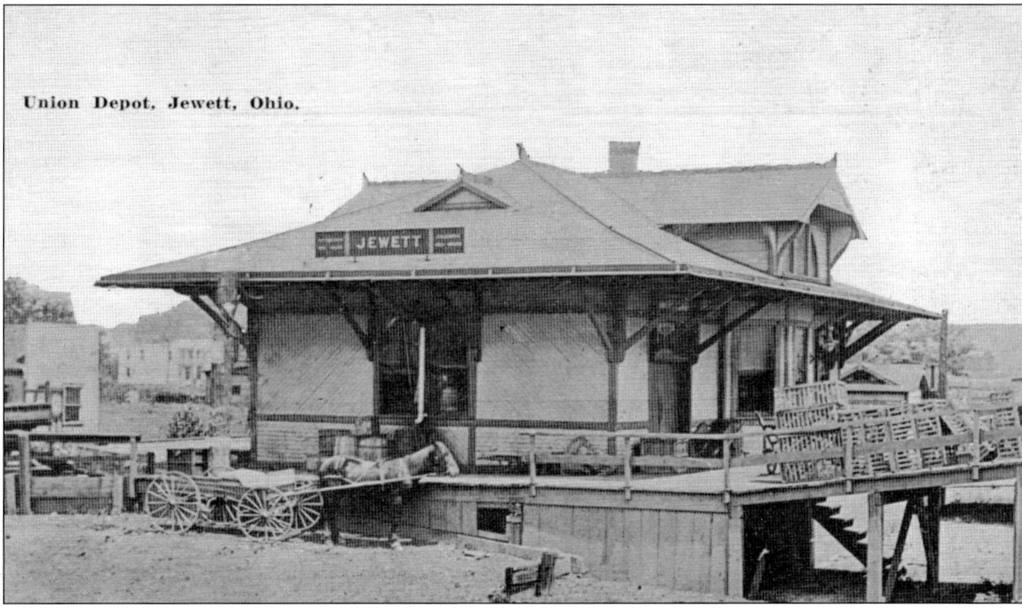

The Wheeling & Lake Erie Railway crosses the PC&StL at Jewett and heads southeast to Pittsburgh Junction. The W&LE built this depot and in 1890 agreed to a joint use of the building with the Pittsburgh, Cincinnati, Chicago & St. Louis Railway. This c. 1910 postcard shows the elevated wooden loading platform on the PRR side of the building. This was still in use in 1927. Jewett was also home to the Jewett Car Company, a maker of streetcars, from 1894 to 1904. By the late 1960s, only a PRR interlocking tower remained. (Author's collection.)

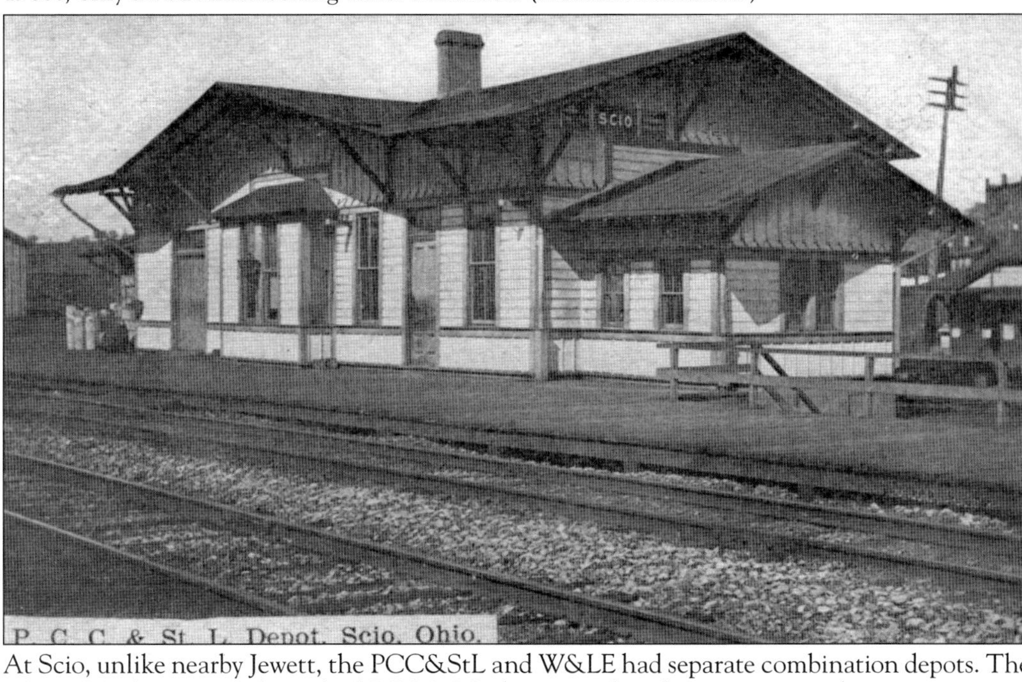

At Scio, unlike nearby Jewett, the PCC&StL and W&LE had separate combination depots. The PCC&StL depot was of standard PCC&StL design, a plan that was repeated at many stations along the line. This depot was a busy place during the Scio oil boom. Only W&LE's Scio depot remains in 2017. (Author's collection.)

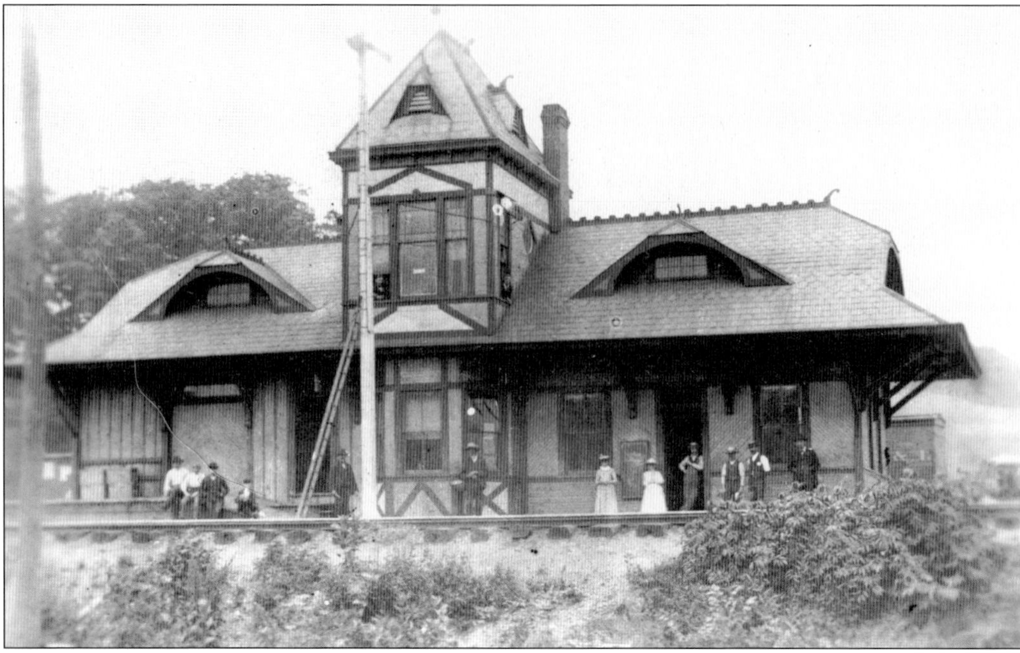

Since the PCC&StL and W&LE paralleled each other from Jewett to Bowerston, the second depot built at Bowerston was a joint one, like at Jewett. These views show the PCC&StL side around 1910 (above) and in 1927 (below). Note the raised plank platform on the PCC&StL side and the second-floor office tower. The below photograph also shows the W&LE side to the right, This depot was replaced by a smaller prefab building by the late 1960s. (Above, author's collection; below, W&LE photograph, Special Collections, Michael Schwartz Library, Cleveland State University.)

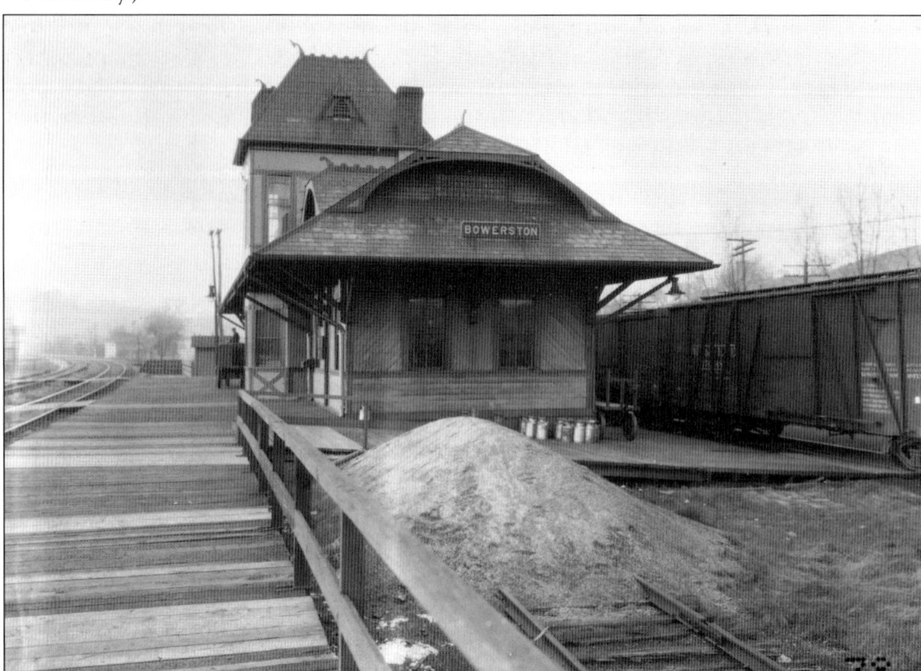

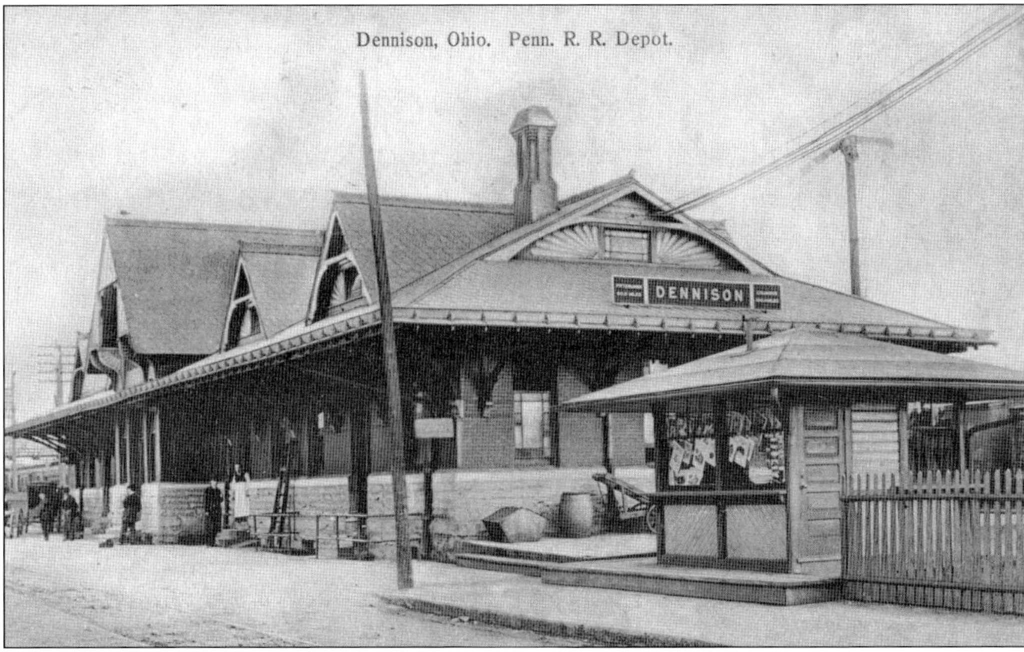

The PCC&StL passes through Fisher and Philadelphia Road on its way to Dennison. The frame building that was converted to a freight house in 1887 when the present brick passenger depot was built was an earlier PCC&StL depot constructed in 1873. Dennison came into existence as a water and fueling stop on the Steubenville & Indiana Railway in 1864. It became one of the largest PRR shops by 1900 and headquarters of the Panhandle Division. Twenty-one passenger trains served the terminal. During World War II, the servicemen's canteen at the depot catered to over a million and a half soldiers as they passed through Dennison on troop trains. Passenger service ended in 1971. The yards were gradually abandoned, and freight traffic shifted to other routes. Most of the service facilities were dismantled or demolished. The depot was probably next. Enter the village of Dennison and a great group of volunteers. The village bought the depot from Conrail in 1984 and, after much work, reopened it in 1989. In 2017, it is a historic attraction: the Dennison Railroad Depot Museum. (Both, author's collection.)

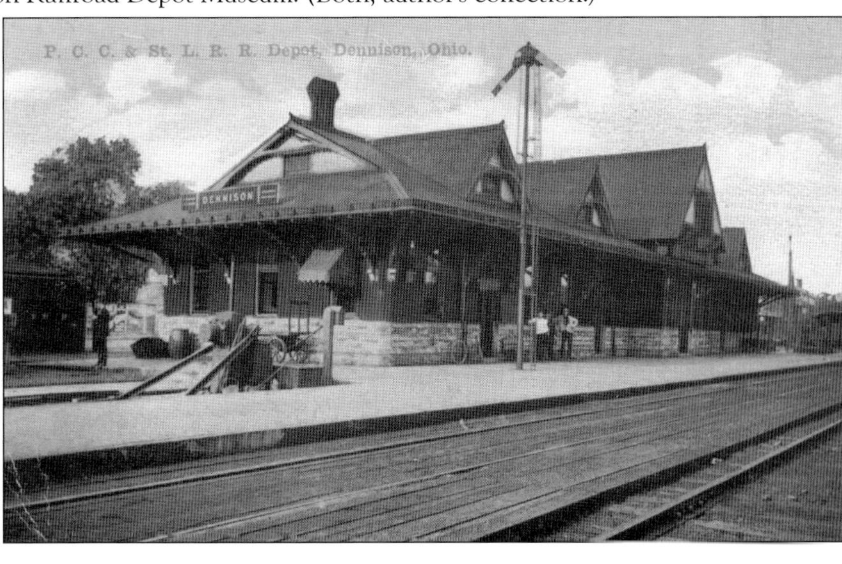

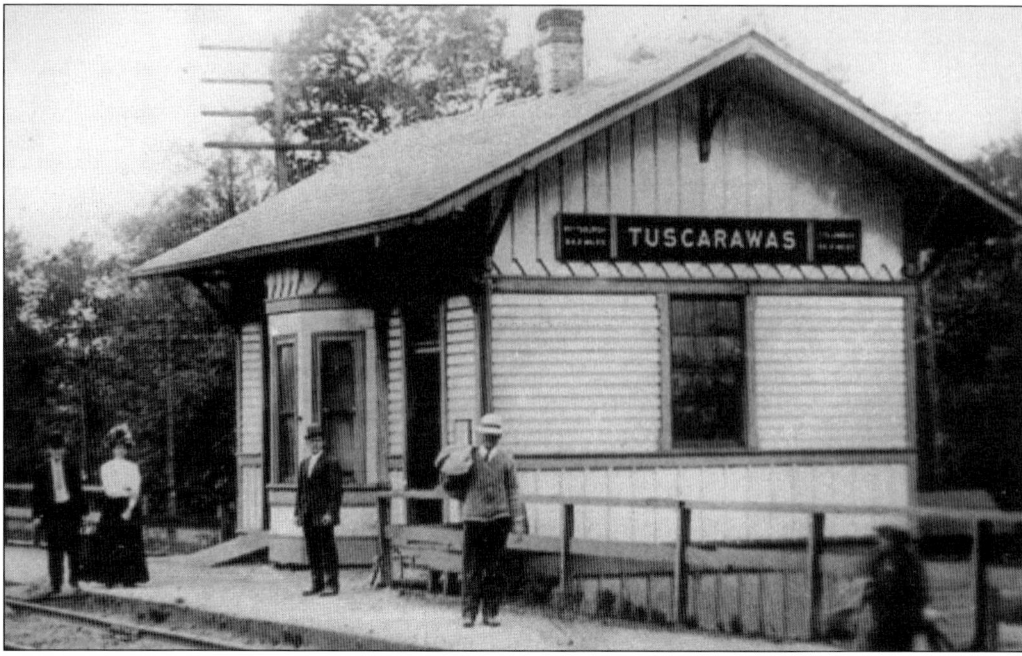

The PCC&StL and B&O shared a passenger depot in Uhrichsville (see page 14). At the next station, Tuscarawas, the PCC&StL built a standard-plan combination depot designed for a smaller community. Note the scalloped eave boards, narrow horizontal siding, and board-and-batten wainscot. This depot was closed by the mid-1900s. (Tuscarawas County Historical Society collection.)

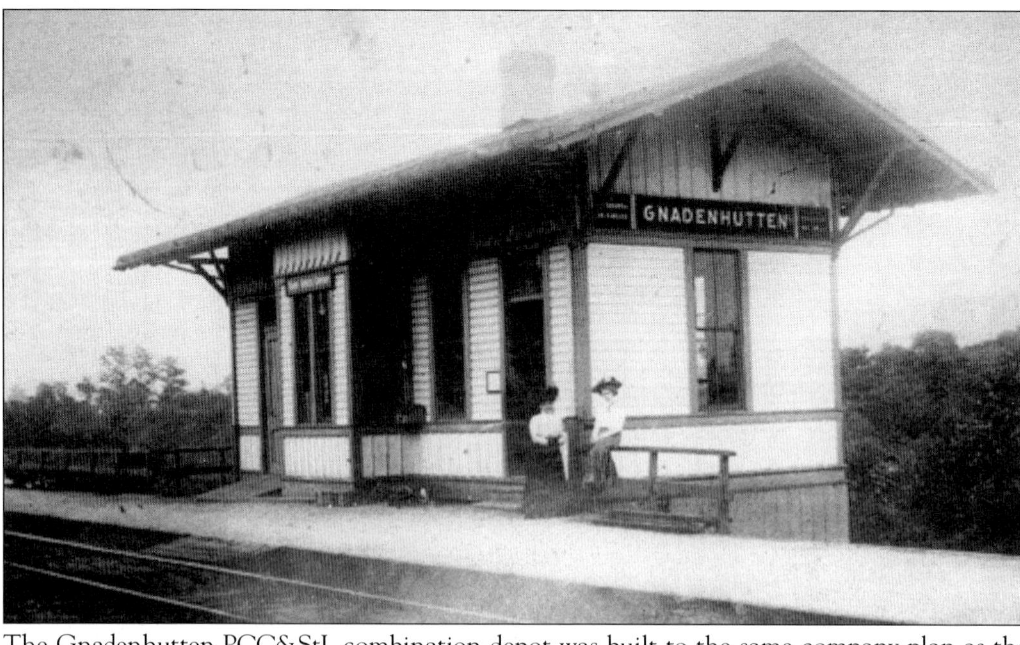

The Gnadenhutten PCC&StL combination depot was built to the same company plan as the one in neighboring Tuscarawas. The big difference is that Gnadenhutten has a squared vestibule, while Tuscarawas has a rounded one. Also, the waiting room in the Gnadenhutten depot is slightly larger. (Tuscarawas County Historical Society collection.)

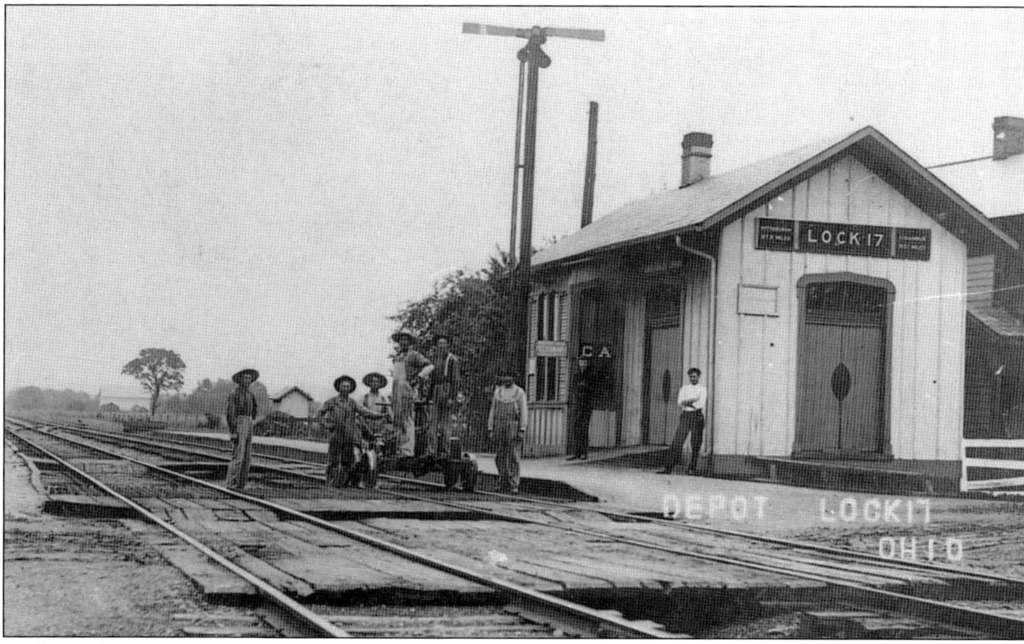

A short distance west of Gnadenhutten is this combination depot at Lock 17, a town obviously associated with the nearby Ohio & Erie Canal. This day, a section crew takes a break from track work to add interest to the postcard photographer's view of the depot. The depot appears to be of an earlier design. The town was here long before the rails came. (Author's collection.)

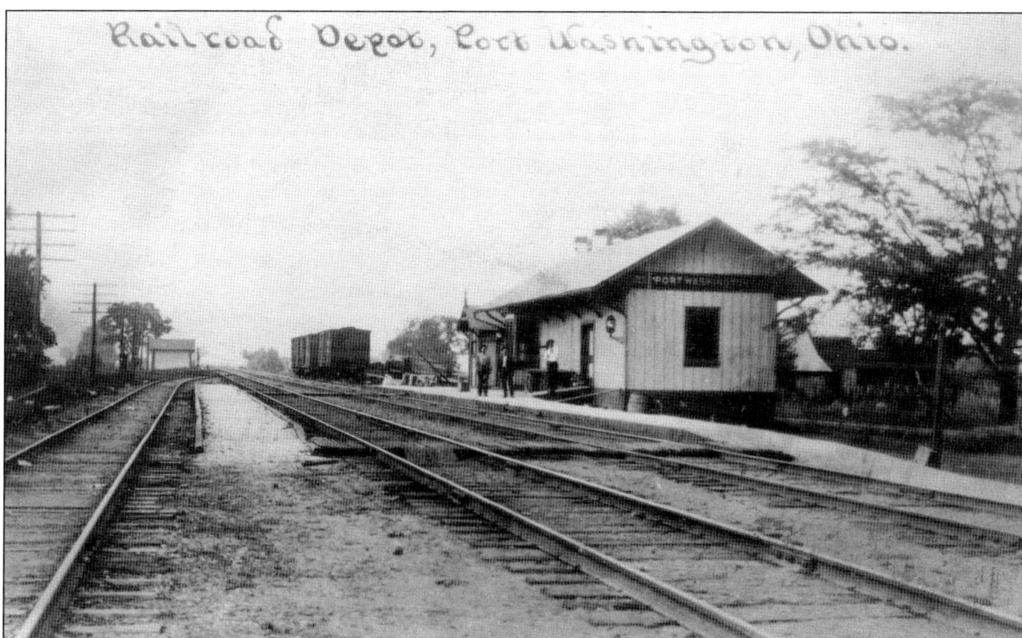

The combination depot in Port Washington was probably also built before PCC&StL days. Look closely for the similarities to the Lock 17 depot. (Author's collection.)

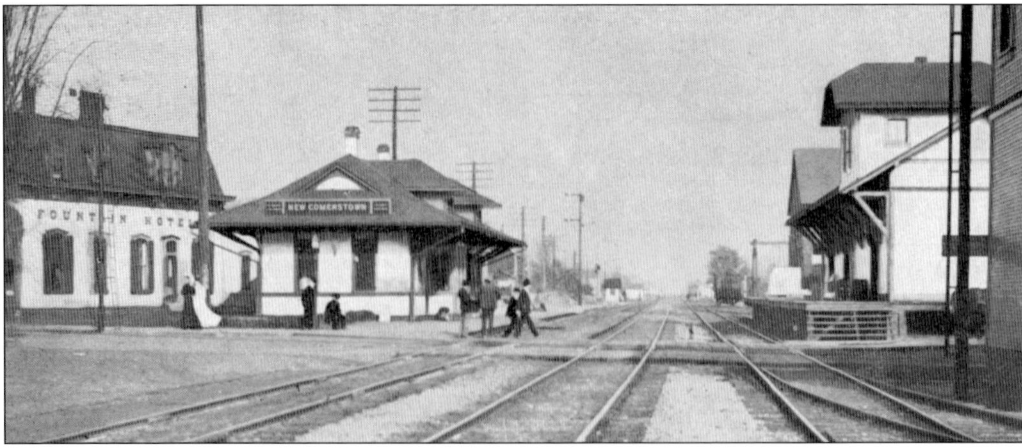

The Cleveland & Marietta crossed the former Steubenville & Indiana (S&I) at Newcomerstown. The above view shows the new PCC&StL passenger and freight depots built around 1900. The C&M diamond is in the foreground, along with the edge of the signal tower to the right or north and the Fountain Hotel to the south. Before the lines came under PRR control and a joint depot was built, the C&M had a freight house with platforms extending along both railroads. The C&M passenger depot was just south of the freight station. The original S&I or PC&StL depot was built to a combination style and apparently was torn down when the PCC&StL built the new depots. The view below, taken in 1973, shows the only survivor to that point in time—the 1900 PCC&StL passenger depot. (Above, author's collection; below, author photograph.)

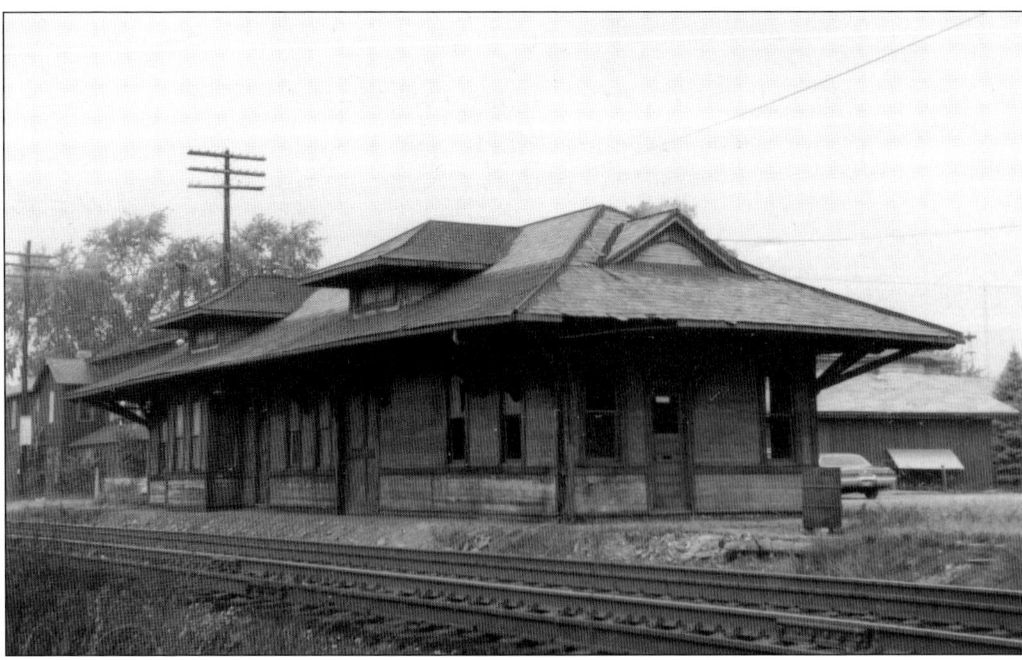

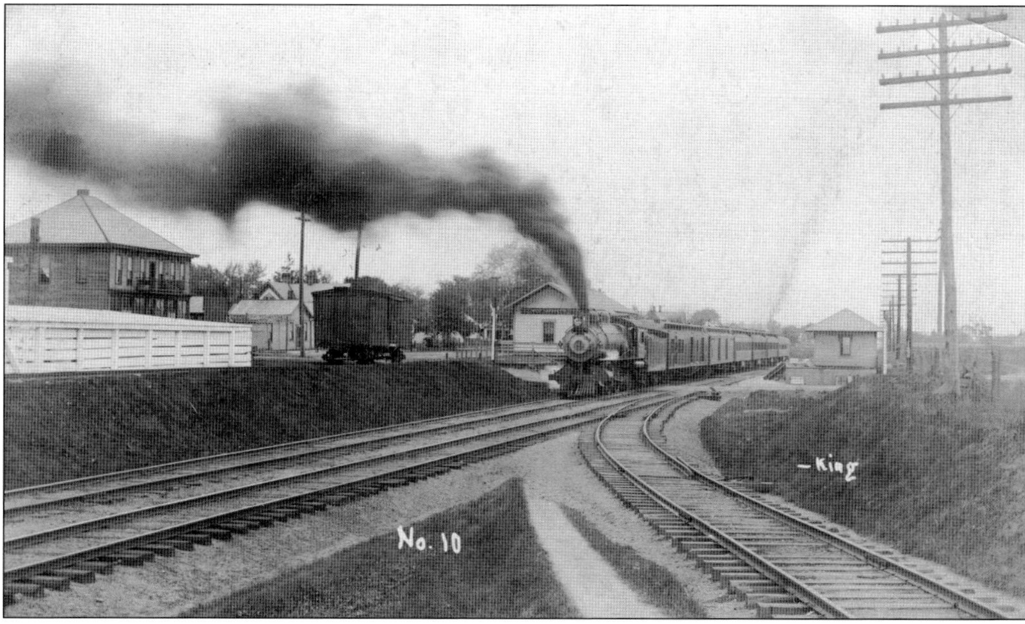

The next station west was Isleta, and then came West Lafayette, which was served by this frame passenger depot and small freight house. The two-story building to the left is the local hotel, catering especially to visitors and traveling salesmen. (Author's collection.)

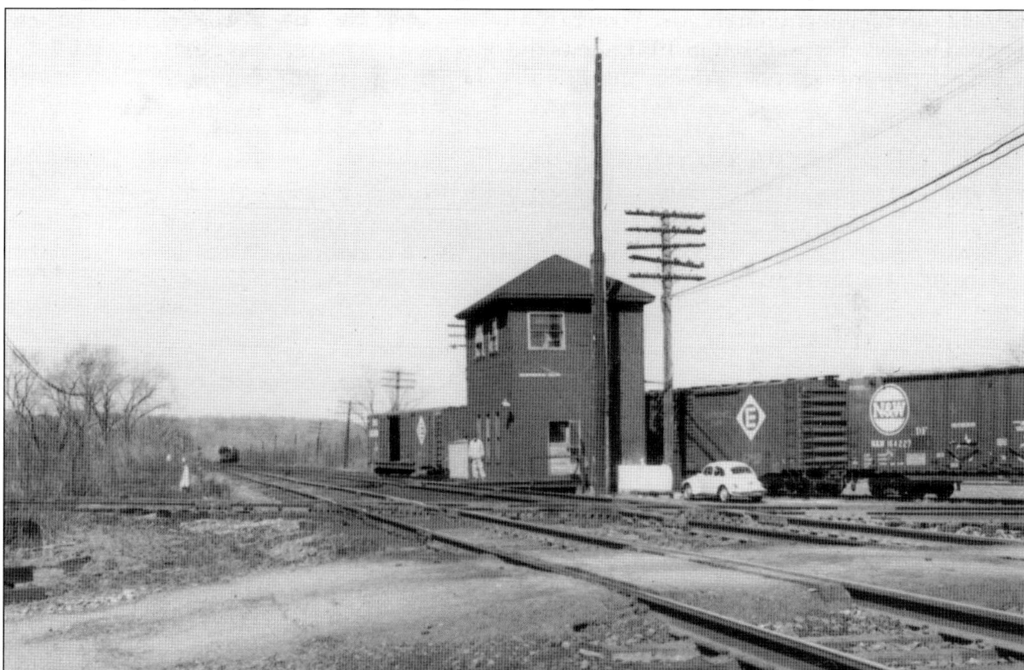

The Wheeling & Lake Erie's Zanesville branch crossed the PCC&StL at Morgan Run. All that was left at Morgan Run in 1967 was the PRR's Morgan Run interlocking tower at the east end of the PRR yards, which extended west to Coshocton. The PRR sided most of its frame towers in the mid-1900s with Insulbrick. Morgan Run was the site of a number of coal mines served by the W&LE. (Charles Garvin photograph.)

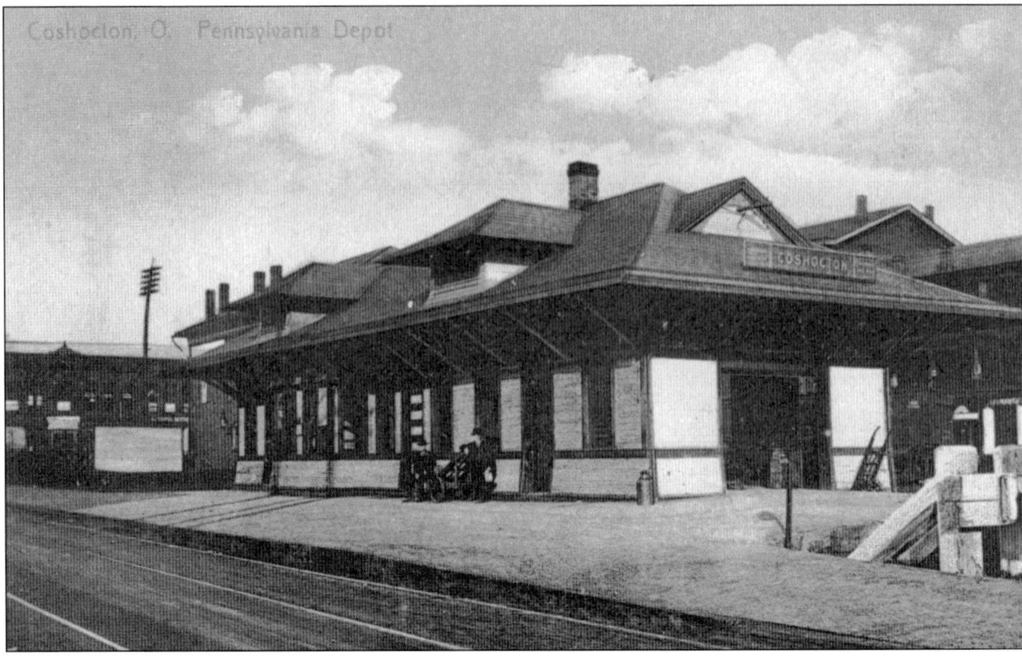

The first regular passenger train of the Steubenville & Indiana Railroad chugged into Coshocton in April 1855. The PC&StL Railway, successor to the S&I, built a frame depot with a square, turreted central tower in downtown Coshocton in 1871. The Connotton Valley Railroad (later W&LE) also used this depot beginning in 1883. The PCC&StL replaced this depot with the frame passenger depot pictured above in 1901. As before, the Connotton Valley ran passenger trains into this new depot until successor W&LE discontinued the arrangement in 1890. At the same time, the new Toledo, Walhonding Valley & Ohio Railroad began running its trains into the depot. The Panhandle depot burned down January 28, 1928, due to a faulty furnace and was replaced by the brick PRR passenger depot, below. The newest depot opened April 1, 1930, and continued to serve passengers until 1971. It now contains offices of the Ohio Central, which also uses the nearby PCC&StL freight house. (Above, author's collection; below, Charles Garvin photograph.)

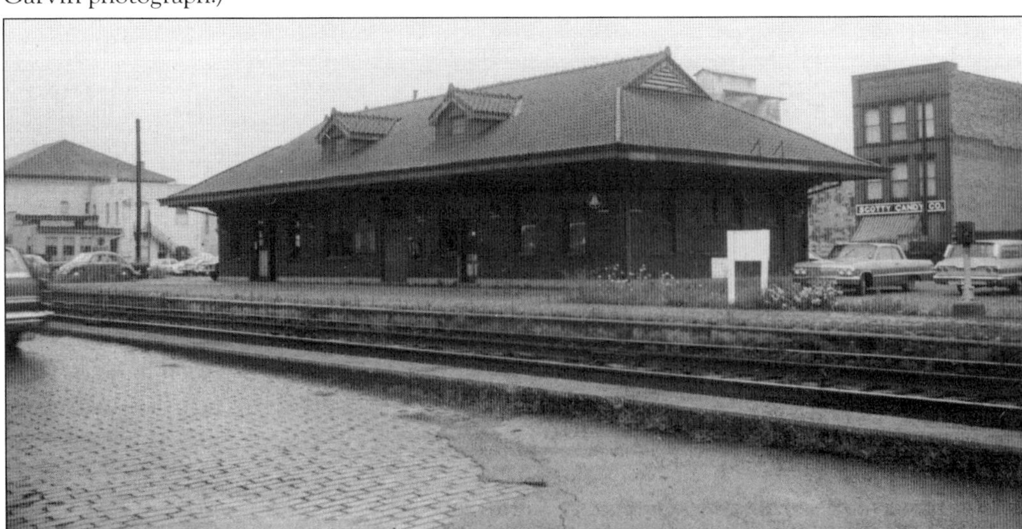

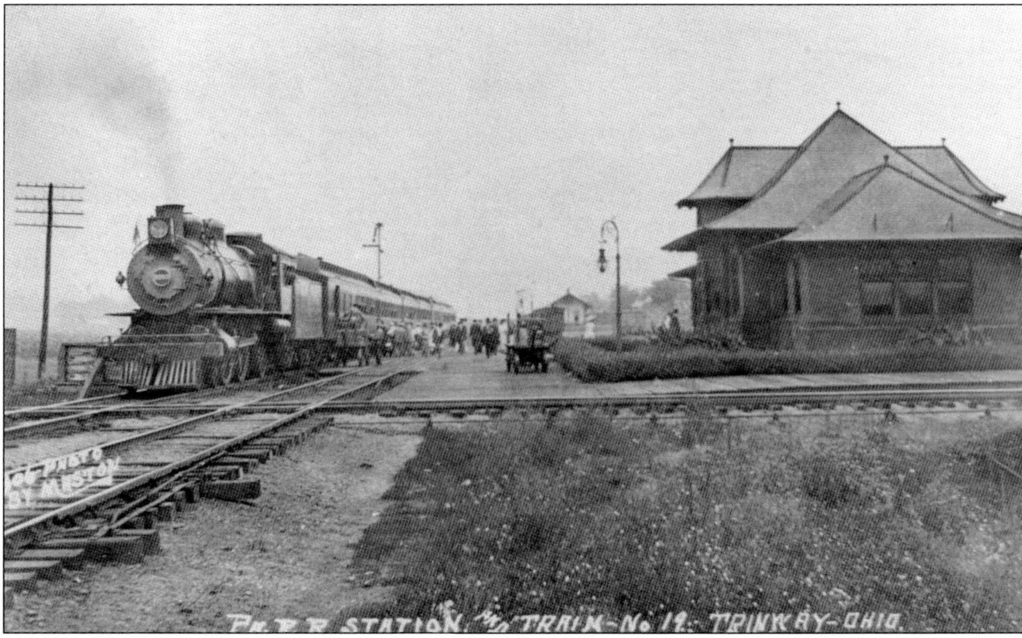

The PCC&StL passes through Rock Run, Franklin, Conesville, and Adams Mills on its way to Trinway, where it crosses the Cincinnati & Muskingum Valley and Cleveland, Akron & Columbus railroads. The first depot to serve this junction, originally called Dresden Junction, became a freight house around 1870 when the PCC&StL erected a frame combination depot-tower. This disappeared before this 1905 brick passenger depot was built by the PCC&StL. A PRR interlocking tower was at the northwest corner of the diamond with the CA&C, and a freight house (a former combination depot) was to the east. In 2017, all are gone. (Both, author's collection.)

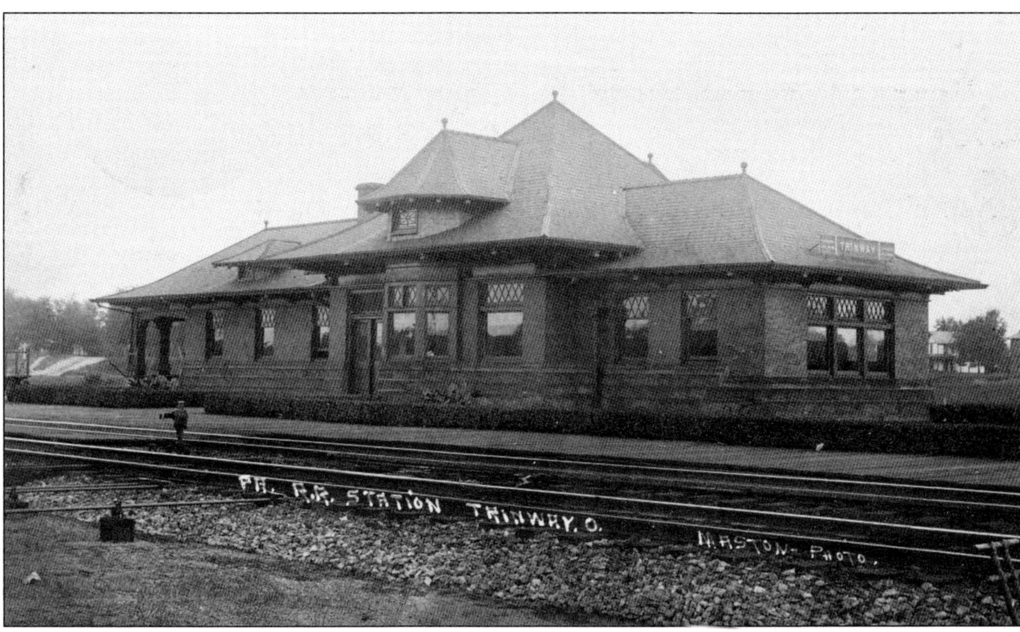

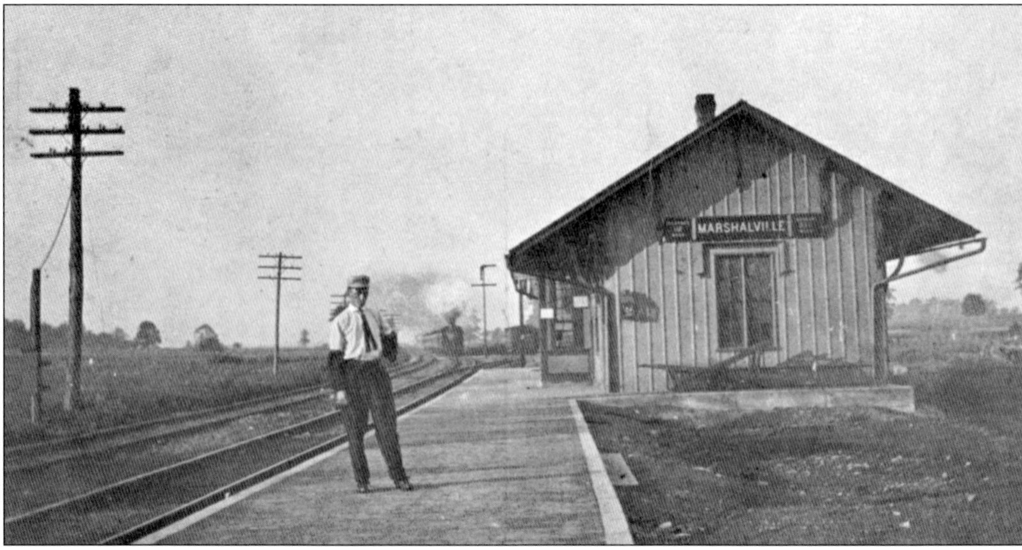

The Cleveland, Akron & Columbus, after the usual reorganizations, eventually opened from Hudson to Trinway in 1888. The portion north of Millersburg was completed much earlier, in 1853. Above, the agent at the CA&C depot in Marshallville, between Clinton and Orrville awaits the arrival of the passenger train. This is a second-generation depot probably dating to the 1880s. Compare it to depots south of Millersburg that were built in the late 1880s. (Author's collection.)

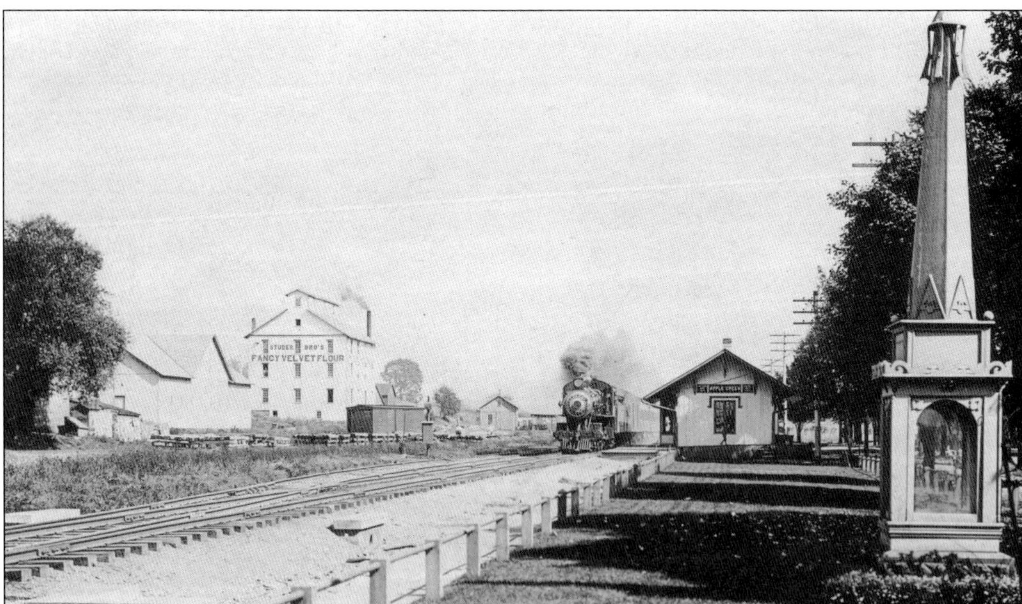

The CA&C used the joint PRR depot in Orrville and proceeded south to Apple Creek, where branches headed east to the coalfields around Sonnenberg (later Kidron) and West Lebanon. These lines were initially associated with the Ashland & Wooster Railroad. The Apple Creek passenger depot had a well-tended park surrounding it. A freight house is visible down the track. As was the practice of the PRR in the 1950s, many depots and towers, including Apple Creek, were significantly simplified and covered with Insulbrick. (Author's collection.)

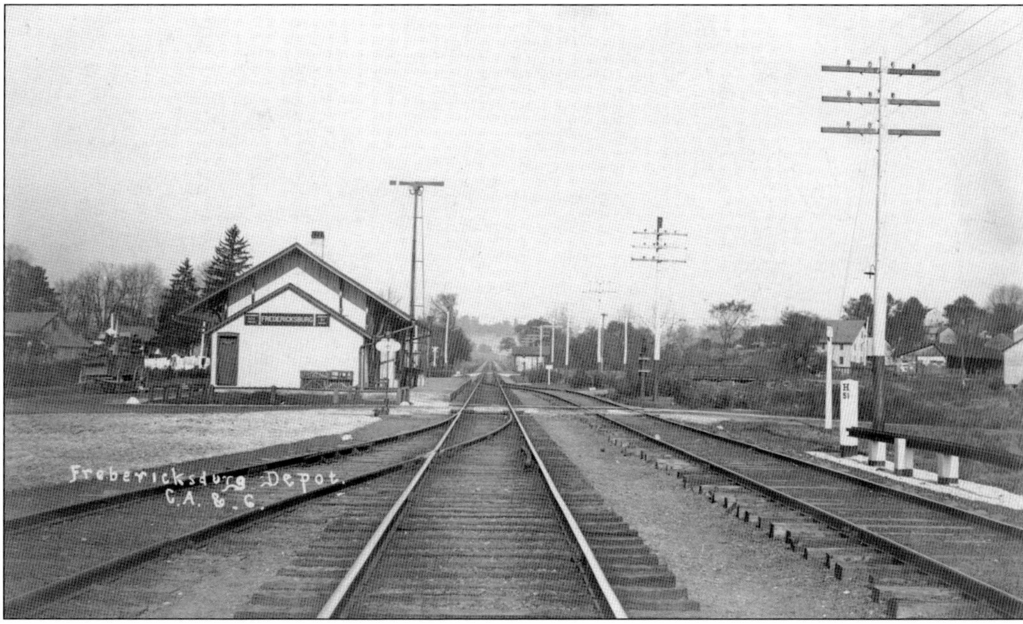

Fredericksburg's CA&C depot is of a similar design. As was common at most CA&C depots, the grounds around the depot were maintained as a park in the 1890s and early 1900s. Note the flowerbed behind the depot The PRR also remodeled this depot in the mid-1900s. (Both, author's collection.)

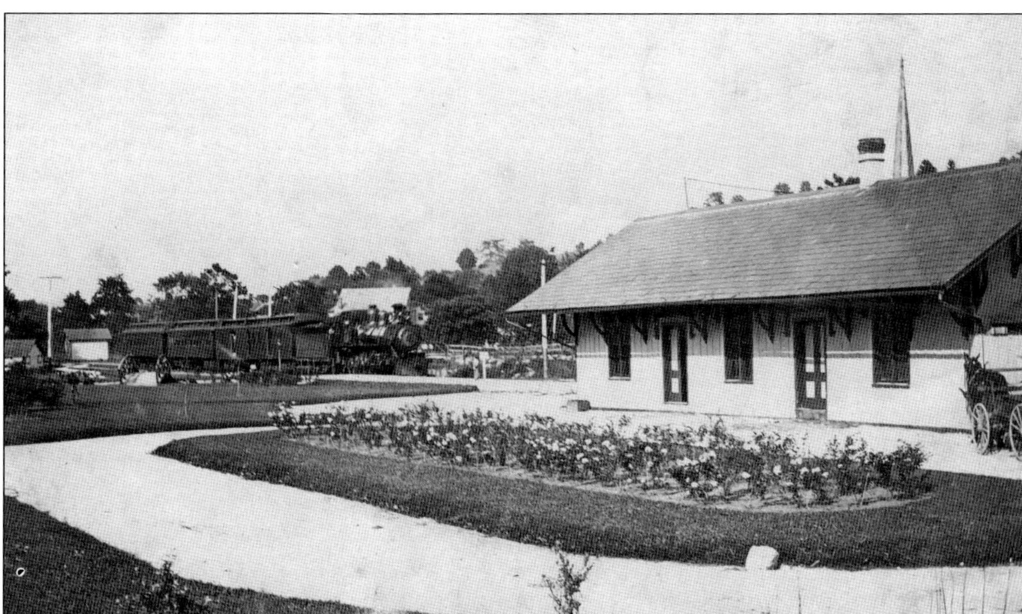

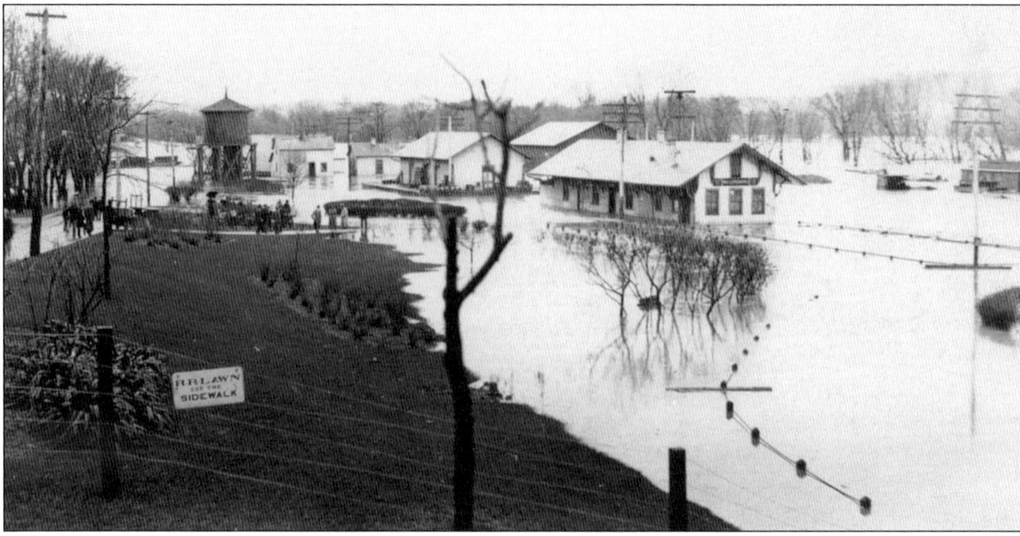

The CA&C and B&O both had frame combination depots in Holmesville. Both were gone by the 1960s. The CA&C and B&O shared this CA&C-designed passenger depot at Millersburg, built on the floodplain of Killbuck Creek. Above, both the passenger and freight depots are submerged. An Insulbrick-sided freight depot was used as the Millersburg PRR facilities beginning in the 1950s. The pictured passenger depot was reportedly relocated in April 2005 as a visitor center on the Holmes County Rail Trail. (Above, Dan West; below, author's collection.)

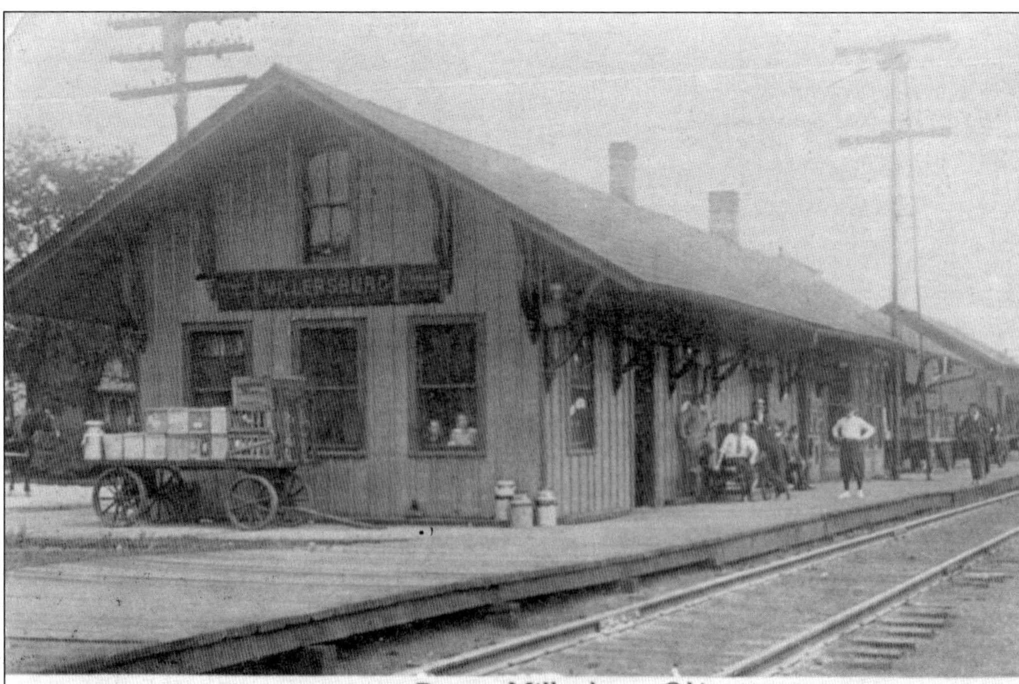

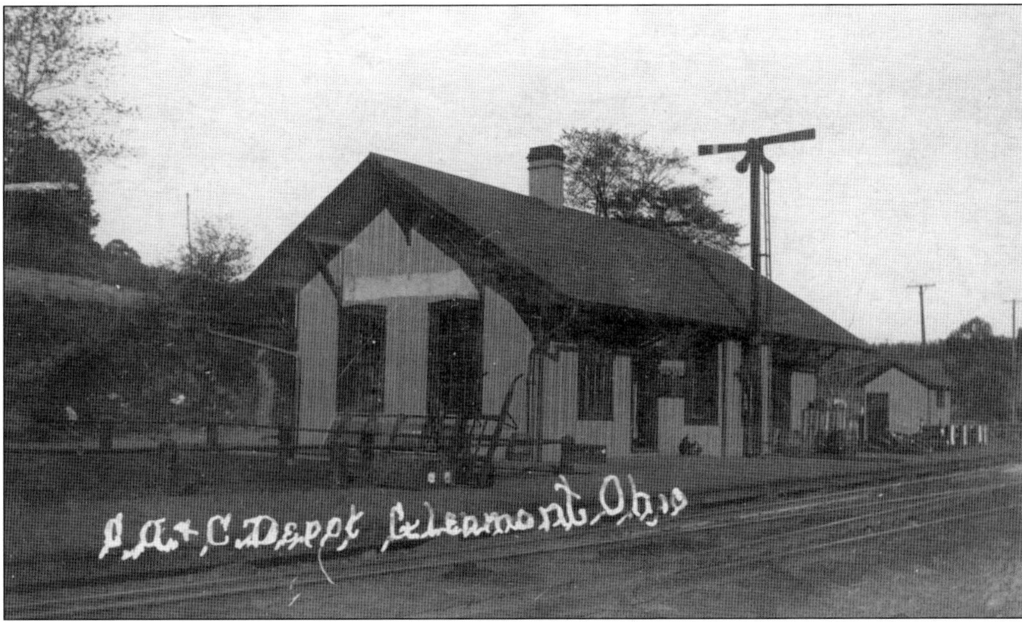

A local sandstone dimension stone quarry and brickyard brought lots of business to Glenmont's CA&C combination depot in the late 1800s and early 1900s. During this time, four passenger trains stopped each day. Railroad crews have removed the town board (notice rectangular patch of lighter color) from this end of the depot for maintenance. Look closely—it is seen resting against the building. Just out of view in the foreground was a water tank. (Author's collection.)

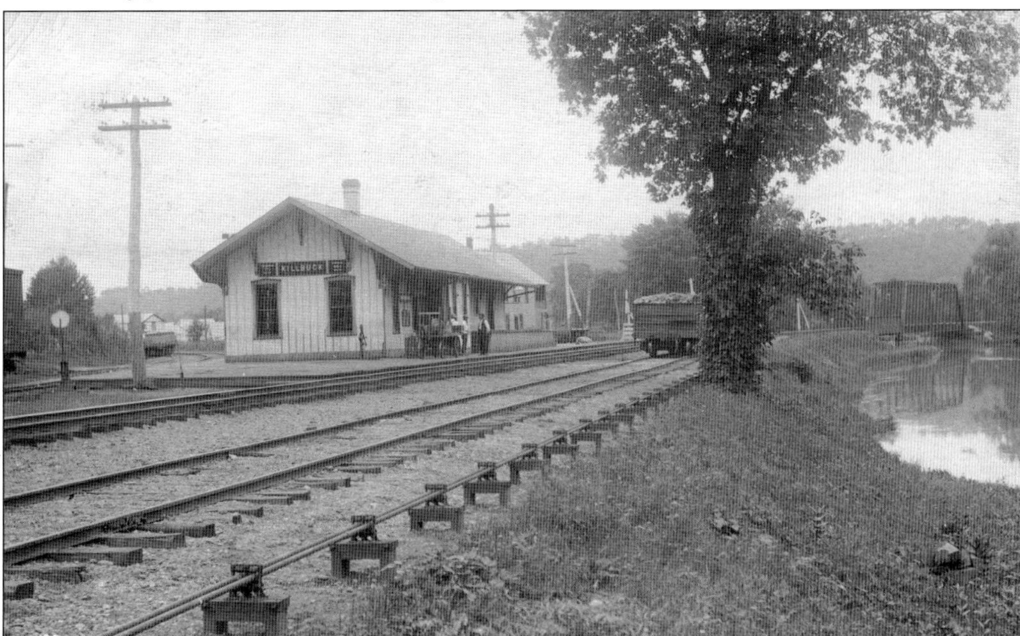

The CA&C lies on the floodplain of Killbuck Creek in the village of Killbuck leading to periodic flooding issues. Killbuck's combination depot was built to a standard plan often repeated along the line. The piping on the lower right is part of the interlocking controlled by the PRR tower, located where the CA&C and Dresden branch of the CA&C meet. (Author's collection.)

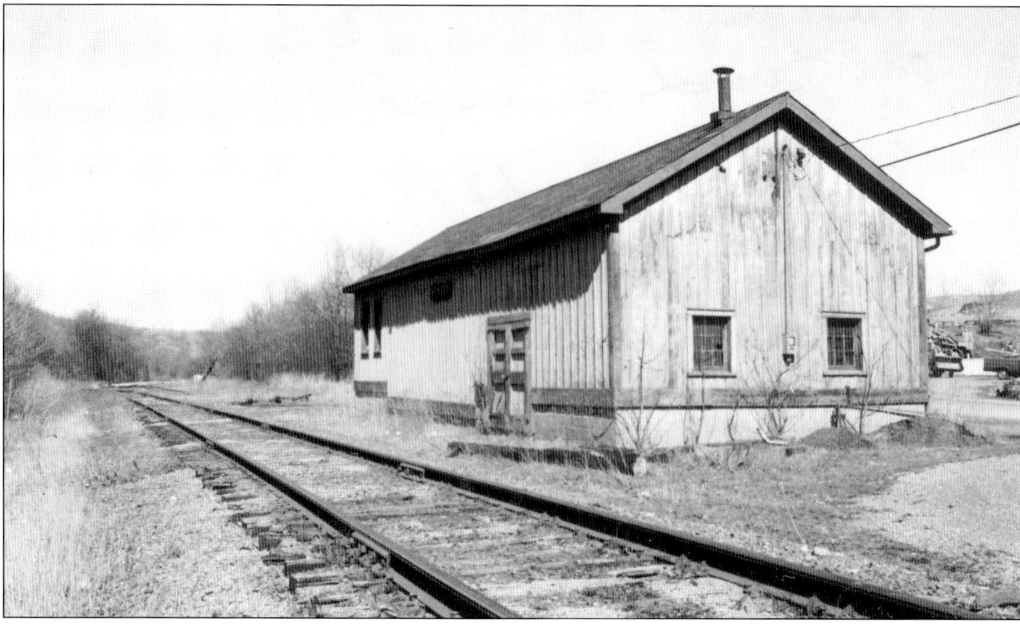

In the late 1960s, Killbuck's depot remained trackside on the north side of town, but stripped of many of its architectural embellishments. After passenger service ended, it was relegated to freight use. The depot remains in 2017, but both the main line and Dresden branch tracks are long gone. This view looks north. (Charles Garvin photograph.)

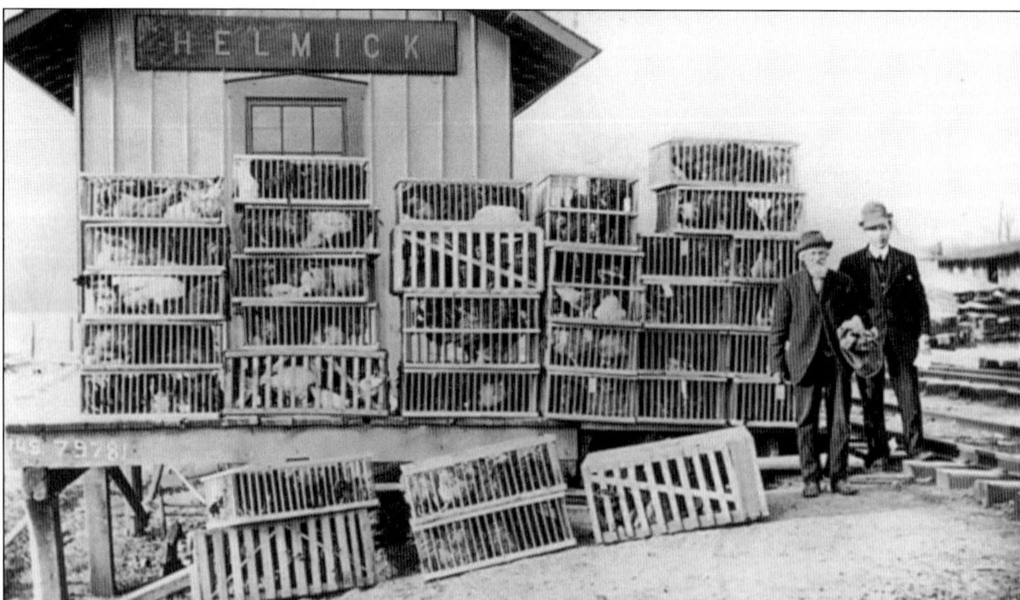

This view of the CA&C depot platform at Helmick on the Dresden branch shows an earlier-style town board before the PRR replaced all with the type giving mileage to the terminals of each line. This is probably the same type of town board that is being replaced in the Glenmont photograph. Farm products were the main source of freight income at Helmick. A load of poultry await shipment. (Walhonding Valley Historical Society collection.)

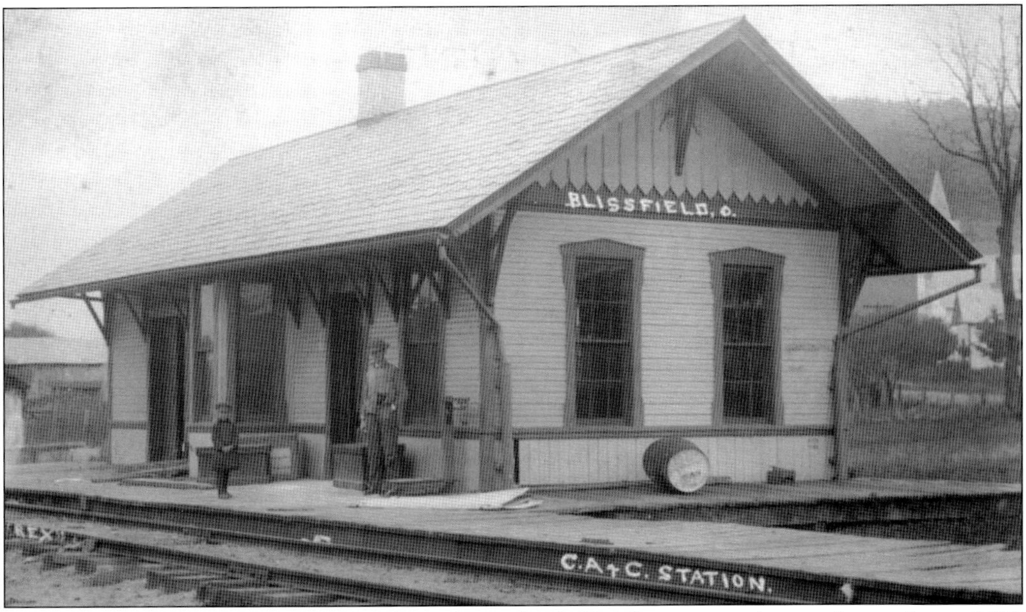

Farther south on CA&C's Dresden branch is Blissfield. This postcard view shows the c. 1888 combination depot before a town board has been attached. The Rex Studio of Warsaw, a local postcard company, has inked "Blissfield" on the original glass plate. The CA&C continued south, crossing the Toledo, Walhonding Valley & Ohio Railroad at Warsaw Junction. South of Warsaw, a resistant rocky ridge necessitated a 1,492-foot tunnel. Work started in 1873 but was not completed until 1887, with the construction of a depot at Tunnel Hill (moved but still there in 1971). (Walhonding Valley Historical Society collection.)

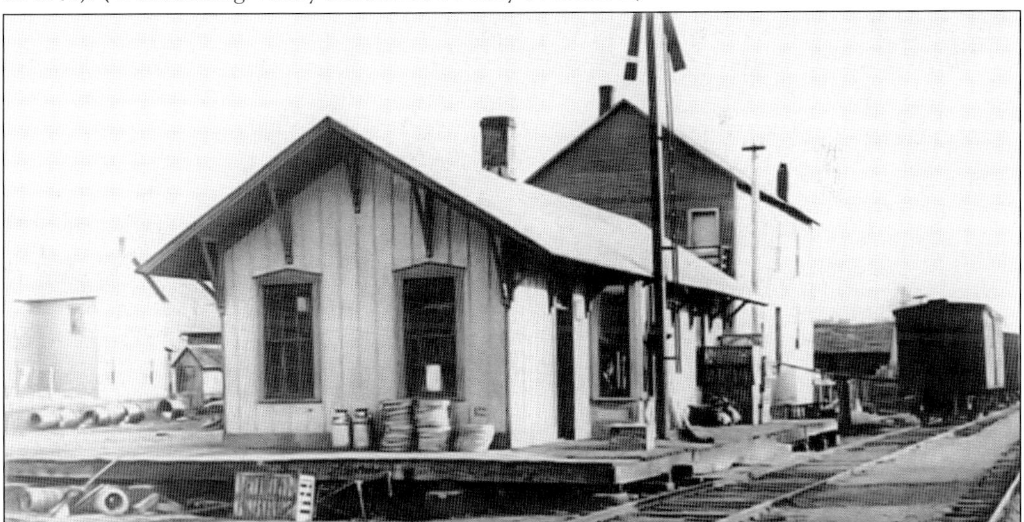

Next stop on the CA&C was Cooperdale. This Coshocton County community was founded in 1888 when the Dresden branch of the CA&C was completed. This view of the new CA&C combination depot shows a cluttered depot platform. Town boards have not yet been added to the structure. Rail service ended in 1935 when Killbuck Creek floodwaters washed out the line in several places and the PRR decided to abandon this line. The Cooperdale depot was relocated nearby, modified, and continues in private use. (Walhonding Valley Historical Society collection.)

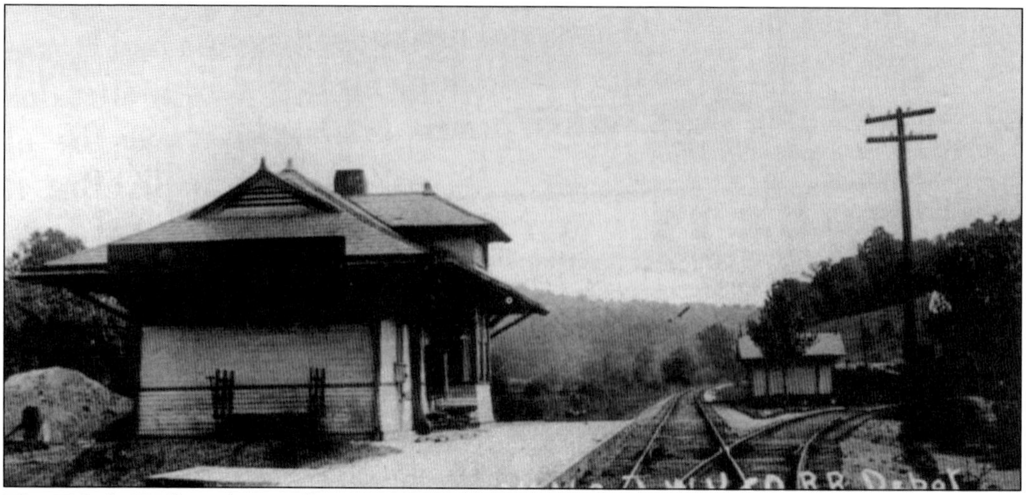

The Toledo Walhonding Valley & Ohio Railroad was opened from Loudonville to Coshocton in March 1893 and soon began running passenger trains in between its coal-laden freights. Copycat combination depots were constructed at each of the main stations along the line. This depot served Loudonville and was ready for use in late November 1892. It appeared as South Loudonville on timetables to distinguish it from the main line PRR stop in downtown Loudonville. It was located just south of the TWV&O-PRR junction in West Loudonville. Hacks regularly shuttled passengers from here to the downtown depot. (Dan West.)

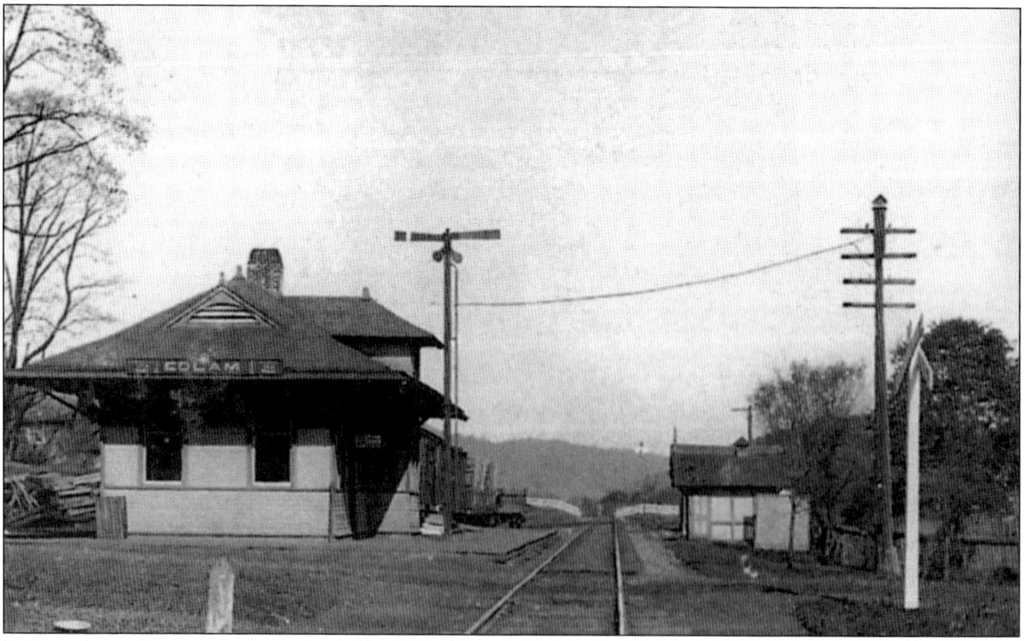

Edlam (now known as Greer) was hit hard by the 1913 flood—track was twisted, ballast washed away, and bridges torn from abutments—but the TWV&O depot survived until the line was abandoned in 1936. (Author's collection.)

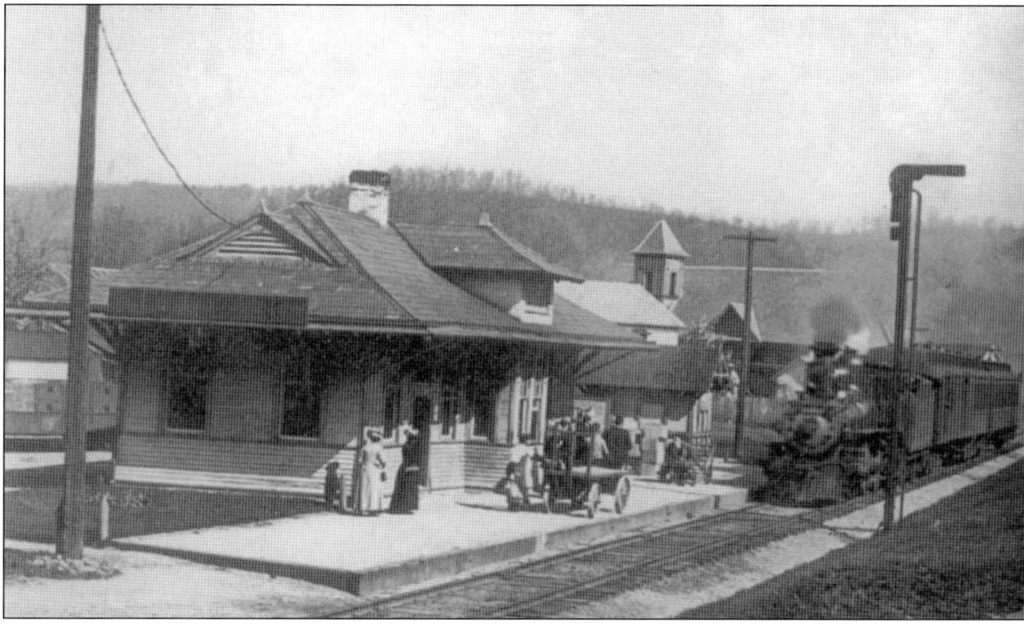

The TWV&O passes across the CA&C in Brinkhaven on a long, high timber trestle. The TWV&O depot, completed in October 1892, was located on the north edge of this trestle. Above, the Wally Flyer pulls into the depot around 1910. It was closed in 1935 when the line was abandoned because of dam construction. (Author's collection.)

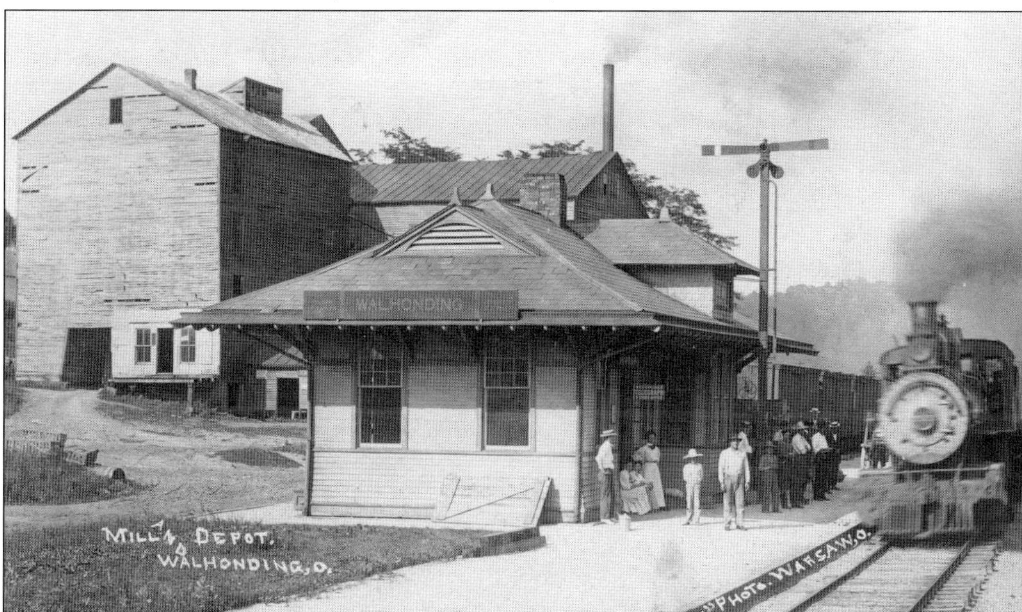

The McVey Mill towers above the TWV&O depot in Walhonding. The depot was completed by October 1892. Walhonding owes its beginning to the Walhonding Canal, a branch of the Ohio & Erie Canal opened in 1842. The Wally Flyer, as it was affectionately known, arrives to a large crowd posing for the photographer. The McVey Mill burned to the ground in a spectacular blaze in 1925. The construction of the Mohawk Dam in the 1930s led to the relocation of many buildings in town and the abandonment of this line by the PRR. (Author's collection.)

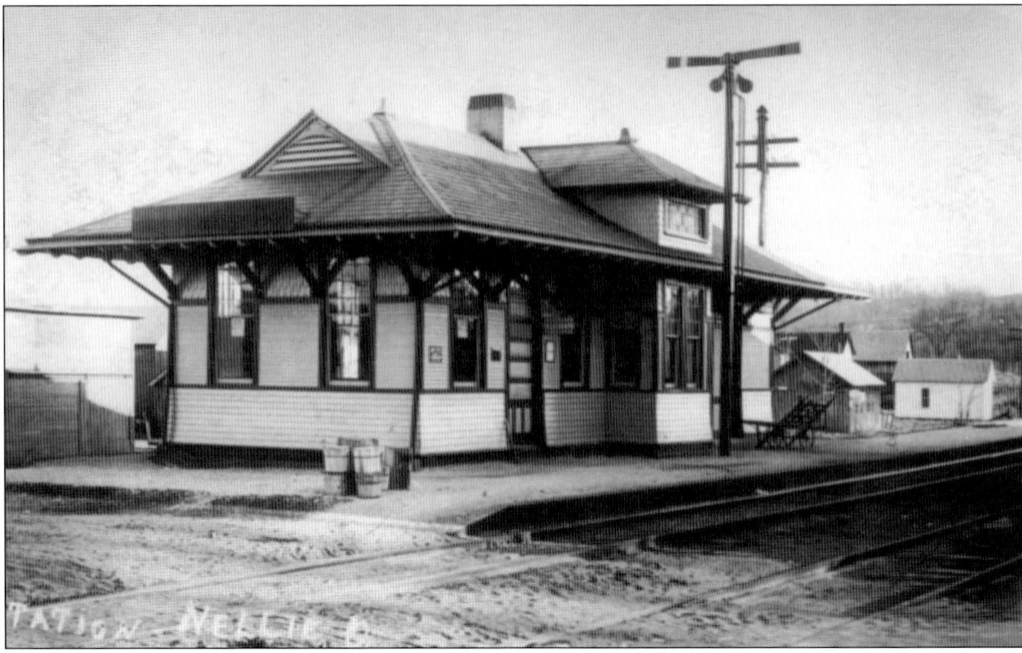

The next stop east on the TWV&O was at Nellie, the station for nearby Mohawk village. This is another example of the pleasing yet efficient plan for TWV&O depots. (Walhonding Valley Historical Society collection.)

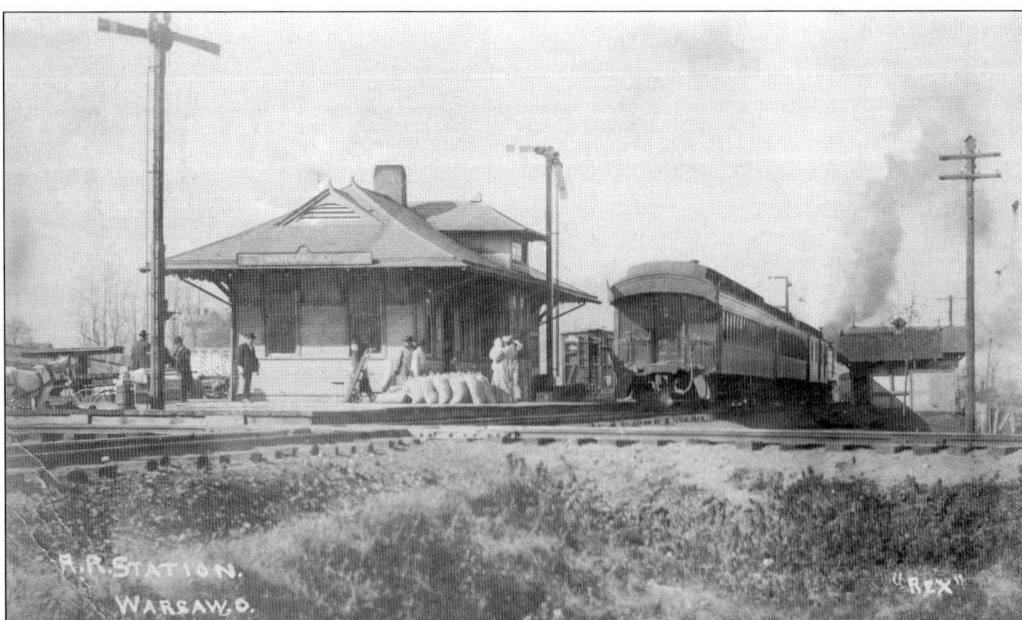

The TWV&O crossed the CA&C at Warsaw Junction and proceeded east into Coshocton. The depot was completed by October 1892. The junction was a busy place around the turn of the 20th century. (Author's collection.)

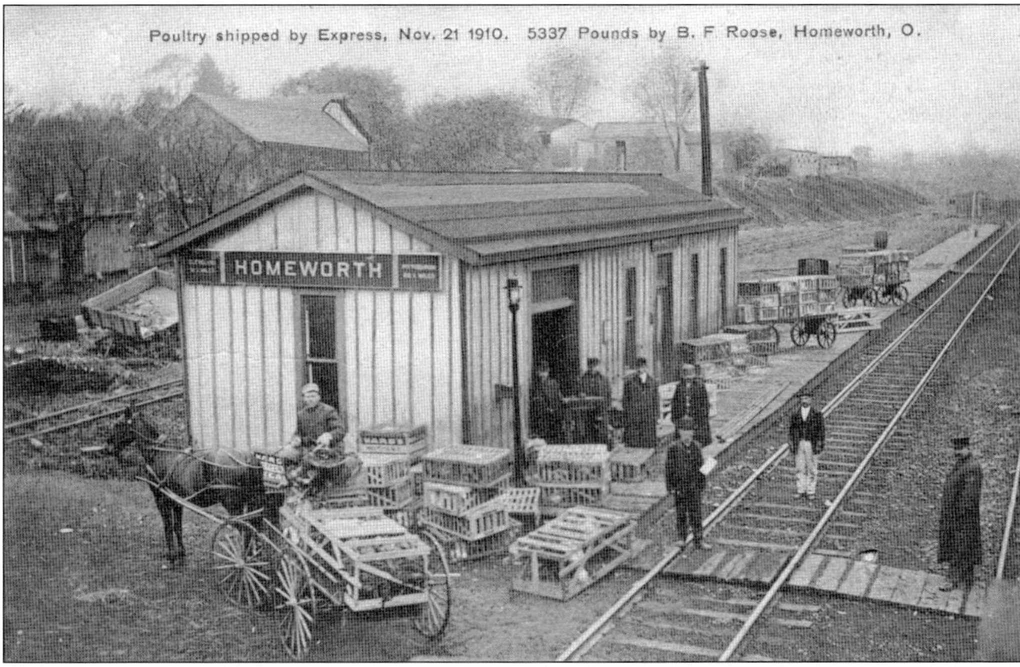

The Cleveland & Pittsburgh Railway opened through Homeworth in 1852. The above freight house was probably an earlier combination depot reconfigured to freight use when the brick passenger depot below was built. The prevalence of brick plants in this area led to the construction of a brick depot rather than the more common and less expensive frame depot. This was certainly an impressive structure for the size of the town. In 2017, both have been gone for many years. (Above, author's collection; below, Dan West.)

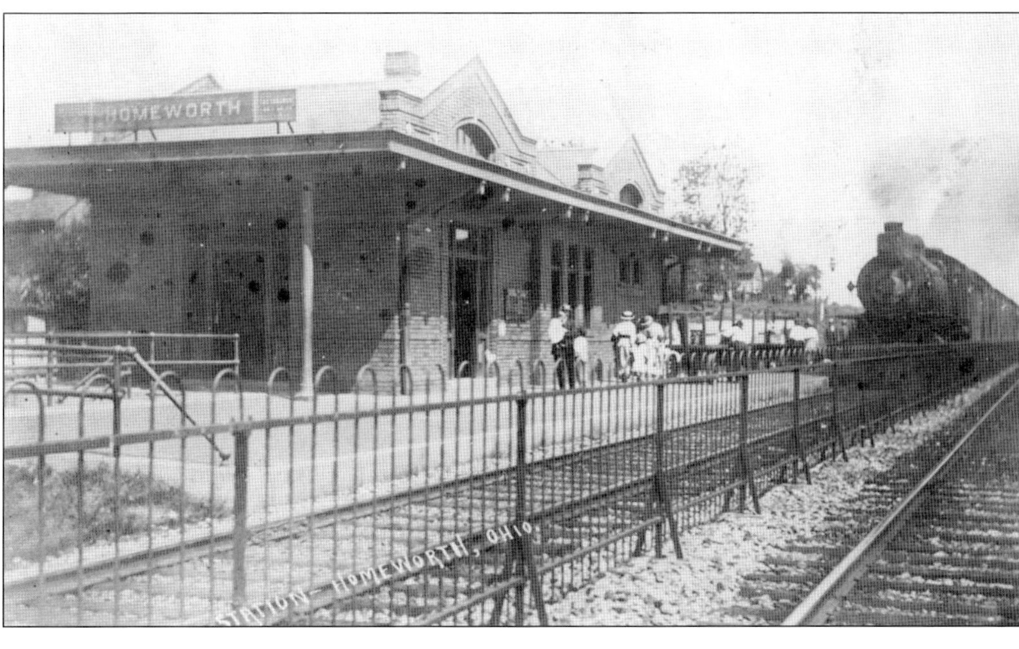

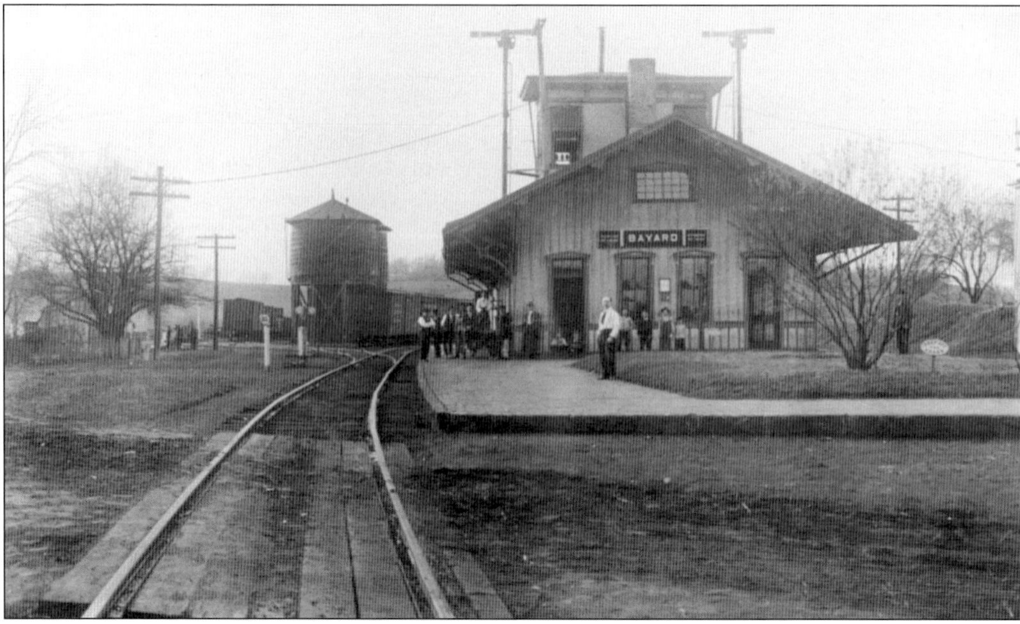

The C&P main line headed southeast at Bayard toward the Ohio Valley, while a branch veered southwest to Minerva. C&P depots tended to be wider, with lower pitched roofs, extended overhangs, and multipaned windows in the eaves. Many initially had second-floor towers above the vestibule. Compare the Bayard structure with the depot at Salineville. These second-floor windows provided an unobstructed view up and down the right-of-way and were commonly present at junctions and both ends of double-track sections. They were removed in later years when separate interlocking towers became favored. A smaller depot served Bayard in the 1970s. (Dan West.)

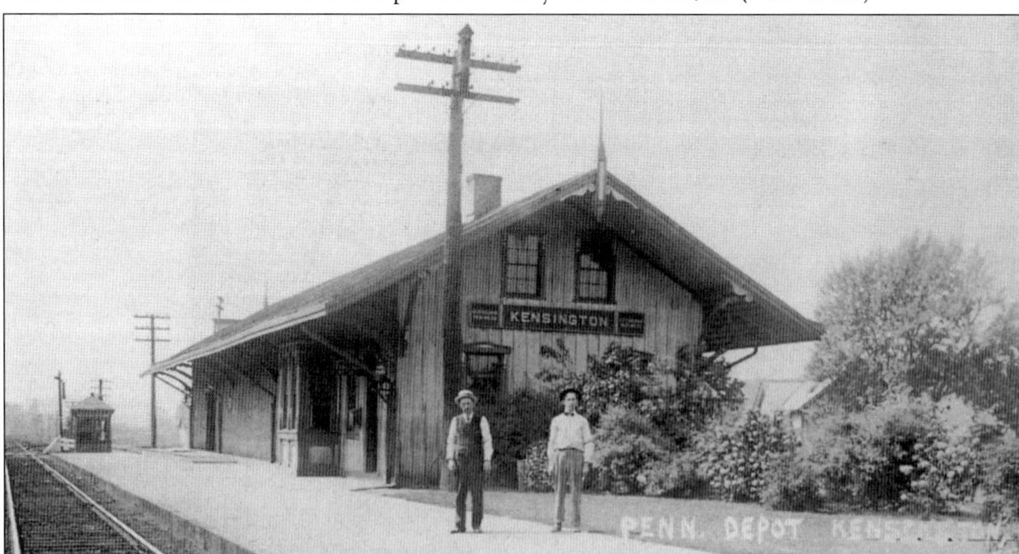

After trains stopped at the frame depot in New Rochester, the next stop was this combination depot in Kensington. Except for the absence of a tower, the building possesses the typical architectural elements of the C&P engineering office. As the C&P headed deeper into coal and clay country, the line passed through Millport and Summitville, both of which had frame combination depots. No trace of these buildings remains in 2017. (Bob Chilcote collection.)

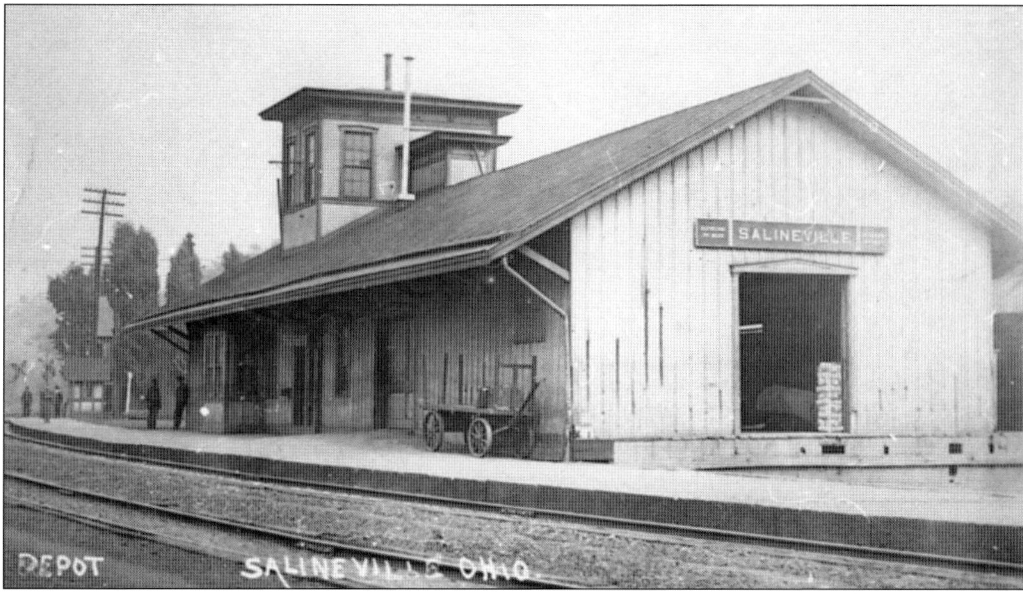

Salt was a much-needed substance in the early 1800s and when water wells drilled in this valley struck brine, a community was established that logically became Salineville. The town also had early coal mines, which by 1852 provided coal for fueling C&P locomotives, some of the first coal to be used in place of wood. By the 1880s, brick manufacturing had become common. A number of short spurs led to nearby coal and clay mines. The C&P combination depot sat at Main and Elm Streets. Compare this combination tower-depot with Bayard. Freight handling was a big part of the daily business; thus, a larger freight room was required. Salineville was near the north end of double-track main line that extended eastward into the Ohio Valley and on to East Liverpool and Steubenville. A PRR-plan crossing watchman's shanty is at the grade crossing just beyond the depot in the view below. Loaded baggage carts and passengers await the next passenger train. (Both, author's collection.)

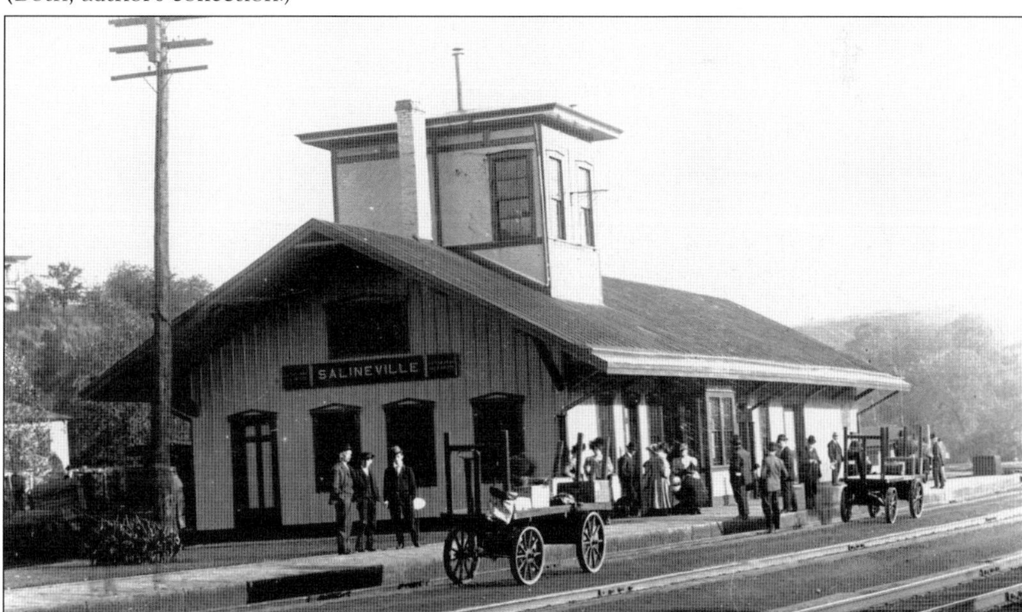

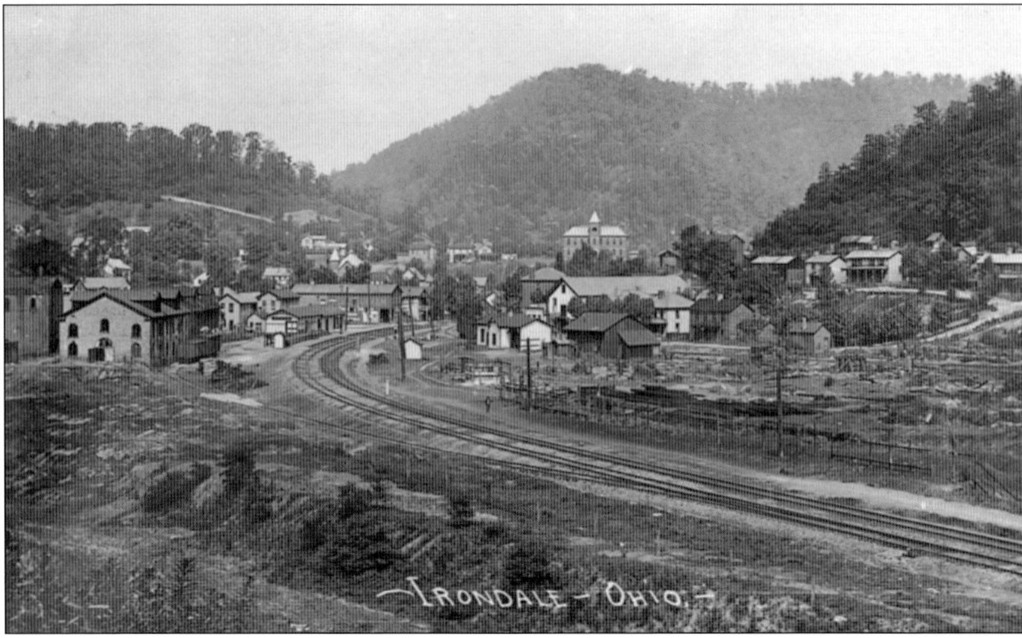

Nestled on the flatland where Salt Run joins North Fork is Irondale. Besides brine, coal, and clay, the bedrock of this area also yielded a low-grade iron ore. An early iron smelter gave the community its name. The depot was uncharacteristically located on a curve. C&P depots were also located at nearby New Salisbury and Hammondsville. (Author's collection.)

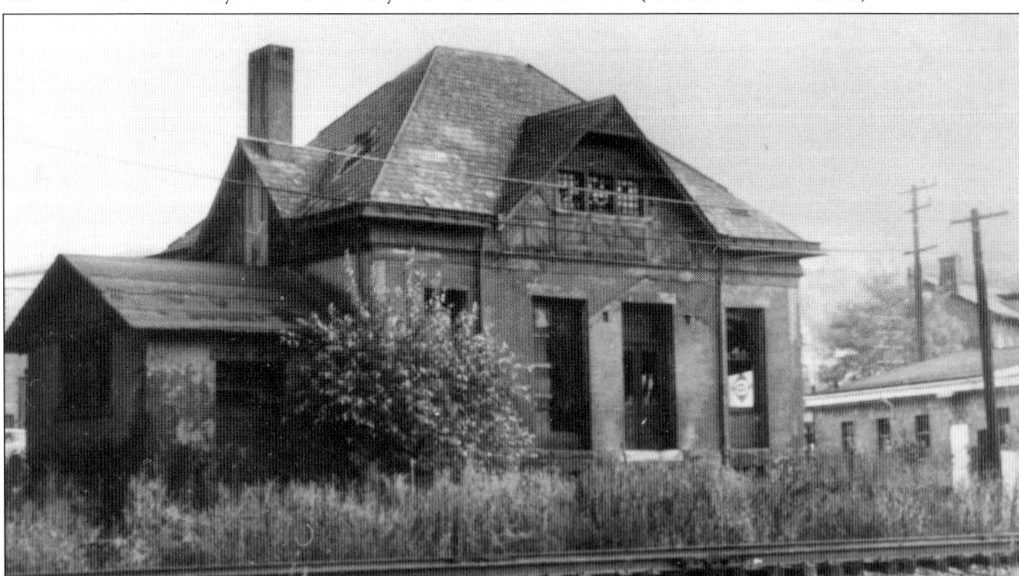

Due to river transportation and the nearby occurrence of several clay beds, East Liverpool grew rapidly and became a center of pottery manufacture. The Cleveland & Pittsburgh Railway reached town by September 1856. The Wabash Railroad, when it controlled the Wheeling & Lake Erie in 1903, contemplated building into East Liverpool, but the plan was eventually abandoned. The C&P's last passenger facility was this brick depot, shown abandoned by the 1960s. As with other river towns, periodic flooding hampered railroad activity. (Author's collection.)

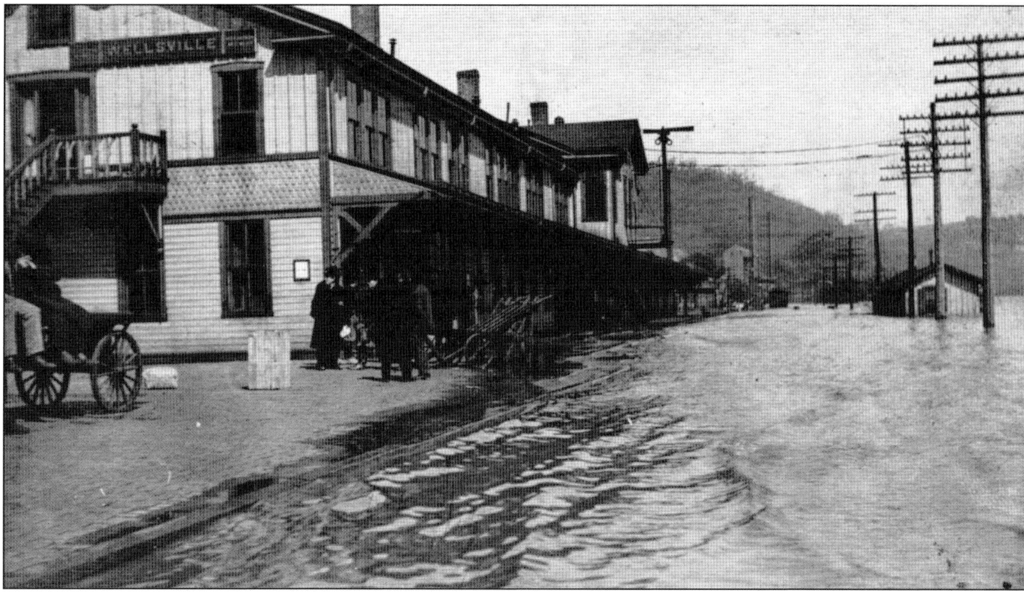

The C&P reached Wellsville in February 1852. With the arrival of the Steubenville & Indiana, the city eventually had two PRR depots. Original C&P depot grounds were located on Broadway until 1853, when they were relocated below Twelfth Street. This large two-story C&P combination depot opened in 1872 at the corner of Twelfth Street and Riverside Avenue. The second floor was used for railroad offices. Built on the Ohio River floodplain, the depot was periodically underwater. The above view shows it during the 1913 flood when the Ohio reached historic levels. In 1905, the PRR yards were extended north along the river to the Yellow Creek area. Below, the depot is seen under drier conditions. (Both, author's collection.)

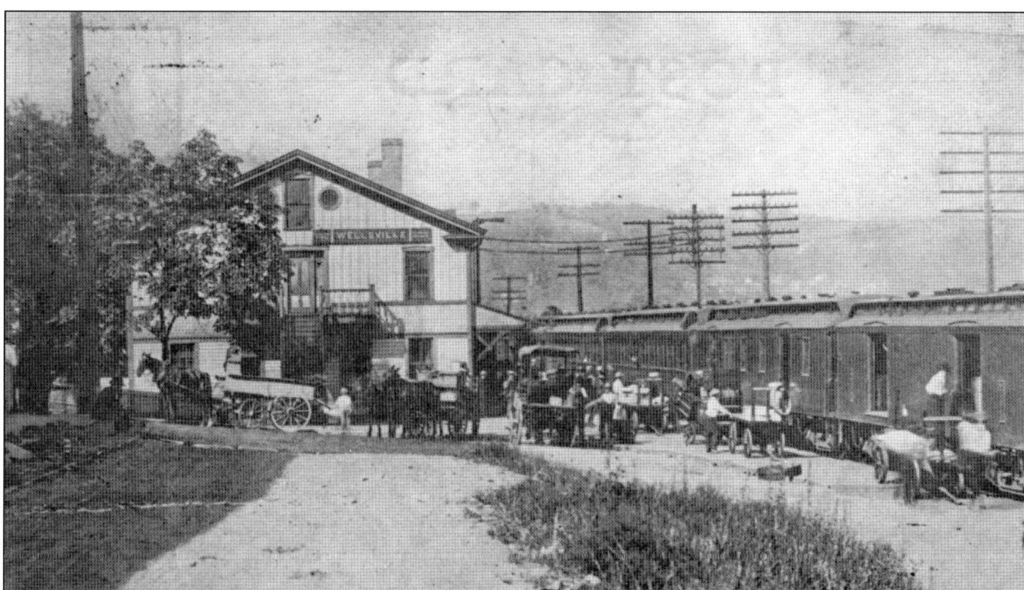

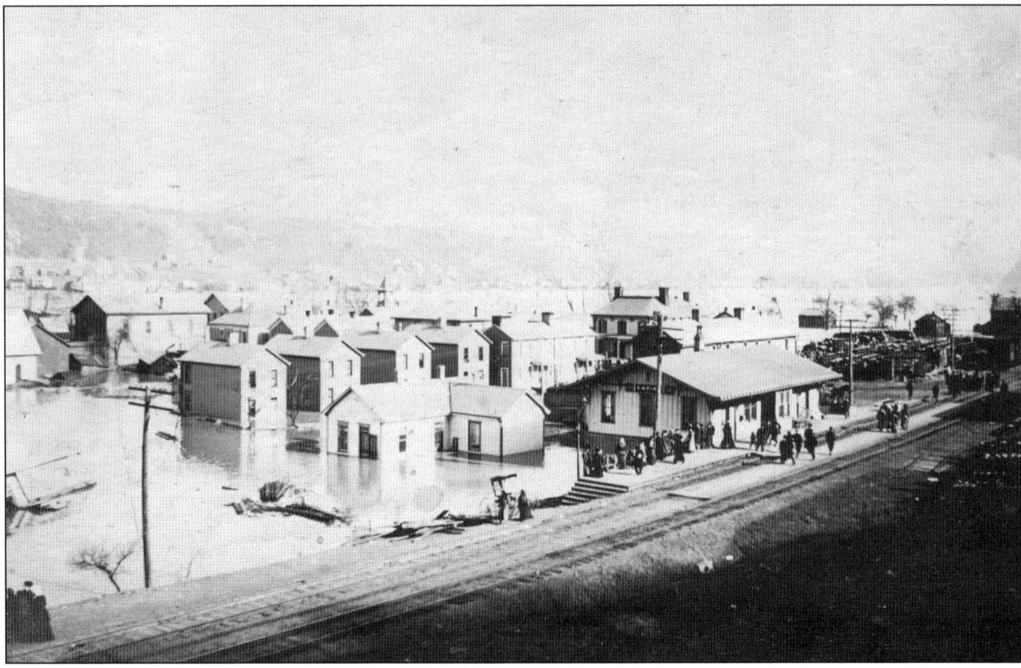

The C&P traversed the Ohio bottomlands from East Liverpool south to Bellaire, passing through numerous river towns. Here is an aerial view of Empire during the 1913 flood. Luckily, the depot was spared great damage since it had been built on a terrace slightly above the floodplain. Here, locals watch the river flow by. At nearby Toronto, a larger frame second-generation combination depot was built around 1900. The freight room of the Toronto depot was later extended due to increased business. (Author's collection.)

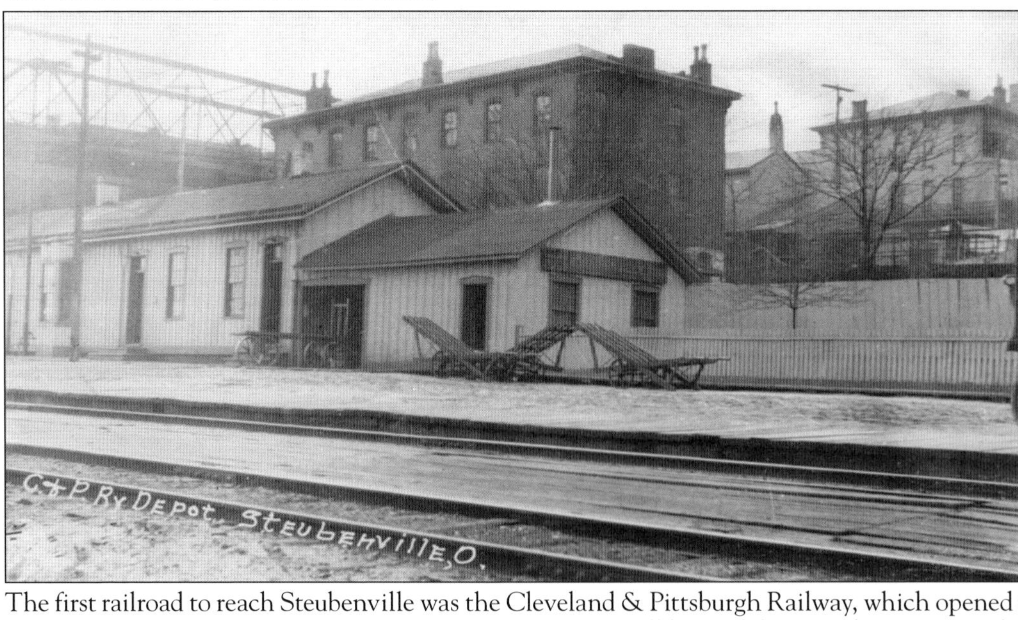

The first railroad to reach Steubenville was the Cleveland & Pittsburgh Railway, which opened a depot in a grain mill in October 1856. Unfortunately, the mill burned down within two months. Until a depot was built, passengers used an old railroad car. The second depot was built in 1857 and replaced in 1864 by the above structure. (Dan West.)

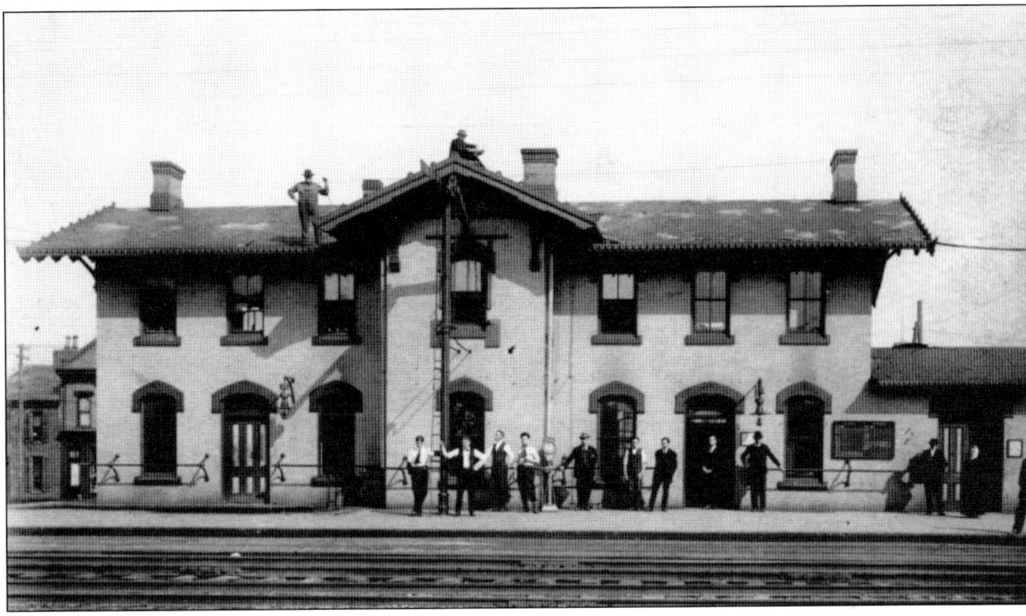

The PCC&StL also used an existing structure as its first depot until the two-story brick depot, above, was built in 1879. This large depot was surprisingly moved off the site to make way for the PRR's 1911 passenger depot. Some seven passenger depots served Steubenville in 1897. Below is a c. 1912 postcard showing the newest depot in Steubenville—the Pennsylvania Railroad passenger depot. A subway allowed the safe passage of passengers to the outer platform. (Both, author's collection.)

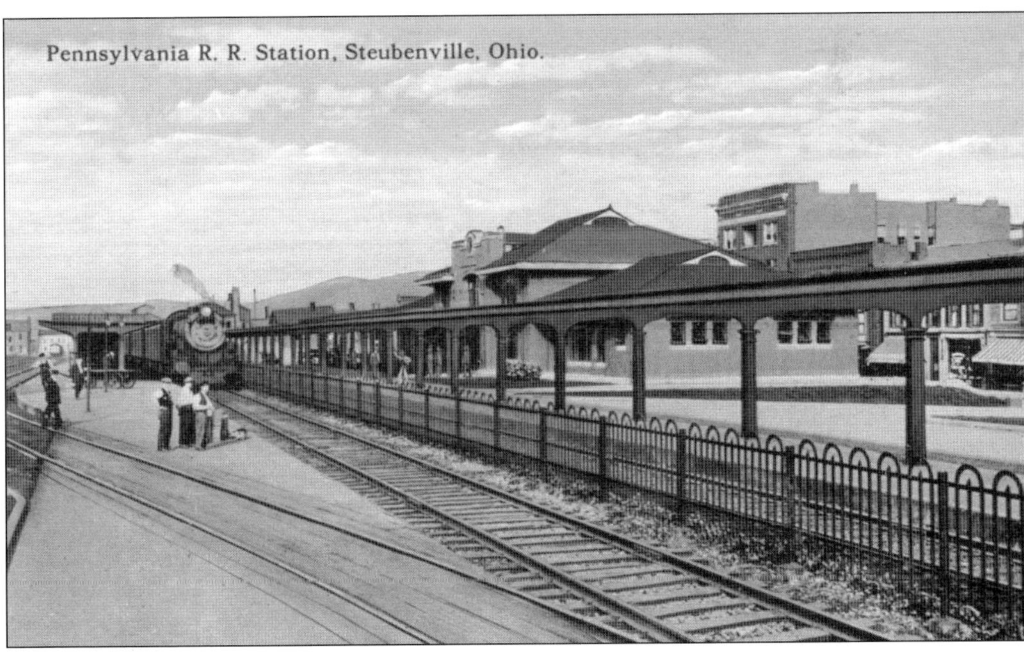

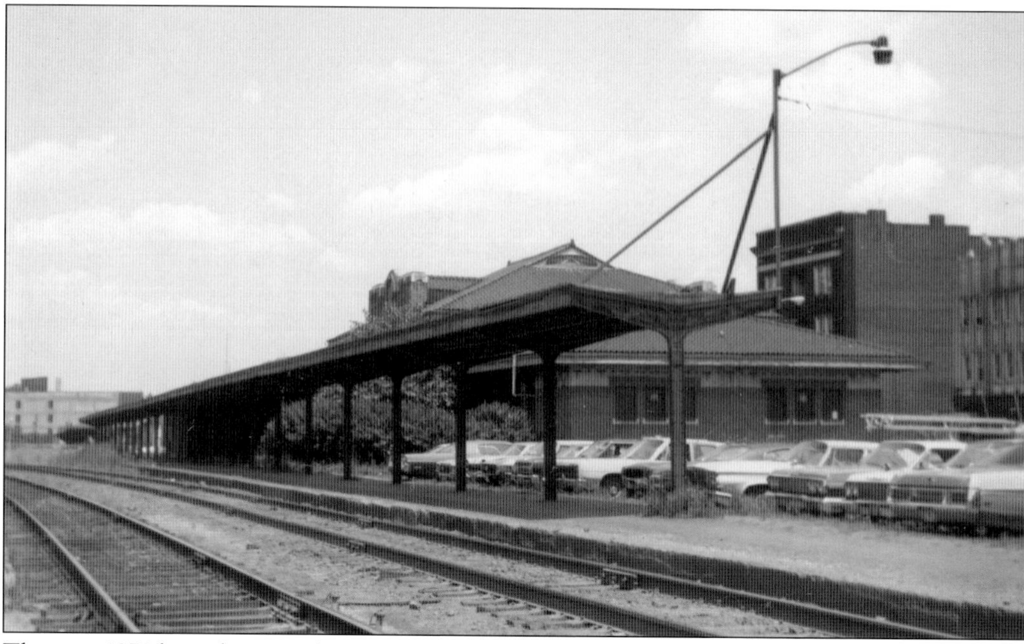

The year 1971 brought an end to Steubenville passenger service. The PRR depot lies abandoned in this 1973 view. It was subsequently torn down. (Author photograph.)

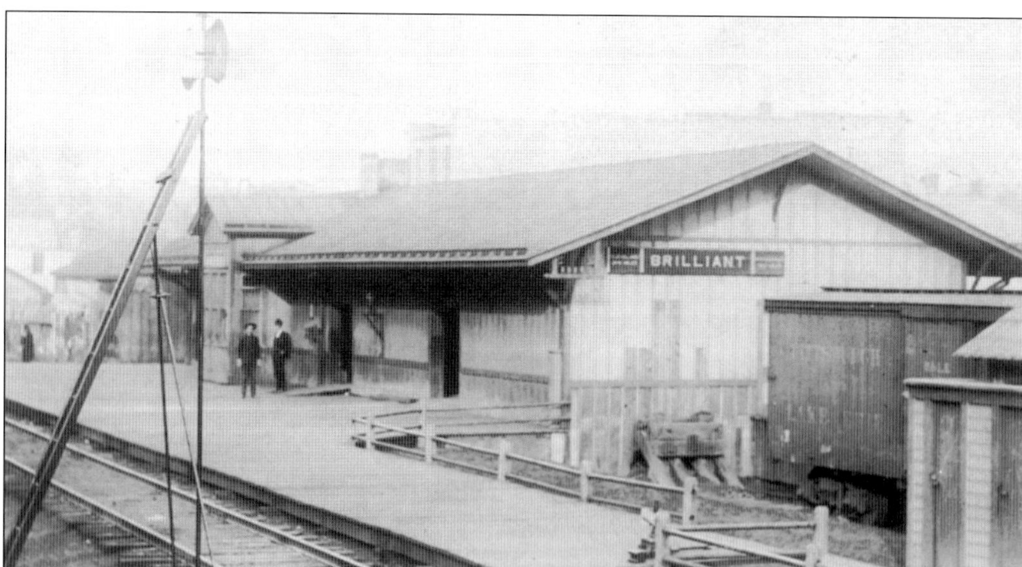

Another classic depot-tower served travelers in Mingo Junction (see page 55). The next station was Brilliant, where this frame combination depot served travelers on the C&P. Of interest are the elevated switch stand and "two-holer" outhouse. The Wheeling & Lake Erie, which roughly paralleled the C&P, also maintained a depot here. Farther south, a similar frame C&P depot stood at Rush Run. (Bob Chilcote collection.)

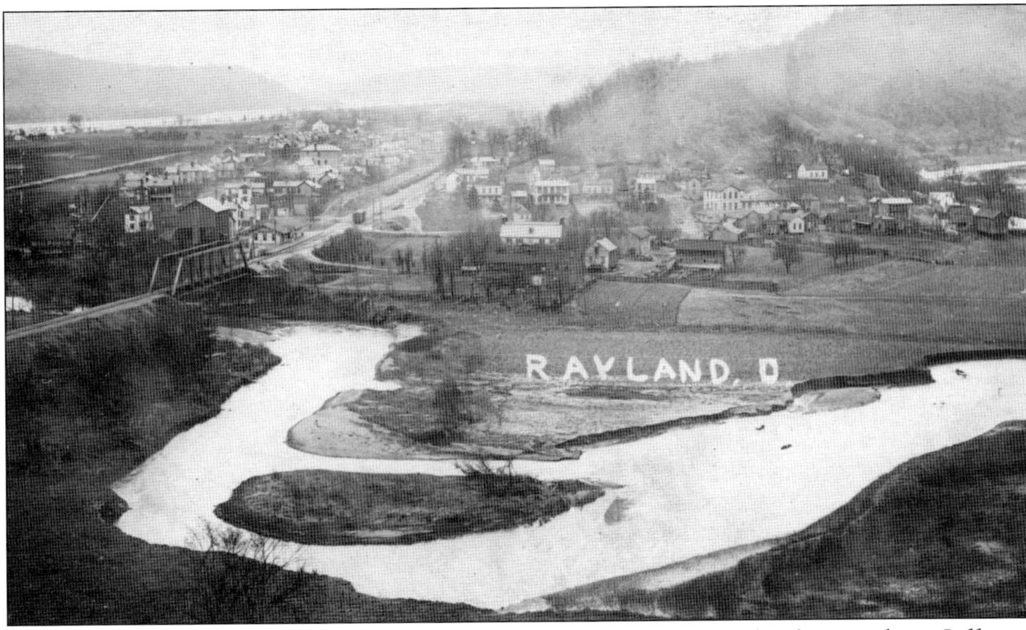

Representative of the smaller river towns is this c. 1910 view of Rayland in southern Jefferson County. The town is nestled on the bottomlands between the rock-capped uplands and the Ohio River at the mouths of Short and Little Short Creeks. The frame C&P combination depot replaced an earlier frame structure probably built in the 1870s–1880s. (Author's collection.)

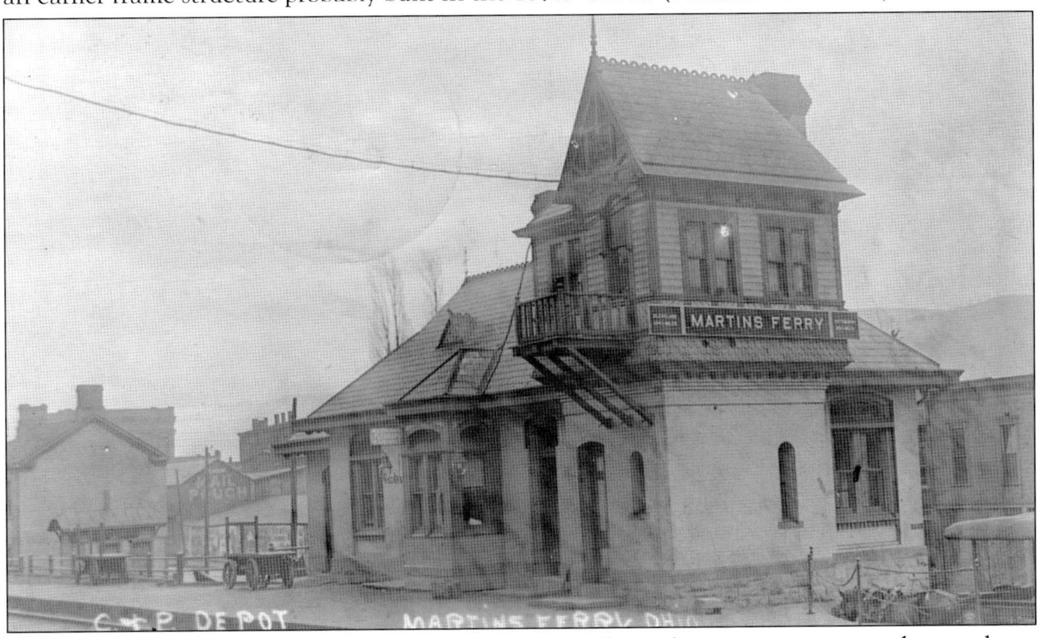

Farther south, the C&P served Tiltonsville and Yorkville. A former passenger coach served as a temporary depot in Tiltonsville around 1900. This brick depot-tower combination was the center of C&P operations in Martins Ferry. Nearby was a C&P freight house. The Cleveland, Lorain & Wheeling, later B&O, had separate passenger and freight depots along First Street in the late 1800s. The Wheeling & Lake Erie's passenger and freight depots were located on Sixth Street. Little evidence remains of these structures in 2017. (Author's collection.)

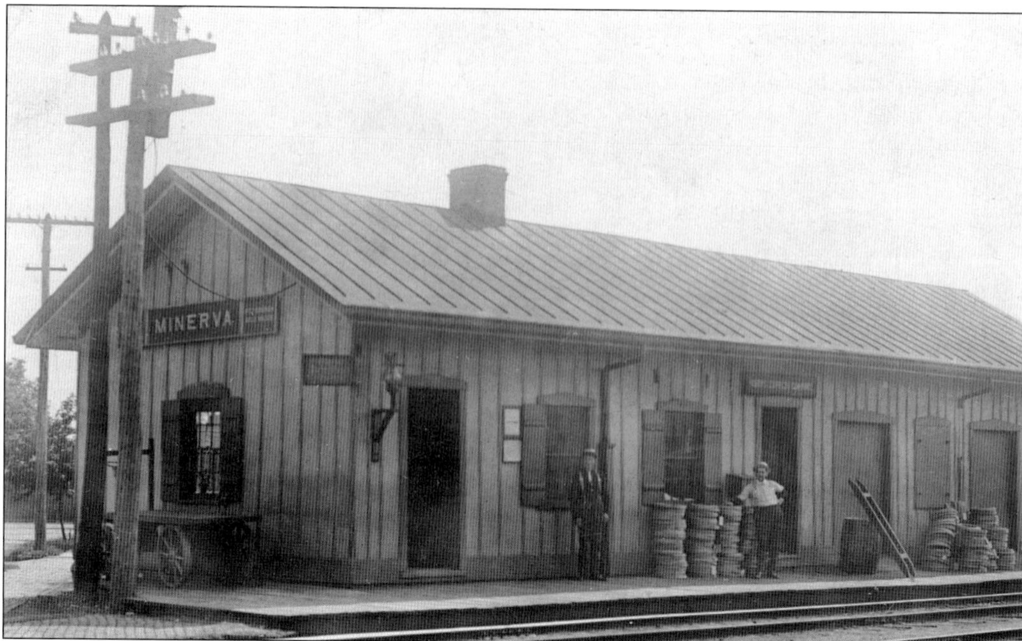

Cleveland & Pittsburgh Railway's Tuscarawas branch began at the Bayard depot. The first depot was at Minerva, shown here around 1910. This second-generation depot was probably built in the early 1870s and shows the general characteristics of a C&P depot. The addition of shutters distinguishes it from most C&P structures. Minerva was also a station on the Lake Erie, Alliance & Wheeling, which crossed the C&P at grade, and the Wheeling & Lake Erie. The PRR modified and sided this building in the mid-1900s, and it served as a freight agency into the early 1970s. (Author's collection.)

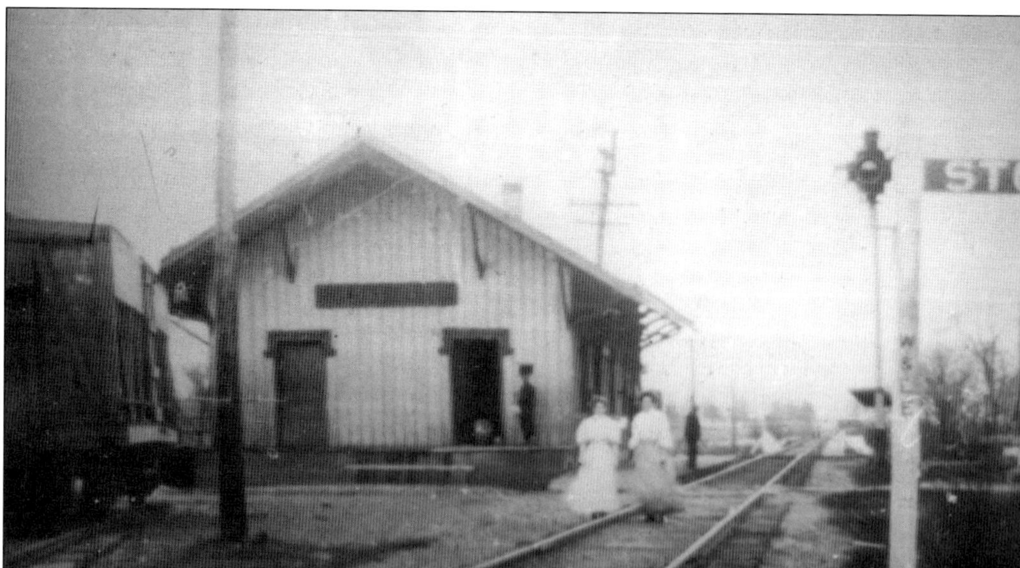
The C&P crossed the Wheeling & Lake Erie at Oneida, the next station south of Minerva. This view looks down the C&P; the W&LE diamond is just beyond the depot. This crossing was not interlocked; the agent-operator was responsible for setting the signal in the foreground. (Author's collection.)

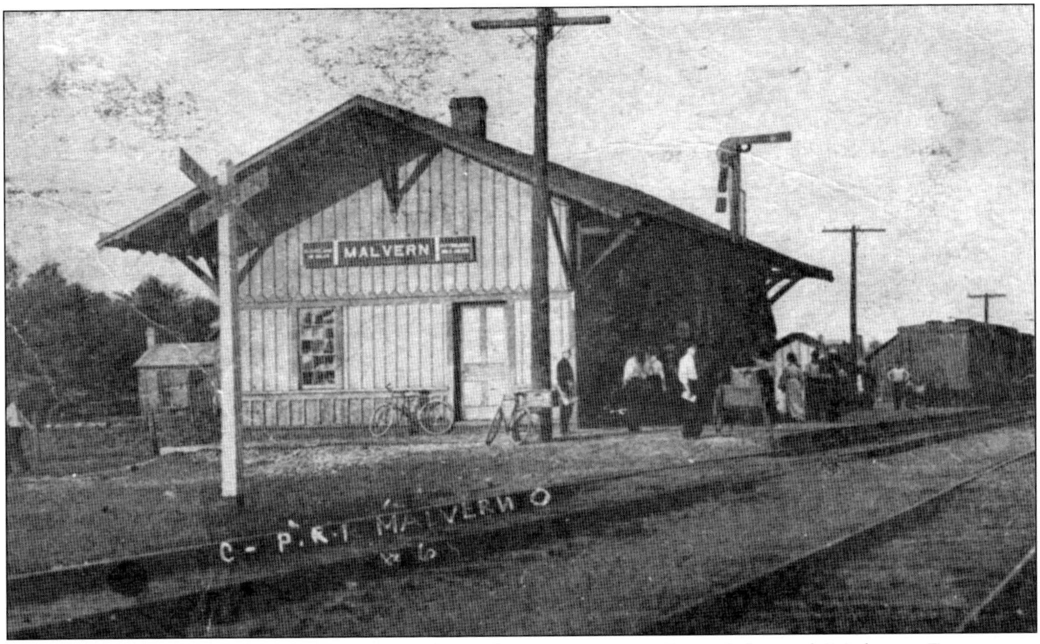

The Cleveland & Pittsburgh Tuscarawas branch continues southward through Malvern. Passengers await the local in this c. 1910 postcard view. A newsboy peddles the local paper. The other bicycle is probably used to deliver telegrams to the townsfolk. A number of brick and tile plants in the area provided lots of work for the freight agent. The Robinson Clay Products kilns are just out of view to the right. (Author's collection.)

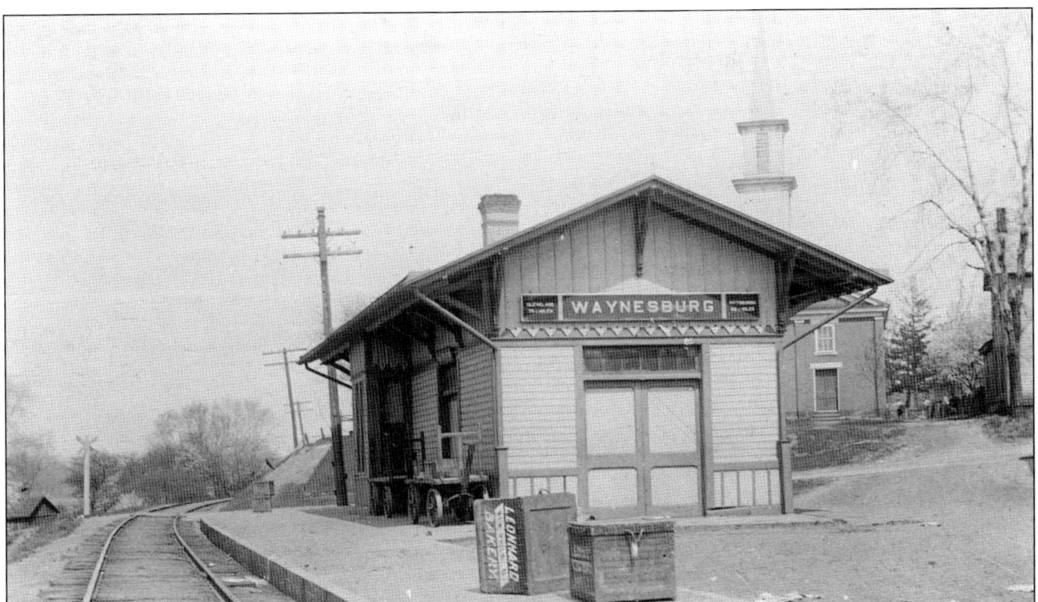

Waynesburg is the next stop heading south and was reached by the C&P in 1854. This second-generation combination depot replaced an earlier frame structure. (Author's collection.)

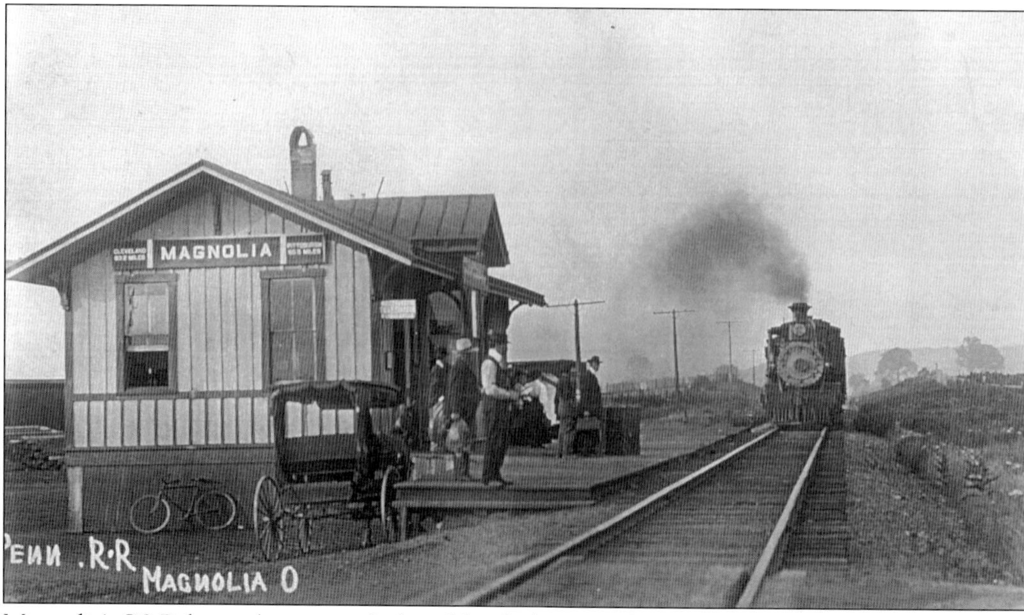

Magnolia's C&P depot also received a lot of freight business from local brick and tile plants. Many a worker used the C&P for transportation to and from work. Magnolia's mills were also a big customer of this depot. The B&O also had a frame combination depot in Magnolia. Luckily, the C&P depot has been repurposed and is located at the Magnolia Mill complex. (Author's collection.)

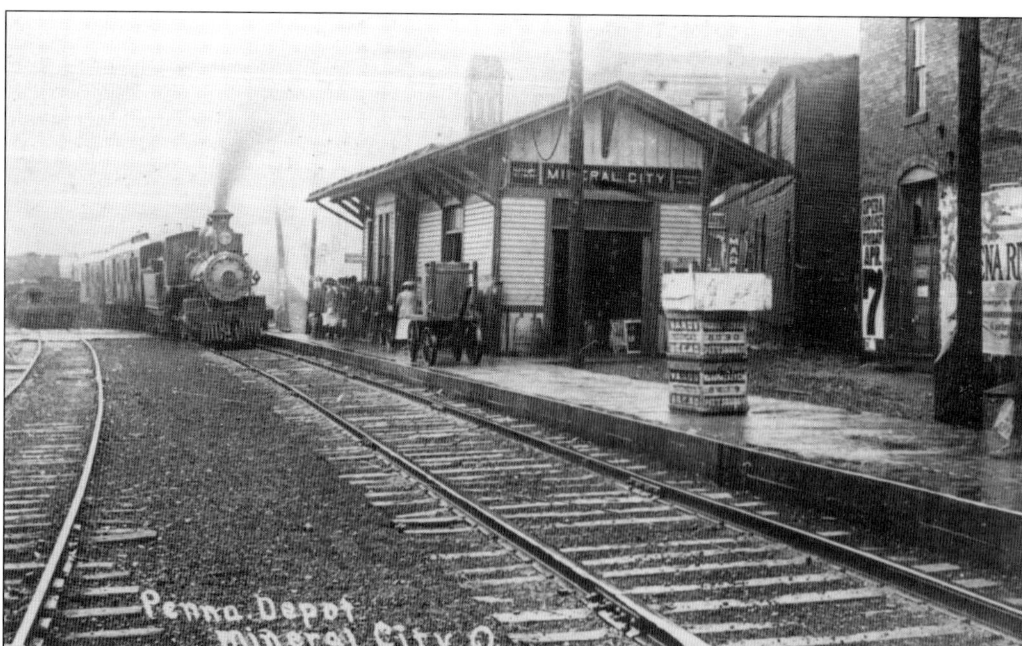

At Mineral City, the C&P essentially parallels the B&O. In the early days, the C&P used a store as its depot. A second-generation C&P depot is shown at train time in this c. 1910 postcard view. This depot appears to have been removed in the 1940s. (Author's collection.)

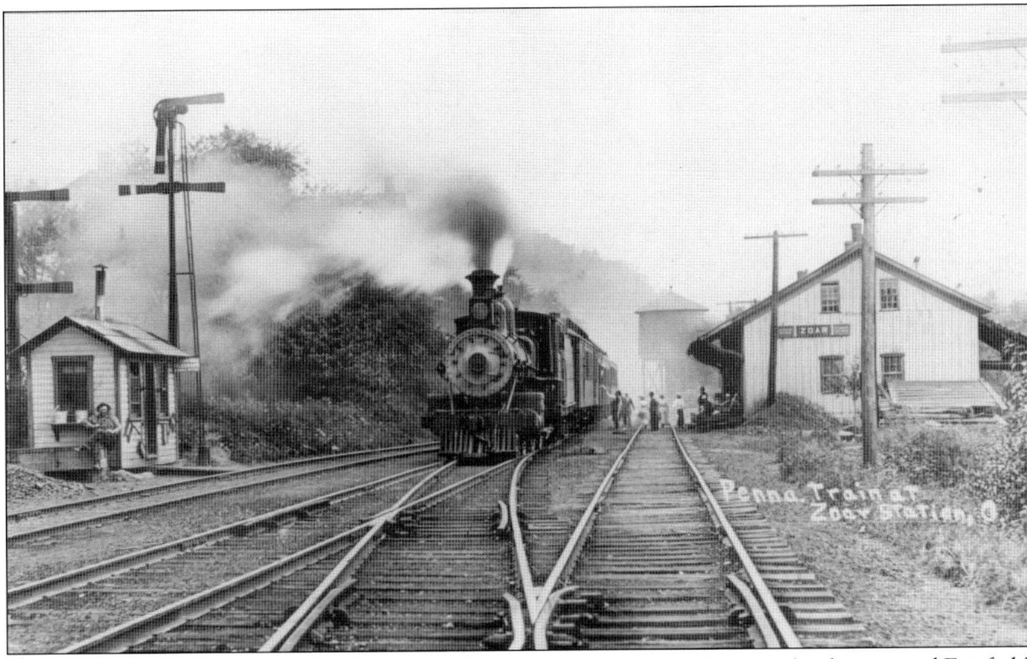

The original C&P line used this frame combination depot at Zoar Station (earlier named Fairfield; later Zoarville). This area was cleared of structures and trees and the PRR line relocated to higher ground in the mid-1930s due to the construction of Dover Dam. A new station was established at New Zoarville, uphill across the Tuscarawas Valley. (Author's collection.)

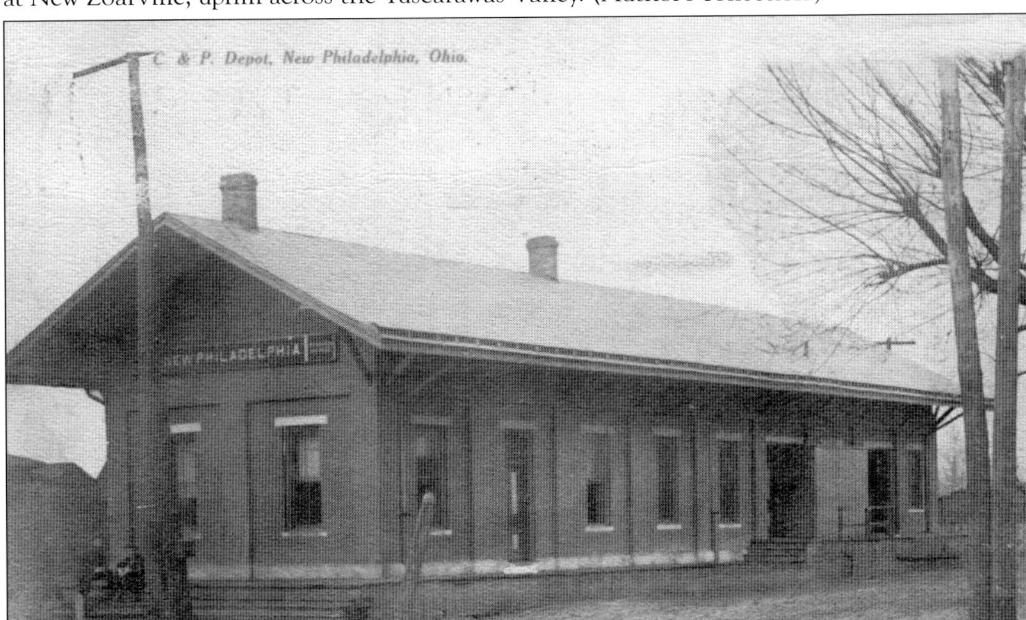

The C&P passenger depot in Dover was demolished by the PRR in July 1956. The next stop to the south was New Philadelphia, the southern terminus of C&P's Tuscarawas branch. The C&P built into New Philadelphia in 1854. This brick depot probably dates to the 1870s. It was torn down in the mid-1900s. The other depot in town, on the B&O line, was still there in the early 1970s. (Author's collection.)

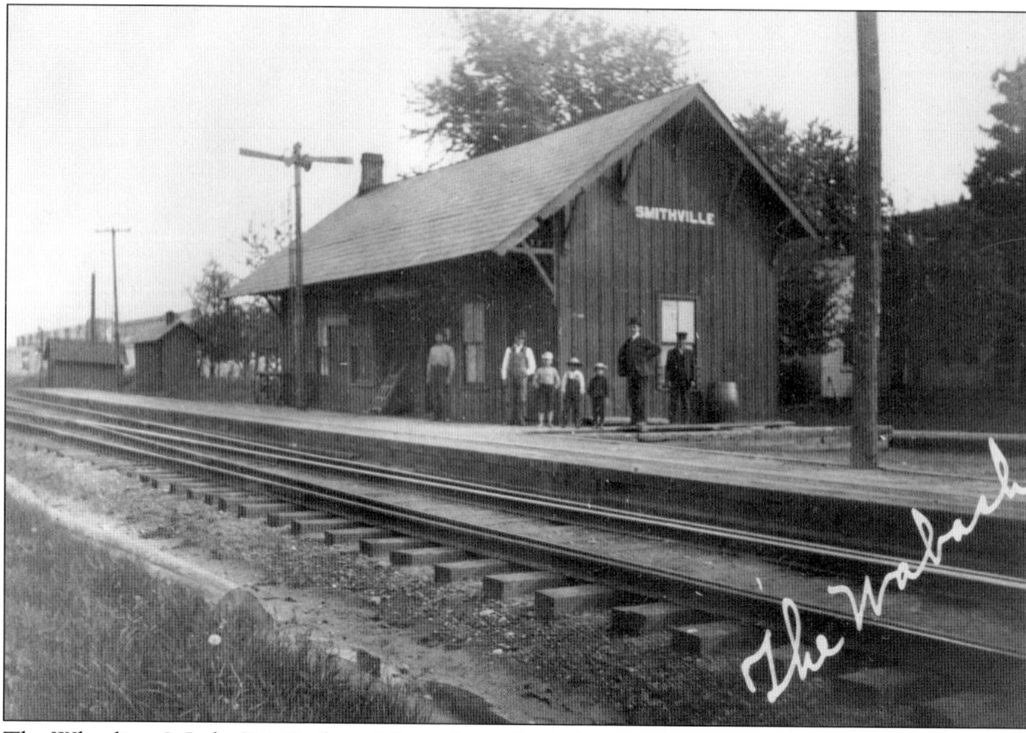

The Wheeling & Lake Erie Railway followed standard plans in the construction of this combination depot at Smithville. The c. 1882 depot is shown above in Wabash colors around 1910 and below in 1925 with a W&LE paint scheme. A characterizing feature of this design is the unequal roof overhang. This provided more protection for waiting passengers. An outhouse and handcar shed are located at the end of the depot platform. The wooden box mounted on the end wall housed a phone that could be accessed by a standard switch key when the depot was not open. It was moved from trackside in the late 1970s to its present location at Main Street and North Milton St. for commercial use. (Both, W&LE collection, Special Collections, Michael Schwartz Library, Cleveland State University.)

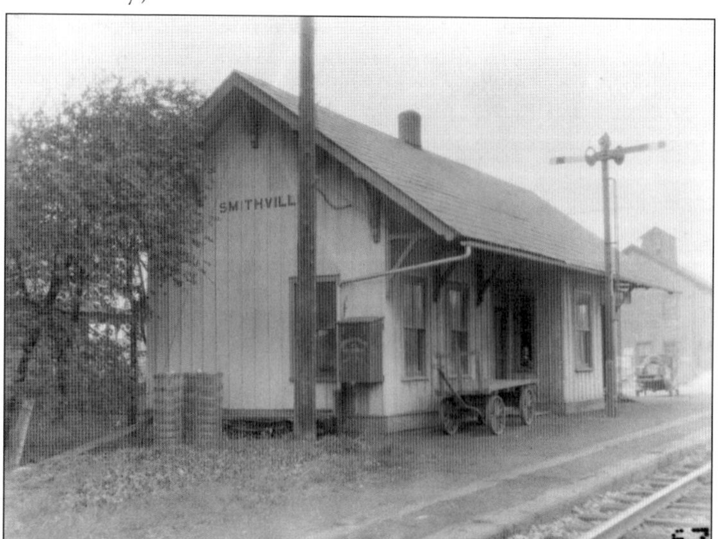

Four

Wheeling and Lake Erie Lines

In April 1871, the Wheeling and Lake Erie (W&LE) Railway was promoted to connect the coal lands of southeastern Ohio with Lake Erie; however, finances were short and little progress was made. With renewed monetary support, the tracks reached Massillon in 1882, Martins Ferry in 1891, and Wheeling, West Virginia, the next year. At the same time, a narrow-gauge line, the Youngstown & Connotton Valley Railroad, opened a route from Minerva to Canton in May 1880 and, as the renamed Connotton Valley Railway, added an extension to Sherrodsville in January 1882 and built into Cleveland in November 1882. The Connotton Valley then built southward to Coshocton and finally, as the renamed Cleveland, Canton & Southern (CC&S) Railroad, to Zanesville in June 1889. The reorganization as the CC&S resulted in the conversion to standard gauge in November 1888. After another reorganization, the W&LE was able to take over the Cleveland, Canton & Southern Railroad in 1899. It became the W&LE's Cleveland Division. The Cleveland Division crossed the Toledo Division, which stretched from Toledo to the Wheeling area at Harmon.

W&LE depots on the Toledo Division were constructed from standard plans and featured mainly frame combination depots. The Cleveland Division retained many frame combination depots of Connotton Valley design. Larger brick passenger depots served Brewster, Carrollton, Coshocton, Dillonvale, Minerva, Steubenville, and Wheeling, West Virginia. The largest structure was located in Canton.

In 1949, the W&LE became part of the New York, Chicago & St. Louis Railroad, better known as the Nickel Plate. In 2017, a good portion of the old W&LE is operated by the new Wheeling & Lake Erie Railway.

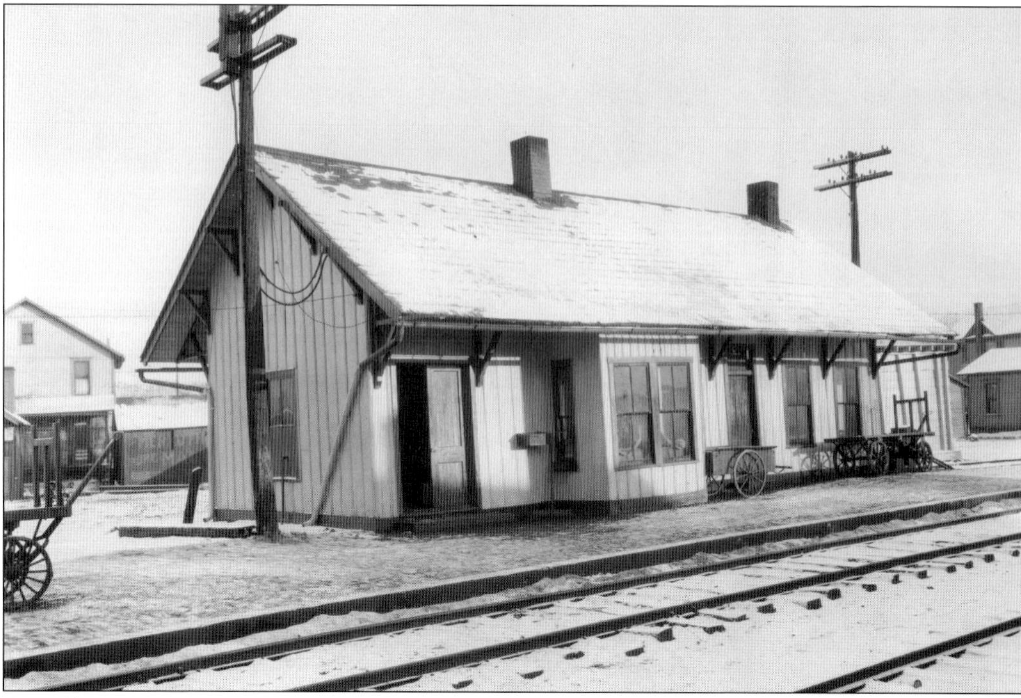

Orrville's W&LE passenger depot was built to another standard plan. The depot is longer, with equal roof overhangs, a two-window vestibule, and a larger waiting room separated from a baggage room by a railroad office area. A frame freight house was nearby. Both were gone by the early 1970s. Orville was also home to a PCC&StL-CA&C passenger depot. (W&LE photograph, Special Collections, Michael Schwartz Library, Cleveland State University.)

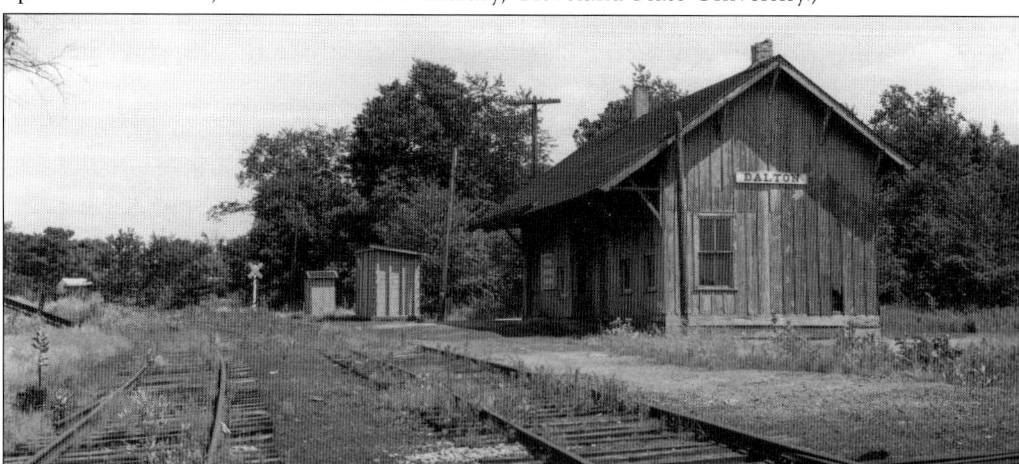

Compare the standard plan W&LE combination depot at Dalton to the images of Smithville. Except for window arrangement, they are very similar. This was certainly a popular and efficient depot style and was repeated at many stations along the system. The depot dates to around 1882. Dalton was initially on the main line, but was shifted to a branch line when the Brewster cutoff was opened between Orrville and Navarre in 1909. Originally, the W&LE followed a route from Orrville east to Burton City, Dalton, Summit, and on to Massillon and then south to Navarre. (Herb Harwood photograph.)

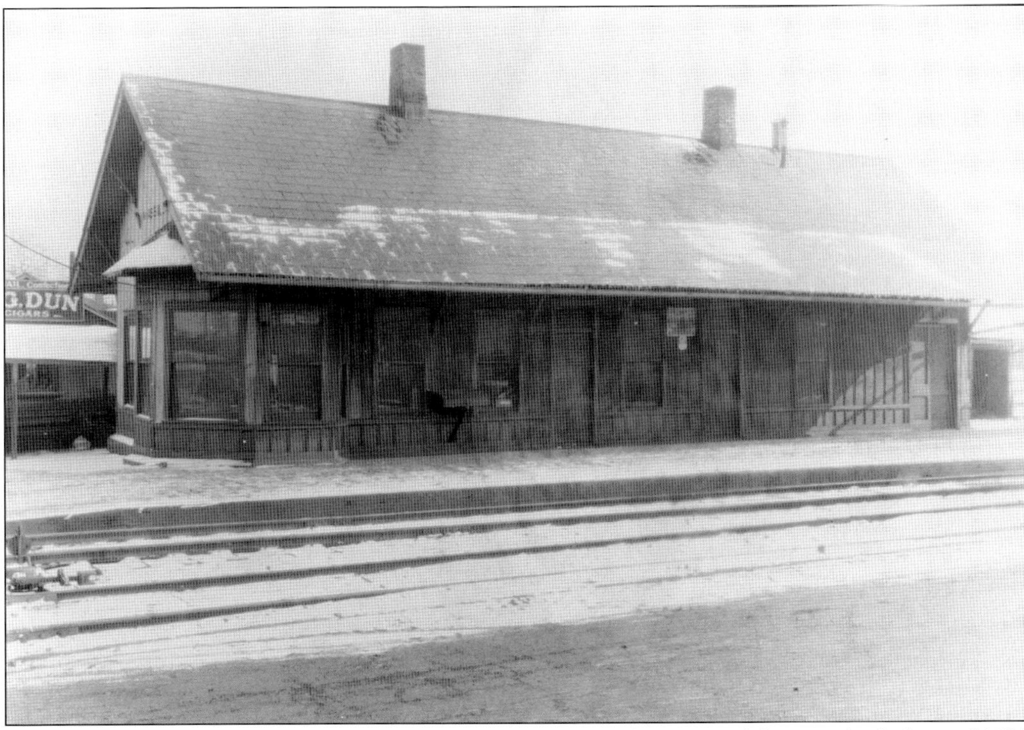

Massillon's frame passenger depot seems to be an elongated version of the standard plans of 1881. As was common in larger communities, a lunch stand was located near the depot for the benefit of travelers. The depot was a busy place in the early 1900s. Flooding was a problem since the track was laid along the Tuscarawas River floodplain. The river channel was straightened through the downtown and the track realigned in 1941. Since passenger service had been discontinued, the depots were not replaced. (Both, W&LE photographs, Special Collections, Michael Schwartz Library, Cleveland State University.)

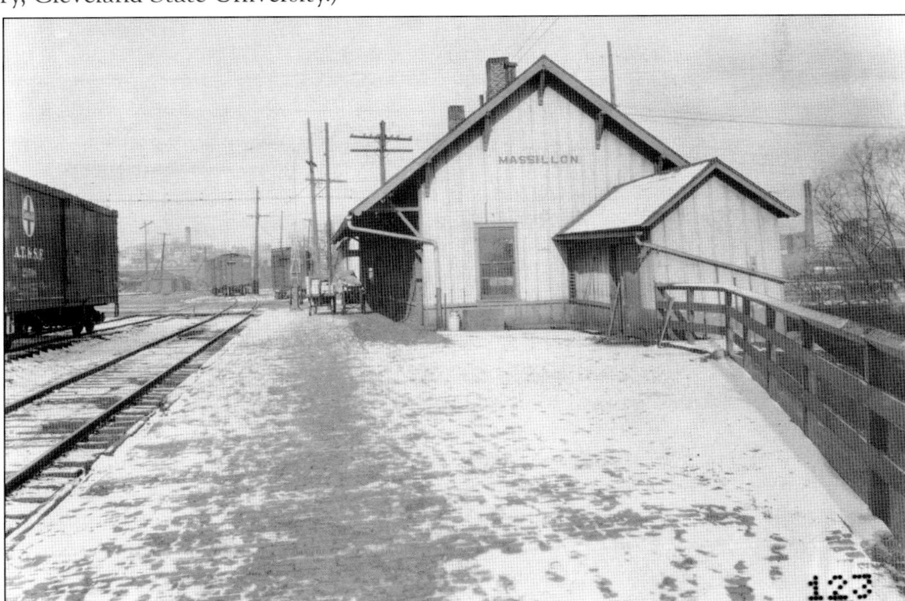

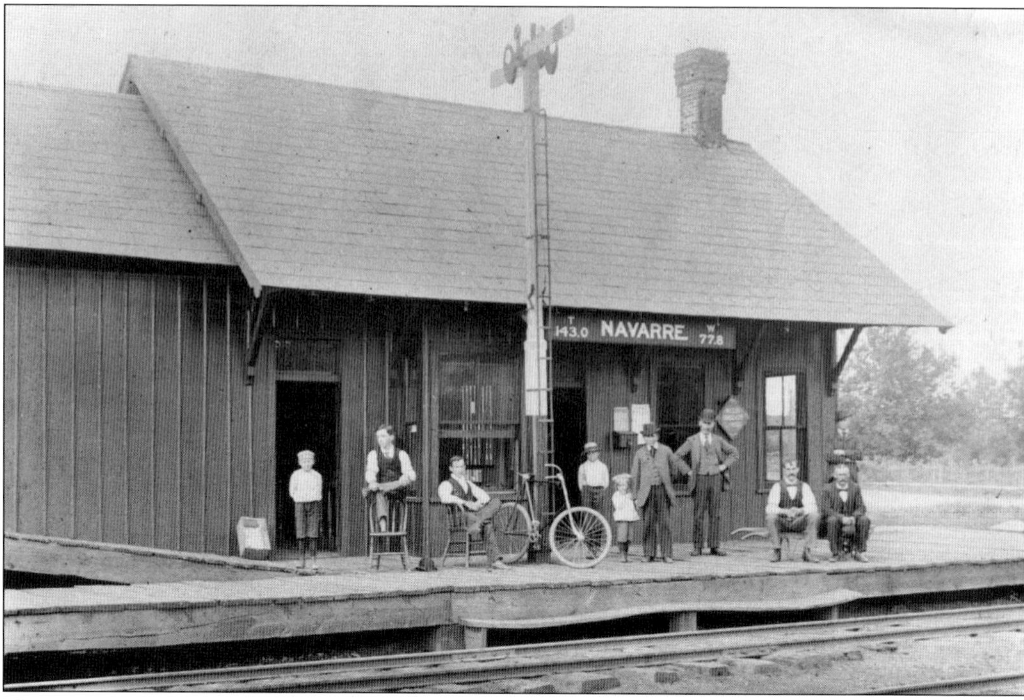

Navarre was a station on the original line of the W&LE, which reached Massillon in 1882, and also later became a station on the Connotton Valley. The above combination depot was built to standard 1881 W&LE plans. When the W&LE took over the Cleveland, Canton & Southern line, Navarre became an important transfer point for travelers heading to all corners of the state. During the time of Wabash control, the depot was modified so that it could handle passenger trains on both sides. A lunchroom was added in 1905. During the St. Louis World's Fair, the depot was often host to two to four trains at the same time and by far the busiest station on the W&LE. When the Brewster cutoff opened in August 1909, Navarre was no longer on the main line. Two months later, the depot was moved to Brewster to serve as a yard office. The below depot, located on the other side of Navarre, was built by the CC&S and was still there in the 1970s. It eventually was torn down after vandals started a fire. (Both, W&LE collection, Special Collections, Michael Schwartz Library, Cleveland State University.)

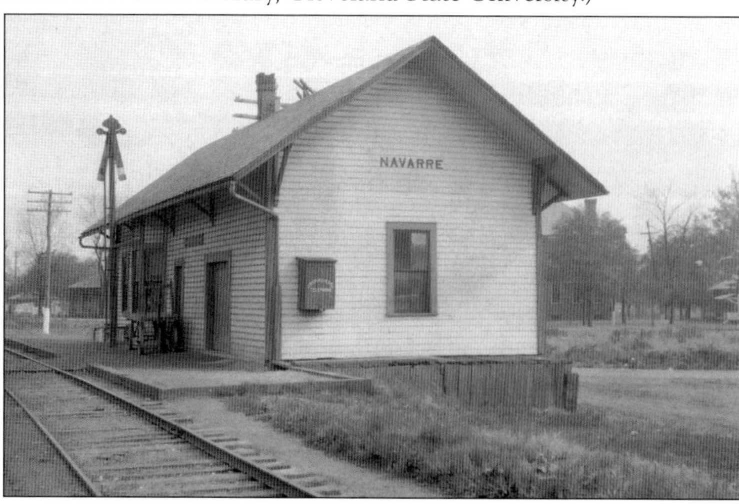

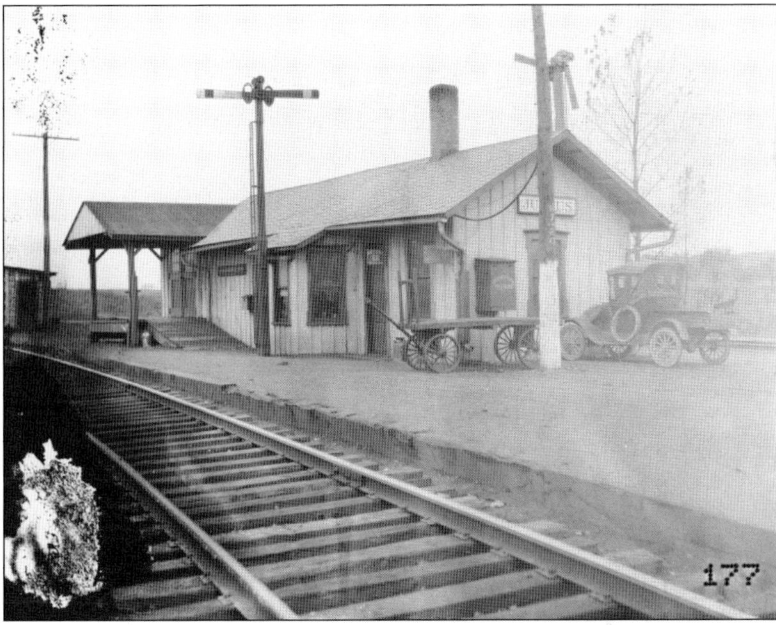

Justus was the station where the Cleveland, Lorain & Wheeling (later B&O) joined the W&LE and paralleled it to Beach City. The Justus depot was a joint facility, used by the W&LE and CL&W. The CL&W track lies behind the depot in this 1925 view. (W&LE photograph, Special Collections, Michael Schwartz Library, Cleveland State University.)

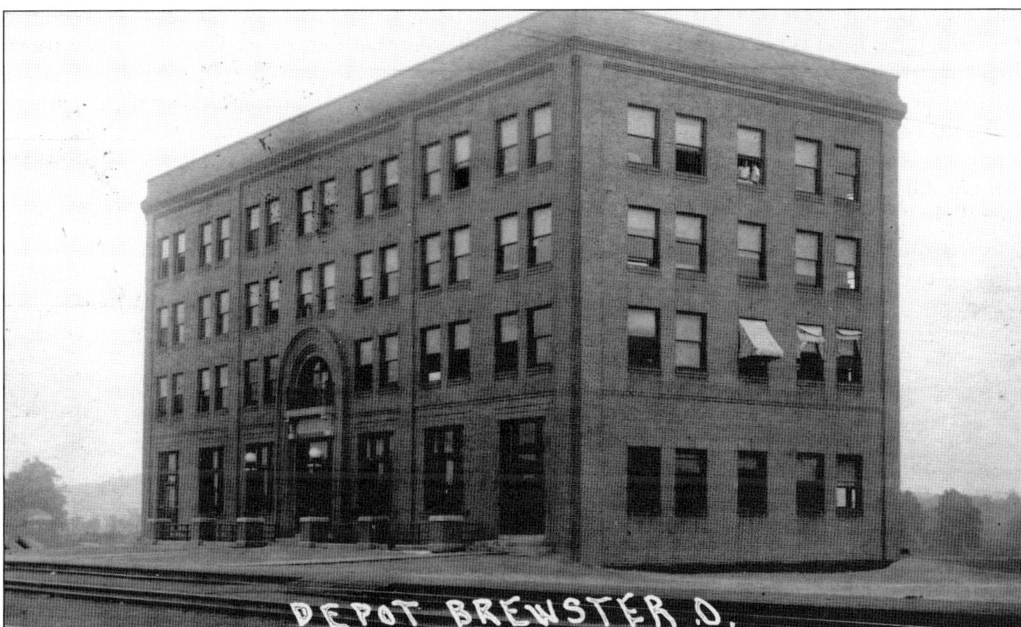

The construction of a low-grade route cutoff eliminating a steep grade west of Massillon between 1906 and 1909 led to the new town of Brewster and the location of new shops and division offices at a central location on the W&LE. This four-story office building/passenger depot was completed in June 1914, replacing the offices in Canton. The passenger waiting rooms and ticket office were on the first floor, railroad offices above. This view is from trackside; there were never any platform shelters. The building remains in use in 2017. (Author's collection.)

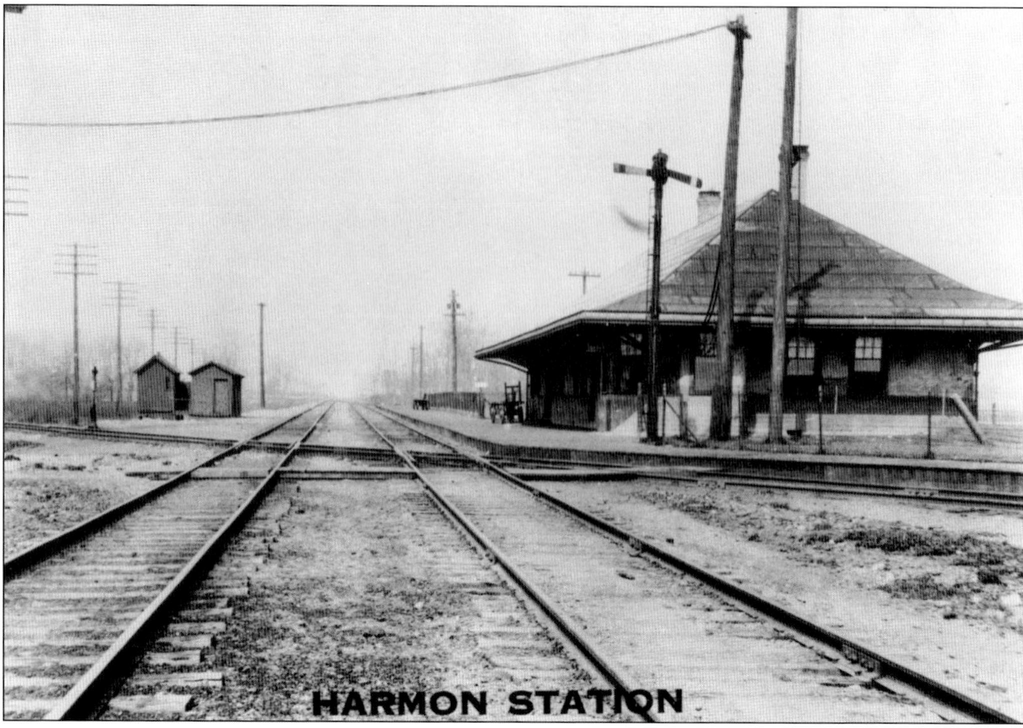

The W&LE built the above depot around 1910 at Harmon, the junction of its Toledo and Cleveland Divisions. The anticipated business at this station failed to develop and it was moved two miles on flatcars to serve as the freight house at Brewster. It was torn down in the 1980s. The view below looks north up the Zanesville branch in 1925. The W&LE replaced the Harmon depot with a smaller telegraph office and waiting room built on the site of the original depot. Across the diamond is a characteristic W&LE water tank. The diamond was removed in 1933. (Both, W&LE collection, Special Collections, Michael Schwartz Library, Cleveland State University.)

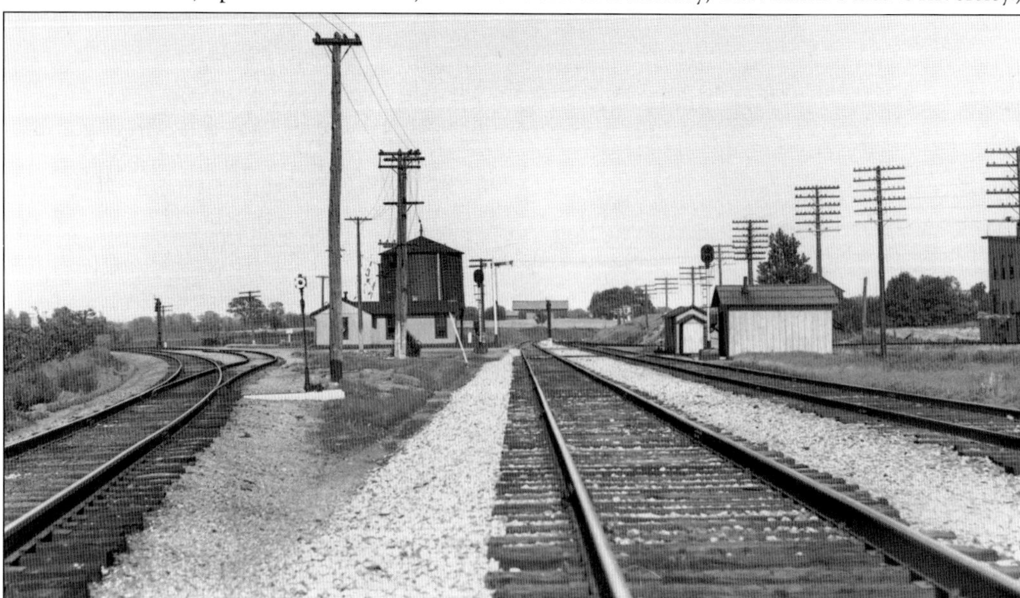

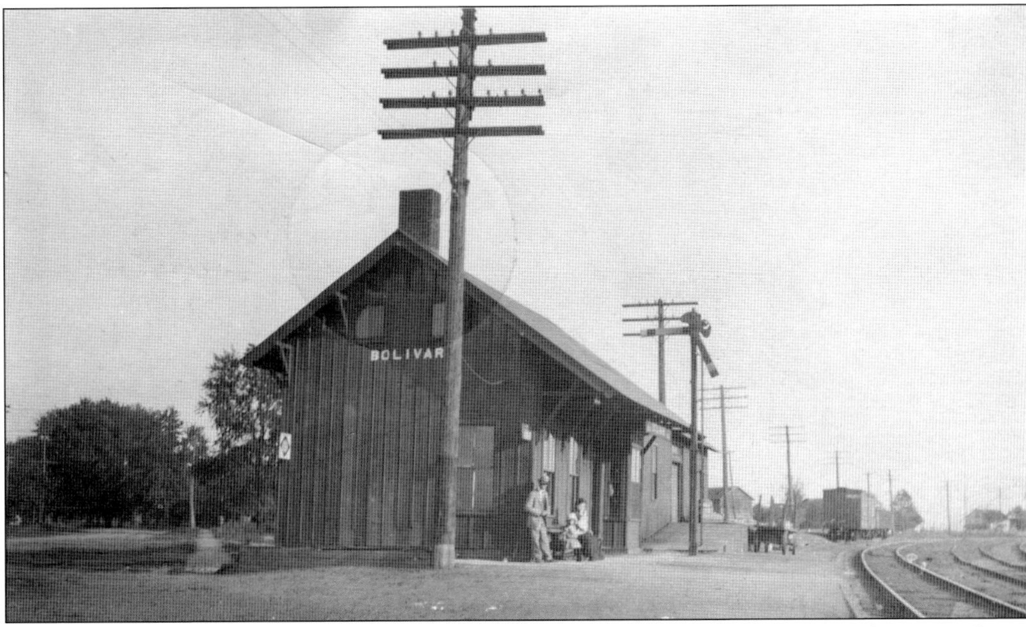

The W&LE's facilities at Bolivar around 1910 consisted of this standard plan combination depot. The freight room was extended around 1900. A nearby brick plant provided additional freight business. The depot was gone by the late 1960s. (Author's collection.)

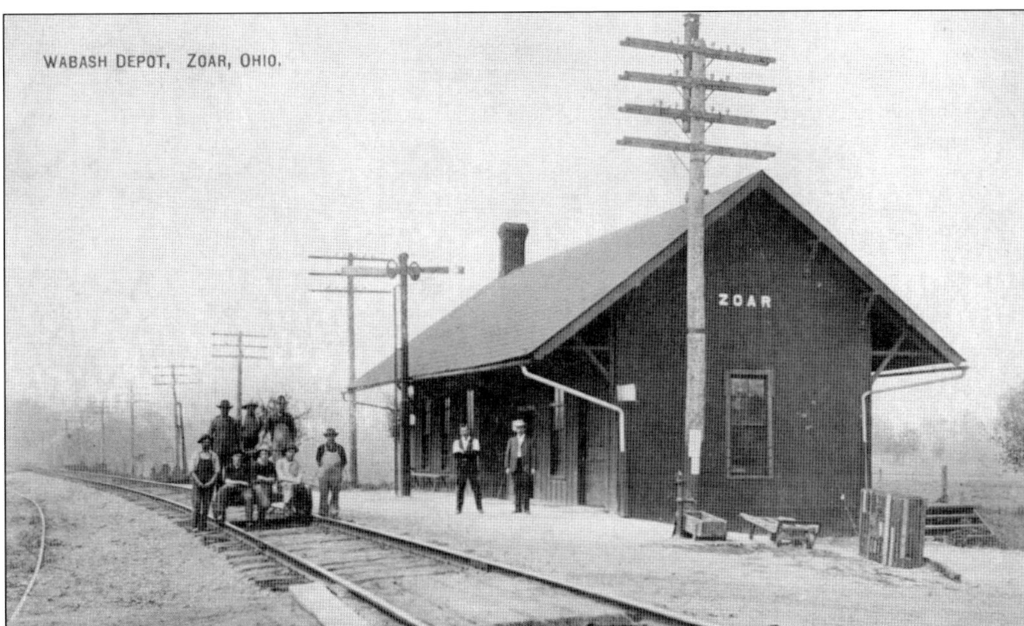

The W&LE built this standard design depot at Zoar around 1882. This c. 1910 postcard labels it as the Wabash depot because this was the time of Wabash control of the W&LE. The Wabash repainted many depots with its gray and green trim paint schemes. This depot was abandoned when Dover Dam was under construction in the mid-1930s. The new alignment included a frame W&LE depot that served as a train order office. (Author's collection.)

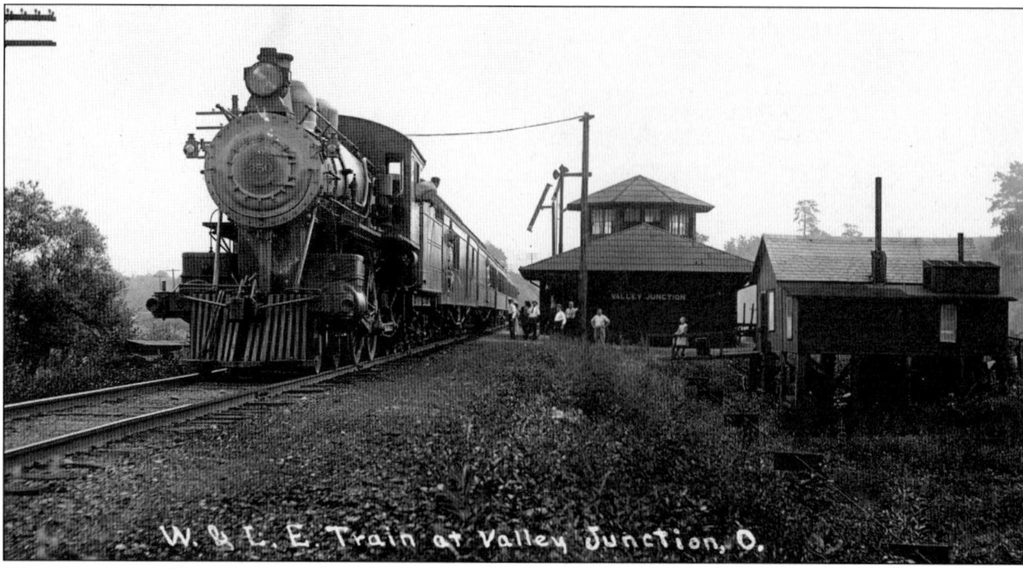

The W&LE Valley Junction depot was situated at the crossing of the Cleveland & Pittsburgh Railway (later PRR) and the Valley Railway (later B&O) on the wide floodplain of the Tuscarawas River and a major tributary—Connotton Creek. This became the second depot at this site when the two-story frame original depot burned down in July 1906. The W&LE opened it in August 1907 with a second-floor tower where operators controlled the signals guarding the junctions. As was standard practice on the W&LE, a boxcar or old coach served as a temporary depot. This c. 1910 view looks southward showing the lunchroom in the foreground. Dining cars were not yet common on passenger trains. This depot was obviously subject to periodic floods. In May 1938, a higher ground rail alignment was completed during dam construction and the depot was abandoned. The below depot was the replacement, completed in November 1937. Its pleasing design seems to be unique among W&LE depots and is attributed to C.W. Taylor & Sons contractors of Zanesville. Unfortunately, it burned and was torn down in the 1980s. (Above, W&LE collection, Special Collections, Michael Schwartz Library, Cleveland State University; below, Charles Garvin photograph.)

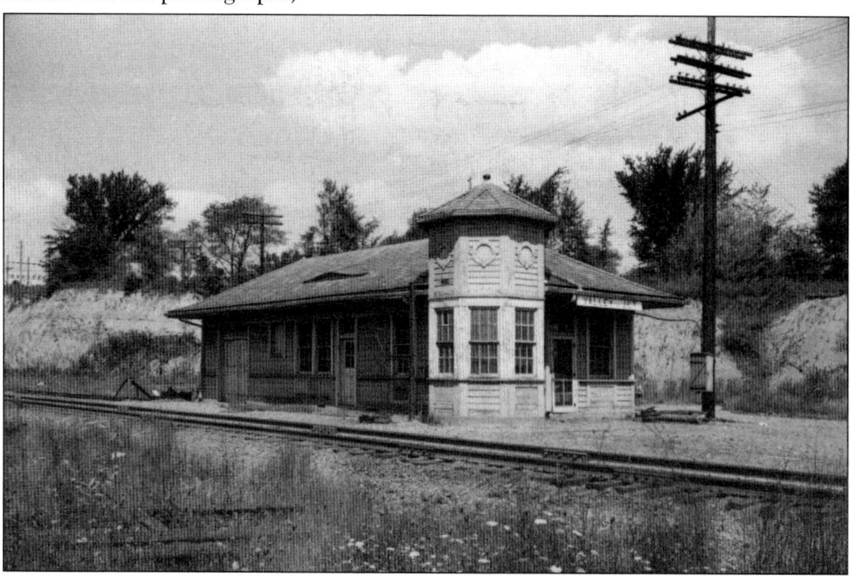

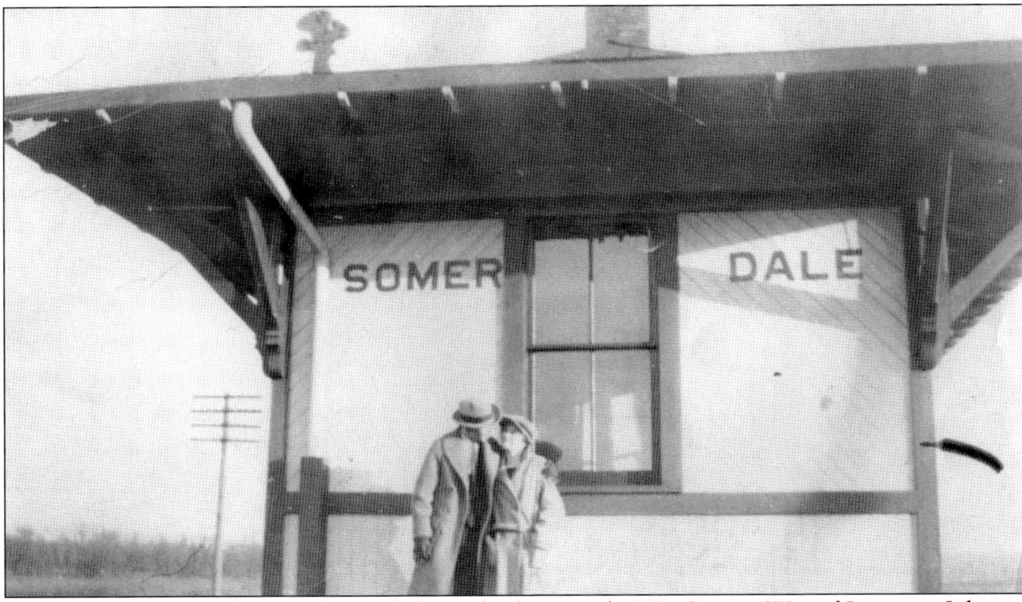

The original W&LE depot at Somerdale was built around 1888. George W. and Lewretta Johnson were photographed at the depot in 1924. The improvements made to flood control in this area led to closing of this depot in 1938 and a relocated right-of-way. The discontinuance of passenger service in 1932 meant that an old coach was more than adequate to serve the needs of local business. (Above, Tuscarawas County Historical Society; below, W&LE photograph, Special Collections, Michael Schwartz Library, Cleveland State University.)

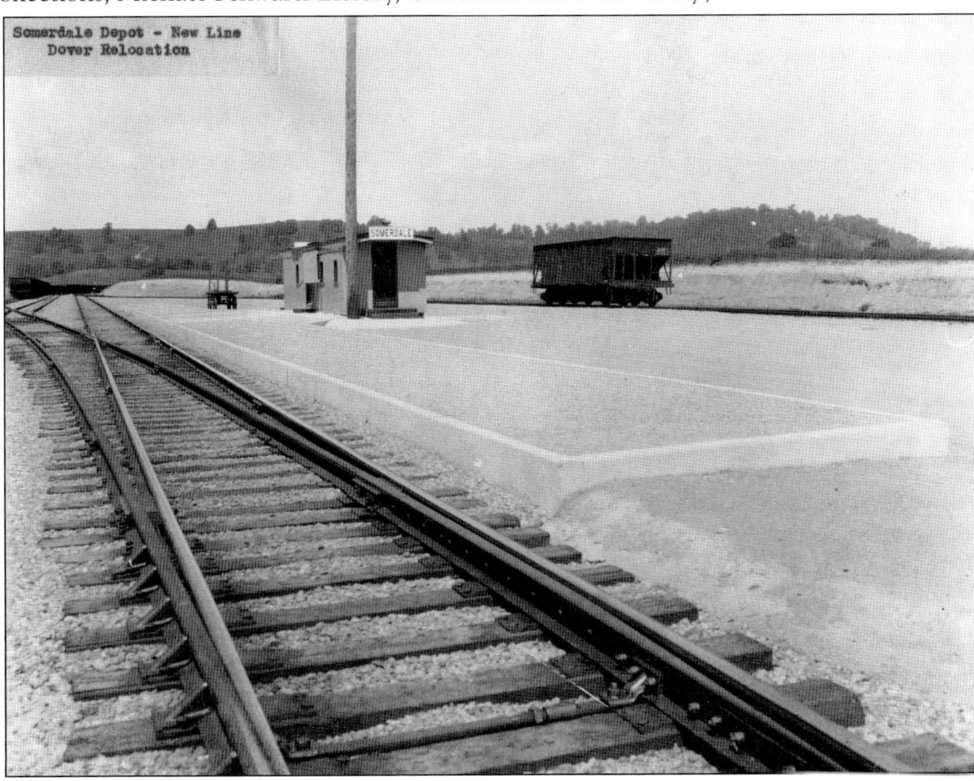

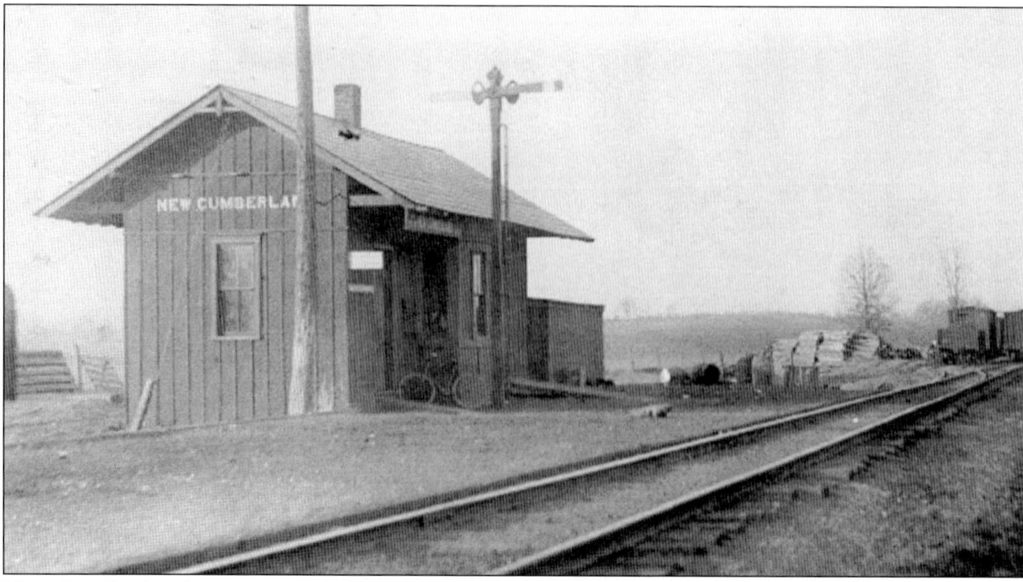

New Cumberland was surrounded by coal mines and thus an important station on the W&LE. The standard plan combination depot seen above dates to 1888. The postcard view is from about 1910. Completion of another flood control project in 1938 led to the closing of this depot, relocation of the main line, and construction of the new depot seen below in 1938. (Above, Tuscarawas County Historical Society collection; below, W&LE photograph, Special Collections, Michael Schwartz Library, Cleveland State University.)

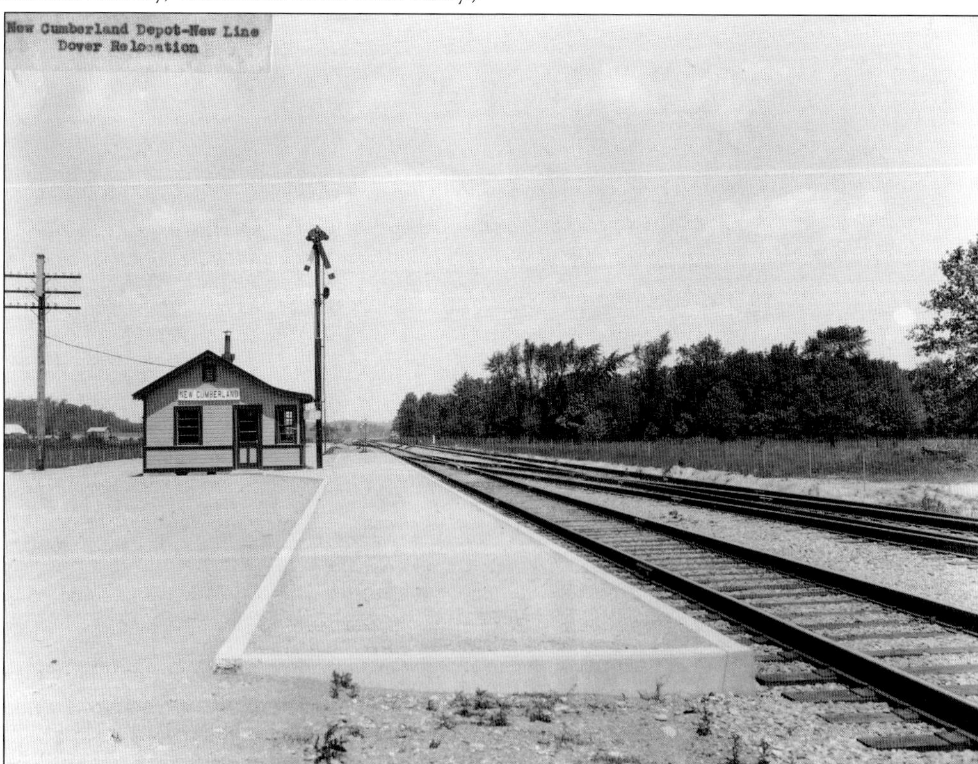

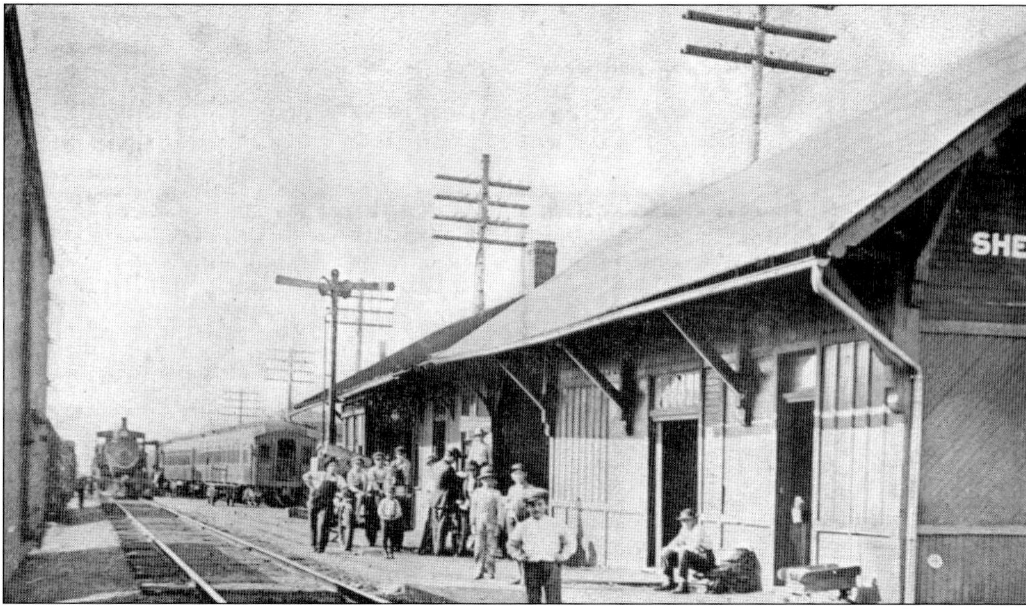

The Cleveland Canton & Southern Railway reached Sherrodsville in 1877. The original depot was gone by 1901. These W&LE passenger and freight depots replaced it. The passenger depot was still there in 1971. (Author's collection.)

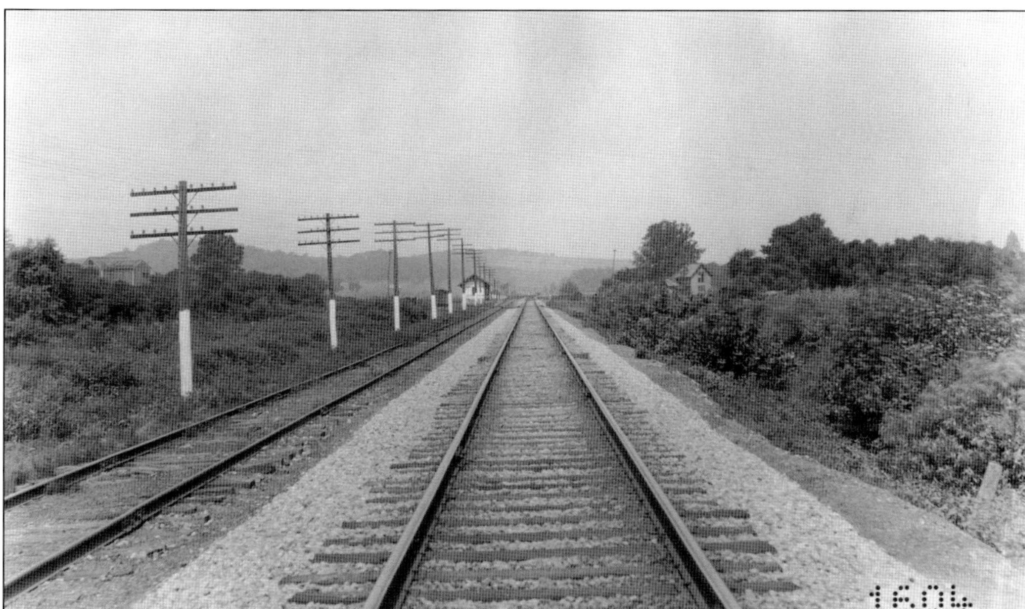

Besides multiple up close views of depots and other structures, the W&LE valuation photographers often took approach views—distant shots showing the surroundings as trains approached a station. Unfortunately, the close views of Leesville are missing. The depot was of a standard design and has been gone since the mid-1900s. (W&LE photograph, Special Collections, Michael Schwartz Library, Cleveland State University.)

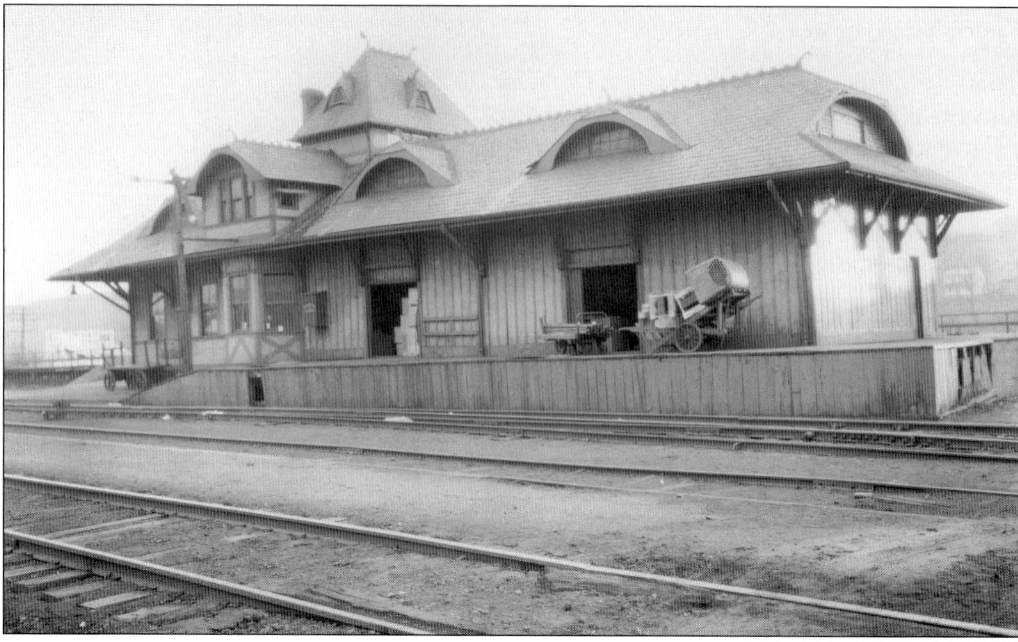

In 1884, the W&LE reached Bowerston and built this joint combination depot between the tracks of the PCC&StL and W&LE in 1885. This view shows the W&LE side in 1925. Note the raised freight platform for ease of loading boxcars. Increased freight business led to an addition to the freight end. The W&LE retired this depot in 1940. It was replaced with a prefab metal freight building in later years. (W&LE photograph, Special Collections, Michael Schwartz Library, Cleveland State University.)

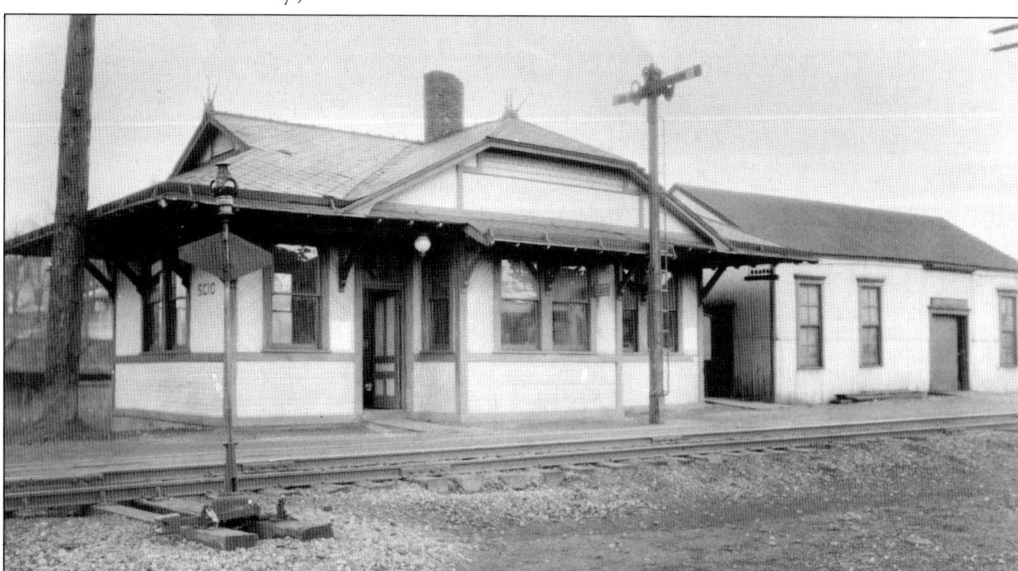

The W&LE constructed the Scio passenger depot in 1889 to a different set of plans than used north of Bowerston. Adjacent was a small freight building. Nearby, the PCC&StL also operated a depot. The Scio depot was closed and sold around 1950 and shortly relocated nearby for commercial use. It remains in 2017. (W&LE photograph, Special Collections, Michael Schwartz Library, Cleveland State University.)

The Jewett depot was built by the W&LE and designed for joint use with the PCC&StL. This 1925 view looks down the W&LE track. By the late 1960s, the depot was gone. (W&LE photograph, Special Collections, Michael Schwartz Library, Cleveland State University.)

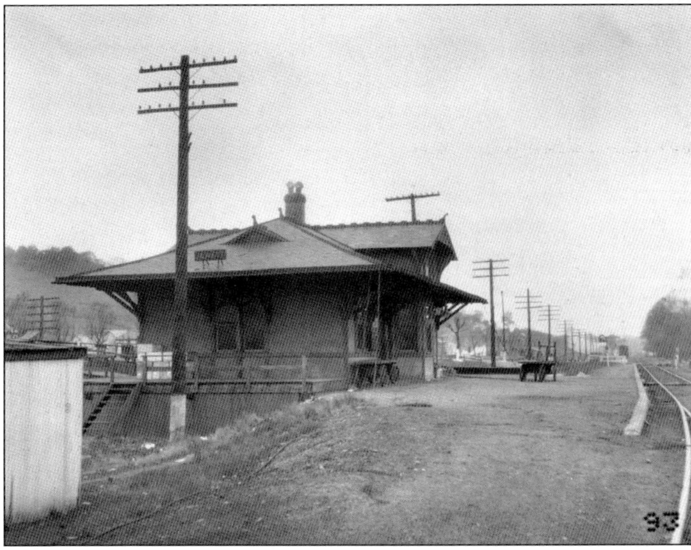

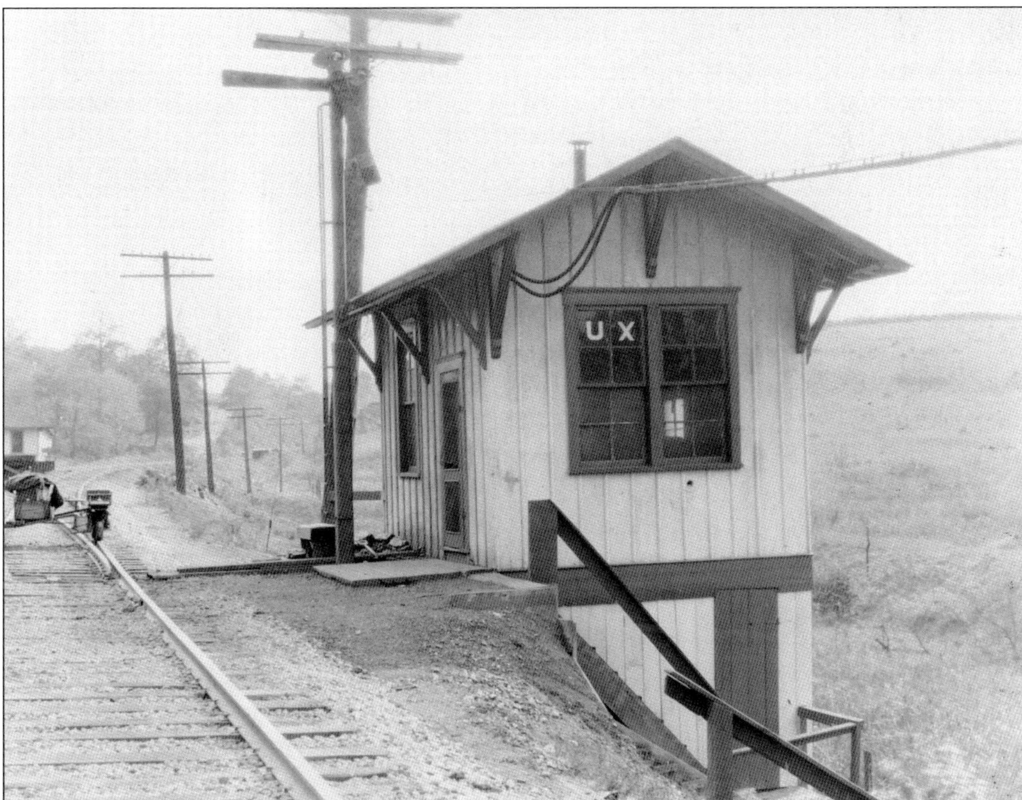

A large frame Pittsburgh & West Virginia Railway passenger depot once served this junction. It was torn down in 1946. The W&LE maintained this small telegraph and train order building. The building actually had two stories; the lower level was for record storage. The "UX" was the telegraph designation of this station. This 1925 view shows the edge of the P&WV's transfer freight house in the distance. The structure was abandoned and vandalized by 1969. (W&LE photograph, Special Collections, Michael Schwartz Library, Cleveland State University.)

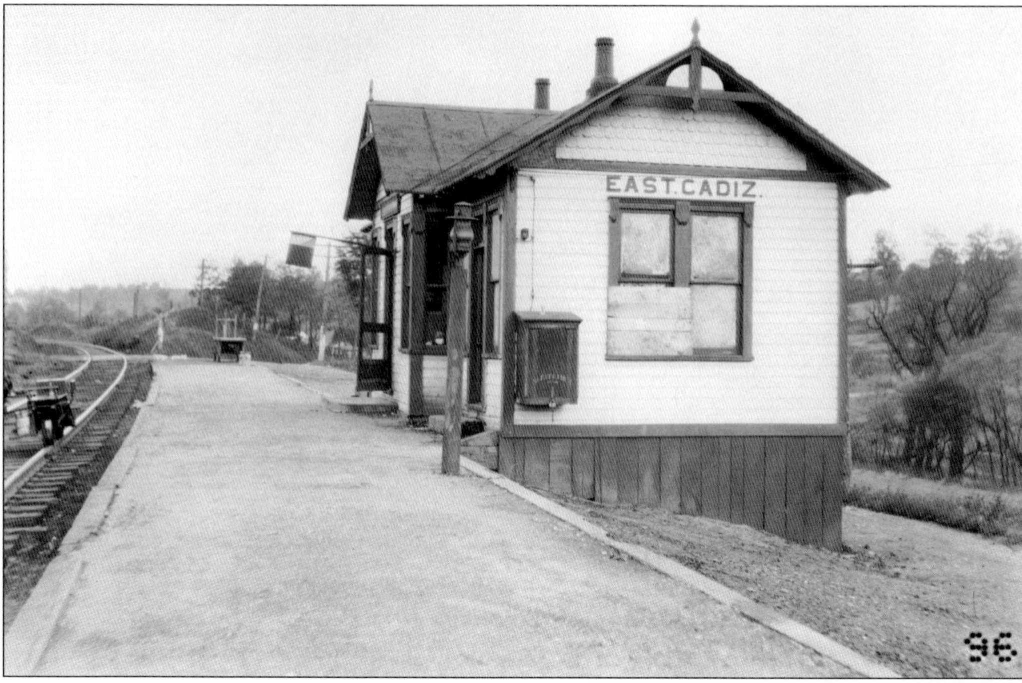

East Cadiz, known formerly as Greenough, was a station on the Toledo Division between Jewett and Adena connected by wagon road to Cadiz. (W&LE photograph, Special Collections, Michael Schwartz Library, Cleveland State University.)

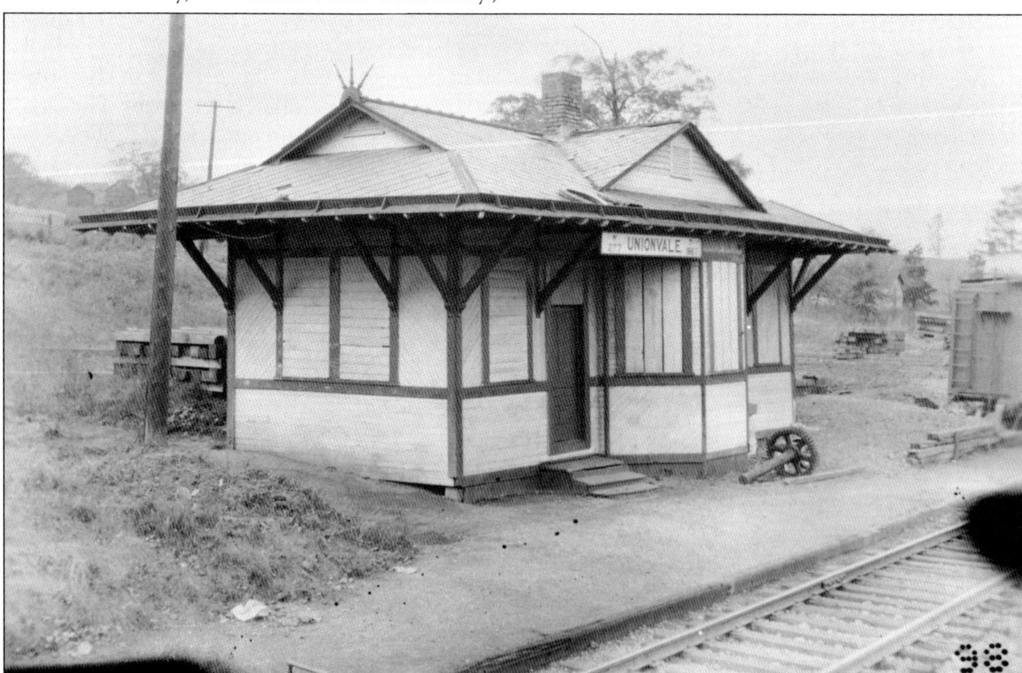

Unionvale was another somewhat isolated depot in the late 1800s–early 1900s. The W&LE had discontinued the agency by 1925. (W&LE photograph, Special Collections, Michael Schwartz Library, Cleveland State University.)

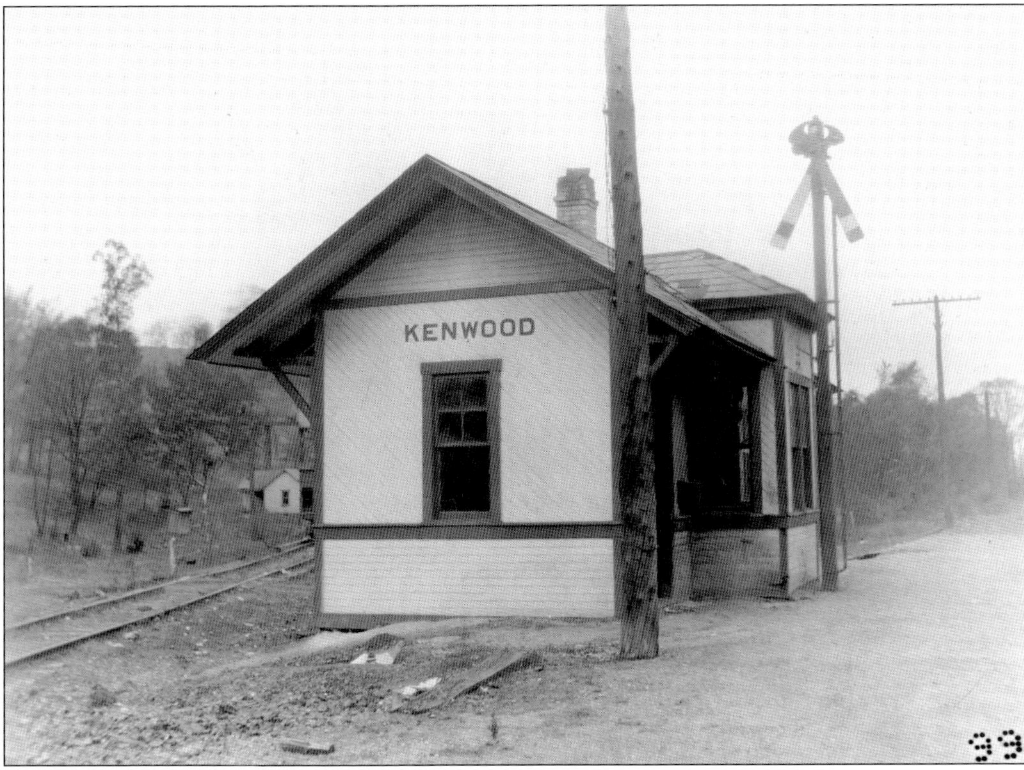

Kenwood was located between Unionvale and Adena. In the 1920s, at least three coal mines were served by this agency. The main mine was the Heil Coal Company. This 1925 view looks northwest toward Jewett. The track behind the depot leads to a coal tipple. Most of the mines were inactive by the mid-1950s but a small yard was still in use for storage of hoppers. The small frame depot was still there in 1975, but in poor shape. (W&LE photograph, Special Collections, Michael Schwartz Library, Cleveland State University.)

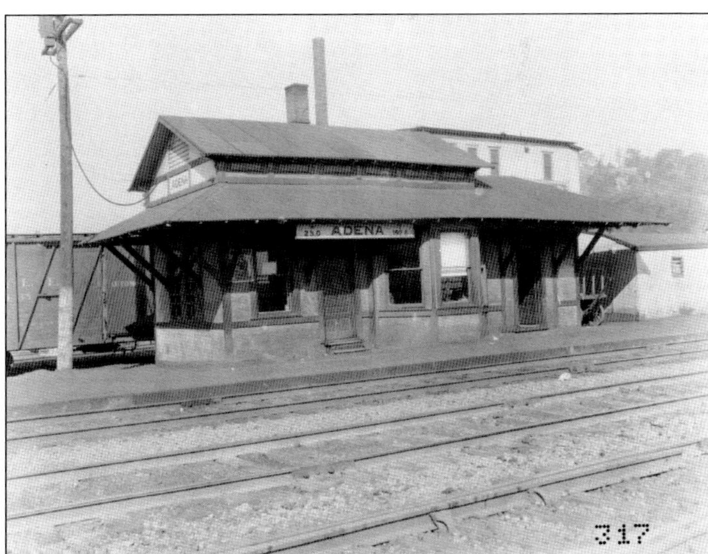

The W&LE depot in Adena dates to 1889. In 1926, a small frame telegraph office with an orderboard was located at the end of the depot platform along with a row of railroad cars converted to maintenance buildings, and further down the track is a water tank. In later years, prefab metal buildings replaced these early structures. (W&LE photograph, Special Collections, Michael Schwartz Library, Cleveland State University.)

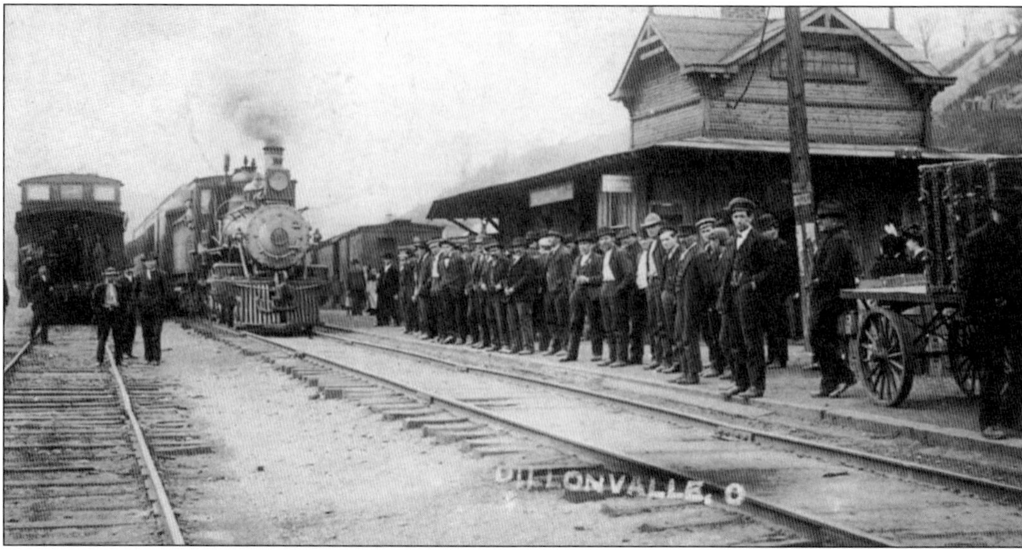

The W&LE reached a location in the coalfields called Dillon in 1890 and erected a two-story frame depot. This and neighboring Pine Valley marked the southern terminal of the line until the W&LE could extend the line into Martins Ferry. The original depot burned down around 1911 and was replaced by a brick two-story depot. (Bob Chilcote collection.)

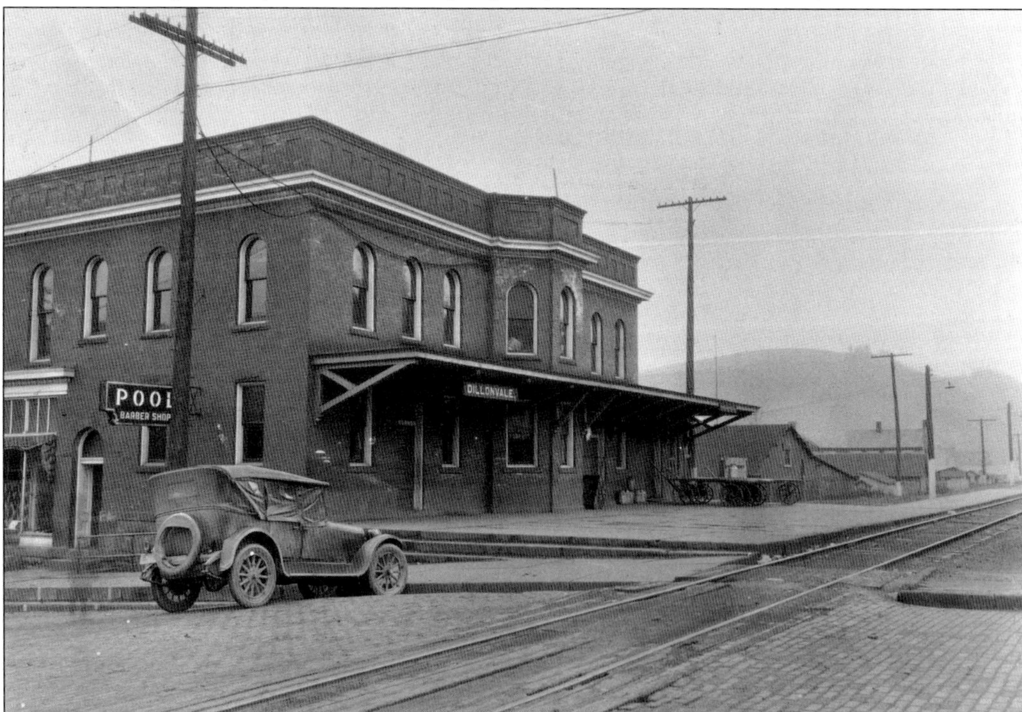

Dillon became Dillonvale around 1912. The depot in 1926 was an early example of a multiuse structure. Railroad offices were upstairs. A number of commercial shops shared the first floor with waiting rooms and a ticket office. At one time, the town board also listed the nearby village of Mount Pleasant. The building was torn down around 1982. (W&LE photograph, Special Collections, Michael Schwartz Library, Cleveland State University.)

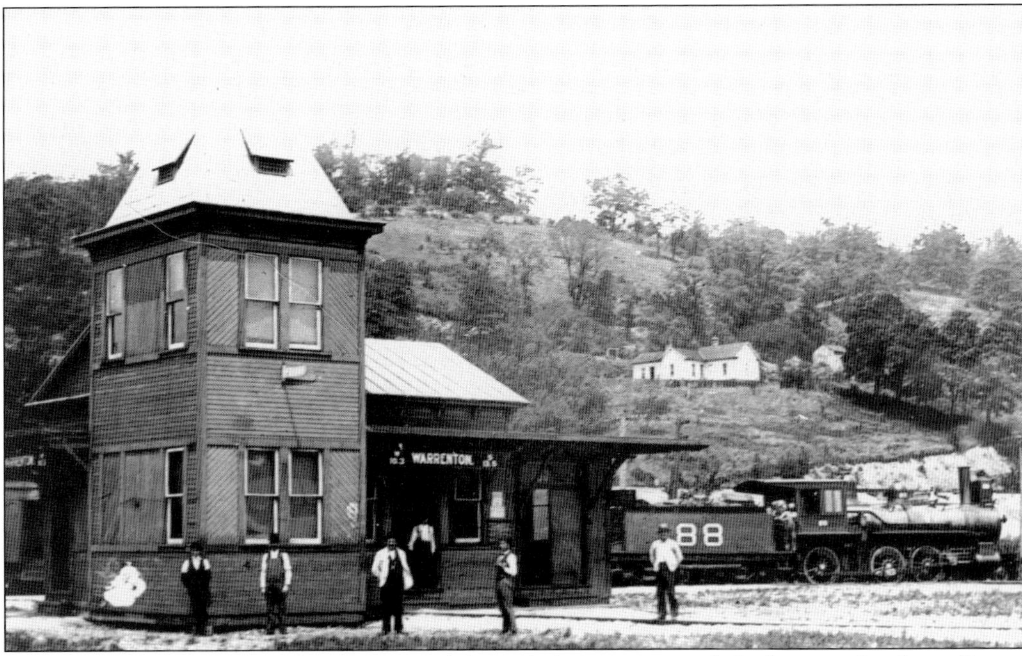

Warrenton was located at the junction of the Toledo Division and the lines to Steubenville and Martins Ferry in the Ohio Valley. The 1913 floodwaters rose to the second story. The depot was removed in July 1945, and an older passenger car served as the depot. At times of flooding, the car could be pulled to higher ground. The passenger train is heading to Steubenville in this c. 1898 view. (Bob Lorenz collection.)

The W&LE depot at Yorkville on the River Division dates to 1891 when the tracks were completed to Martins Ferry. Compare this stucco depot to the one at Baltic (see page 112). The Cleveland & Pittsburgh also had a depot in this river town. (W&LE photograph, Special Collections, Michael Schwartz Library, Cleveland State University.)

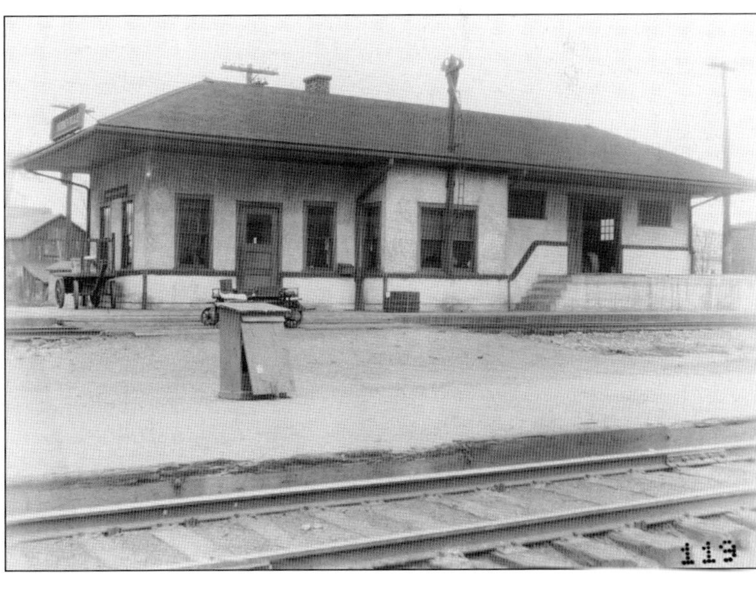

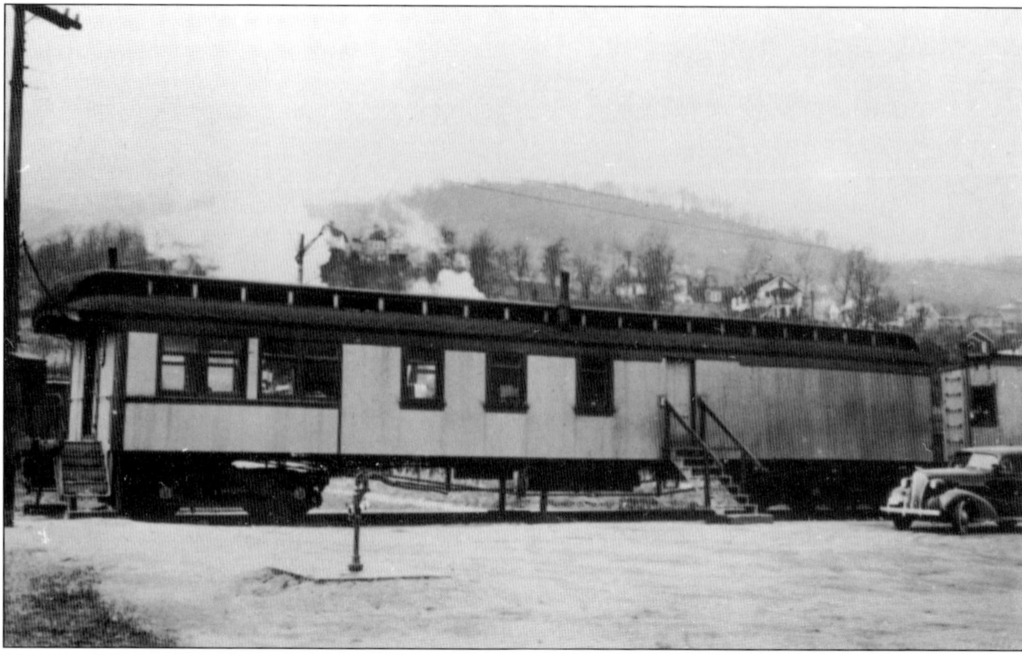

Terminal Junction's depot was an old passenger coach. The W&LE began using these movable depots at spots prone to flooding. With a threat of floodwaters, they could easily be pulled to higher ground. (Gustave Erhardt photograph.)

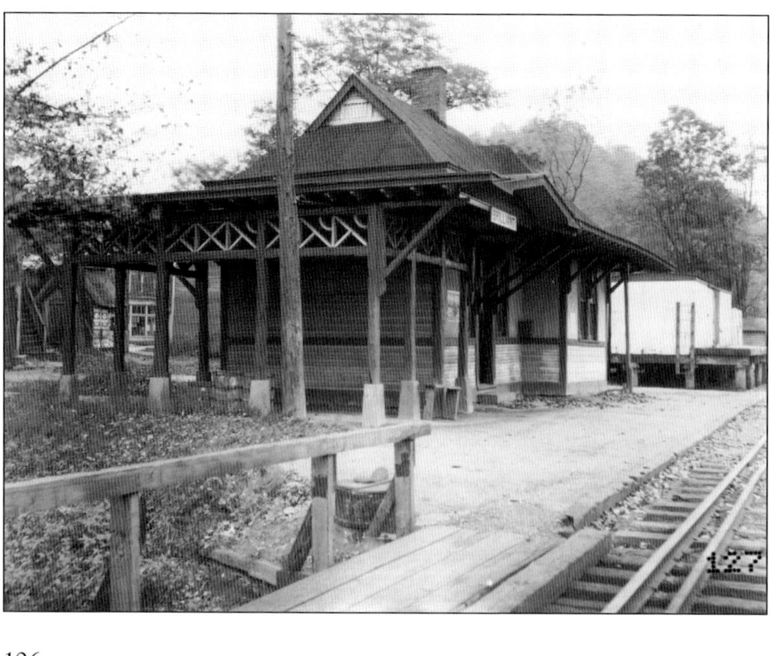

The W&LE opened this trackage in 1891 and built this attractive frame passenger depot at Brilliant. It included a covered outdoor waiting area. Nearby was the depot for the Cleveland & Pittsburgh. (W&LE photograph, Special Collections, Michael Schwartz Library, Cleveland State University.)

Another unique depot was the one at Mingo Junction. A separate freight house was nearby. The C&P also had a depot in this steelmaking town. (W&LE photograph, Special Collections, Michael Schwartz Library, Cleveland State University.)

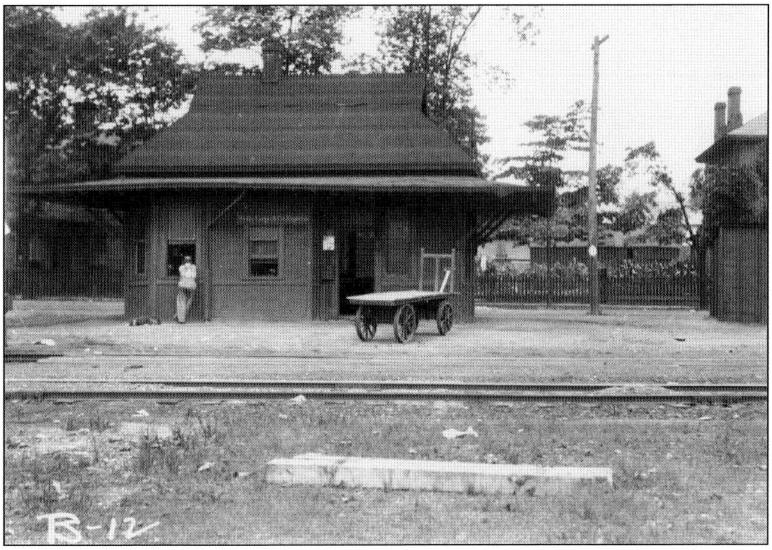

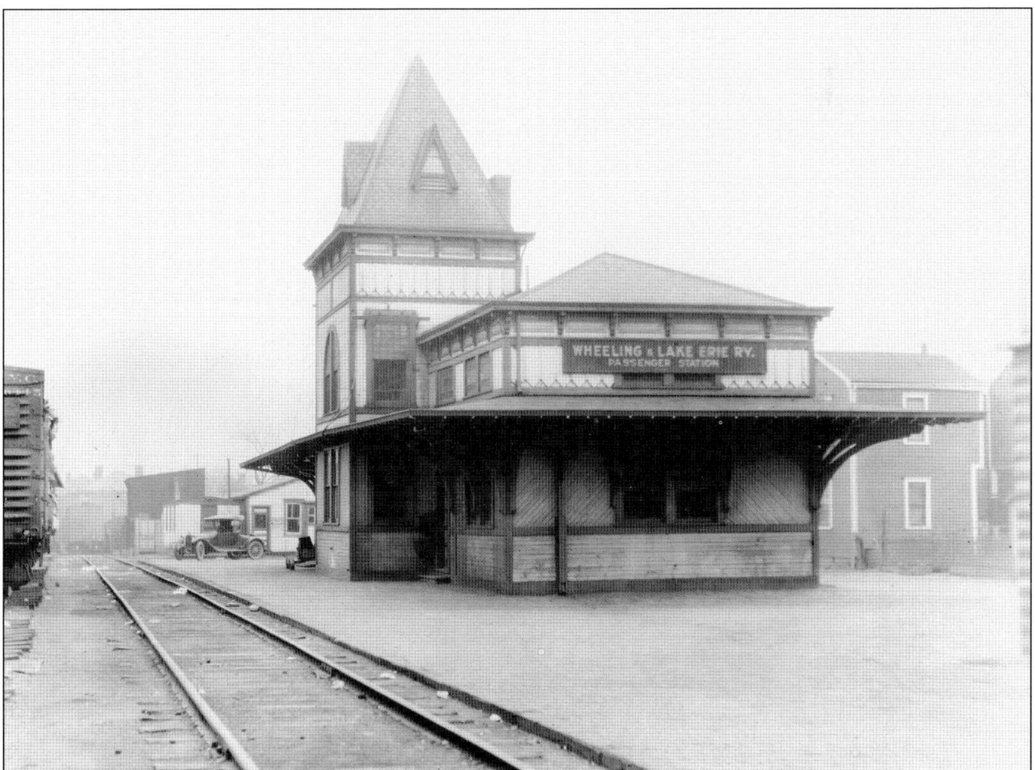

The W&LE completed a branch from Martins Ferry to Steubenville in 1891 and erected this towered frame passenger depot. In its heyday, as many as eight passenger trains arrived and departed each day. It was torn down in the 1930s. Nearby was a frame freight house dating to 1890. The freight house was replaced in 1938 by a metal structure. (W&LE photograph, Special Collections, Michael Schwartz Library, Cleveland State University.)

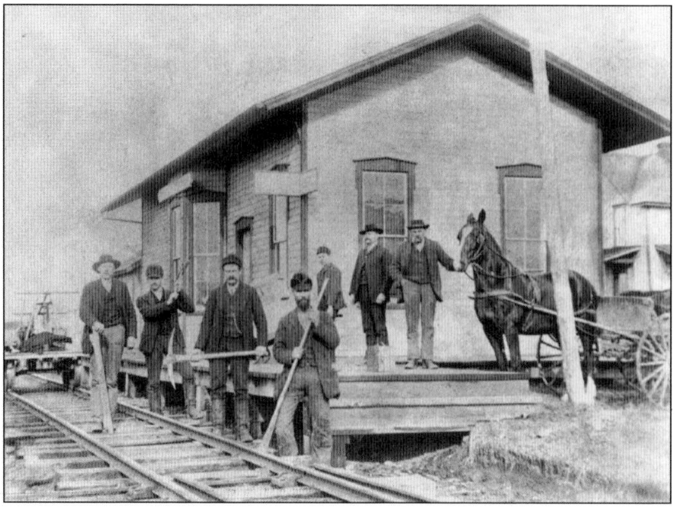

The Connotton Valley completed its Connotton Northern Railway narrow-gauge line from Canton to Cleveland in December 1880. In this early view, a Connotton Valley section crew works on the narrow-gauge track at the 1880 combination depot in Middlebranch. The depot was still in railroad use in August 1967 and torn down in 1969. (W&LE collection, Special Collections, Michael Schwartz Library, Cleveland State University.)

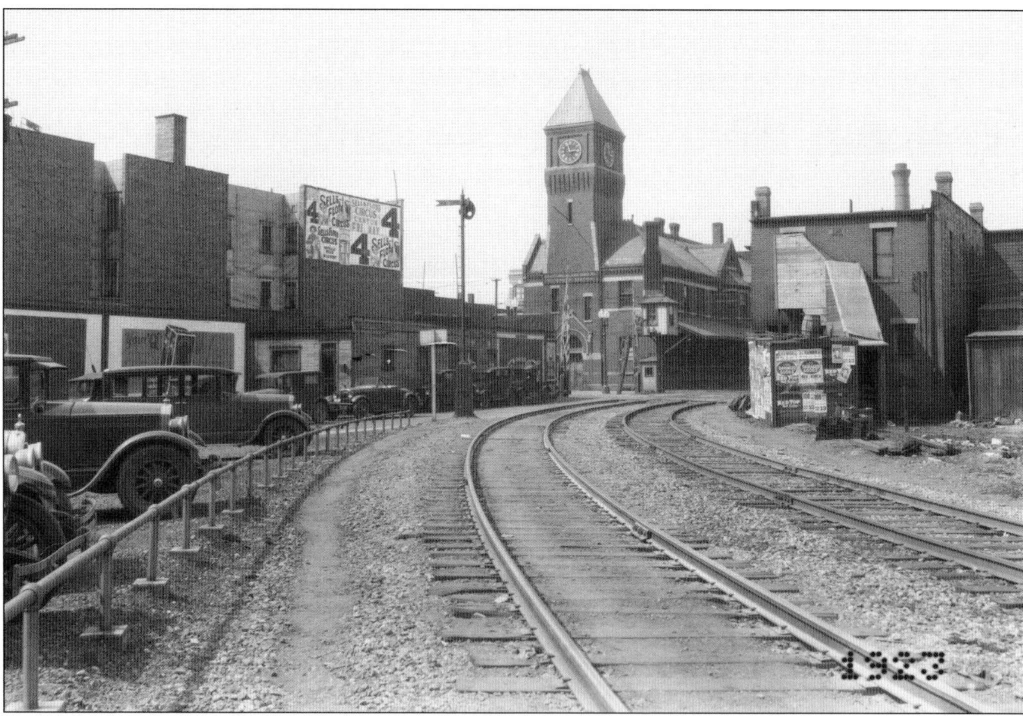

The Connotton Valley began running trains between Dell Roy and Canton by May 1880. The narrow-gauge line was not to be outdone in depot construction. The company built this two-story brick passenger depot with a high clock tower to serve as the general offices in downtown Canton in 1881. It became the proud and joy of the Wheeling & Lake Erie. Within four months of the last passenger trains in July 1938, it was dismantled in November by a local salvage company. (W&LE photograph, Special Collections, Michael Schwartz Library, Cleveland State University.)

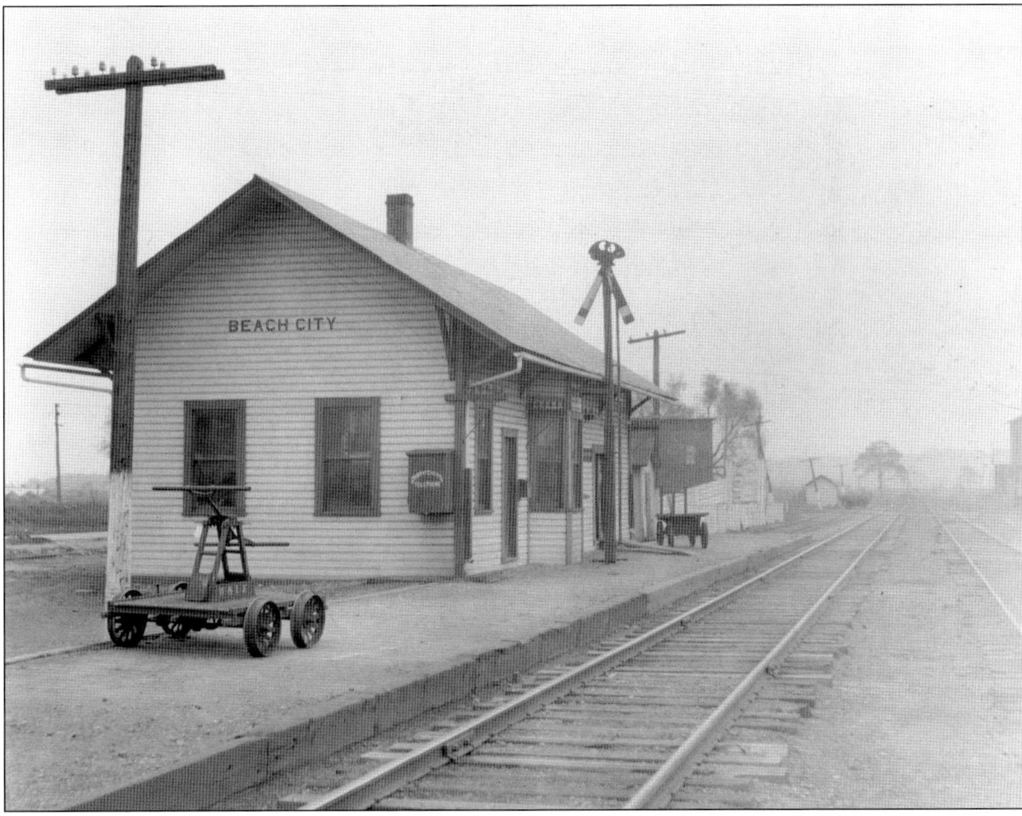

This 1925 valuation photograph was taken looking south in Beach City. The depot probably dates to 1888 when the narrow-gauge Connotton Valley completed this line to Coshocton. The B&O also maintained a separate combination depot in Beach City. Both were gone by the late 1960s. (W&LE photograph, Special Collections, Michael Schwartz Library, Cleveland State University.)

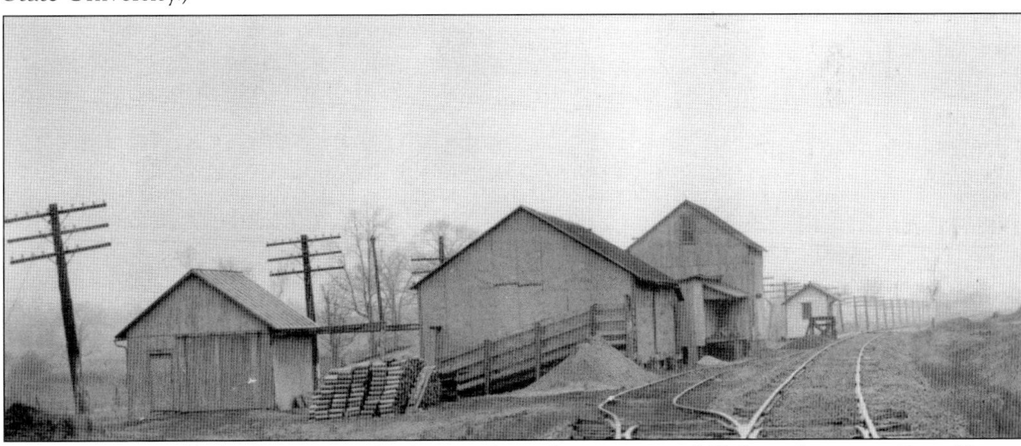

The W&LE established a station for Sonnenberg, later renamed Kidron, between Orrville and Justus on the Brewster cutoff. This valuation photograph records a frame three-sided shelter. It was a two-mile buggy ride down a dusty road into the village. By the 1930s, the shelter was gone, and a town board now reading Kidron was mounted to a new grain elevator. (W&LE photograph, Special Collections, Michael Schwartz Library, Cleveland State University.)

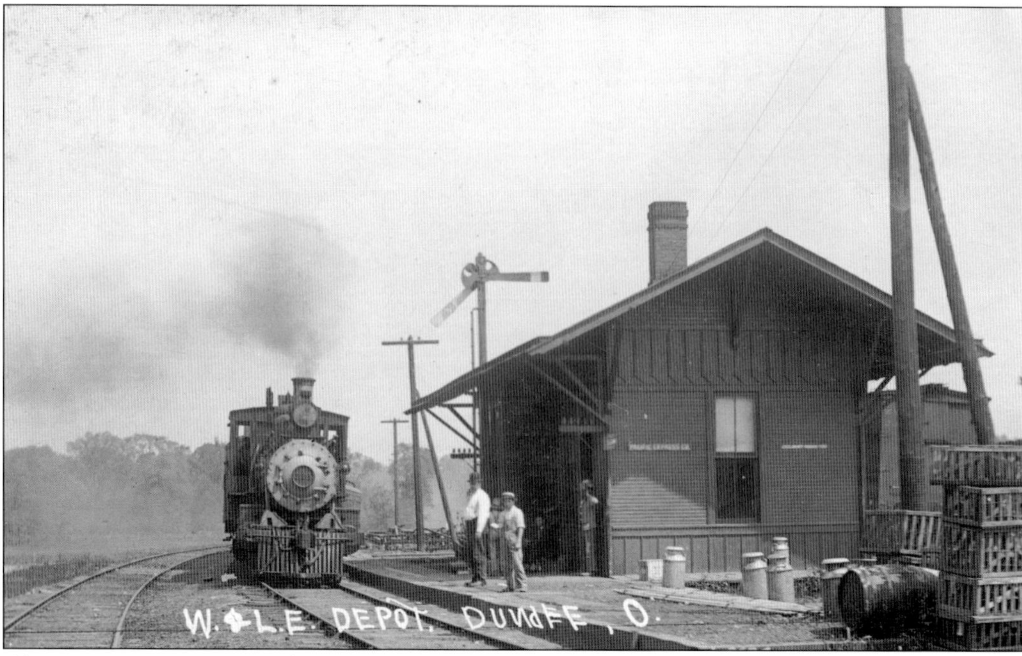

Above is a c. 1910 postcard view of the 1888 Connotton Valley combination depot at Dundee. Compare the architecture of this depot to certain PCC&StL depot plans. Sometimes, plans are very similar and occasionally shared. In 1936, the completion of the Beach City Dam led to a rerouting of part of W&LE's Cleveland Division and construction of a new depot for Dundee by a Strasburg lumber company. The combination depot was opened in November 1936. The earlier depot shows a retirement date in W&LE records of 1938. Interestingly, W&LE passenger service had ended in 1932, and the new depot was built with a passenger waiting room. The photograph below shows it in January 1937. Both are now long gone. (Above, author's collection; below, W&LE photograph, Special Collections, Michael Schwartz Library, Cleveland State University.)

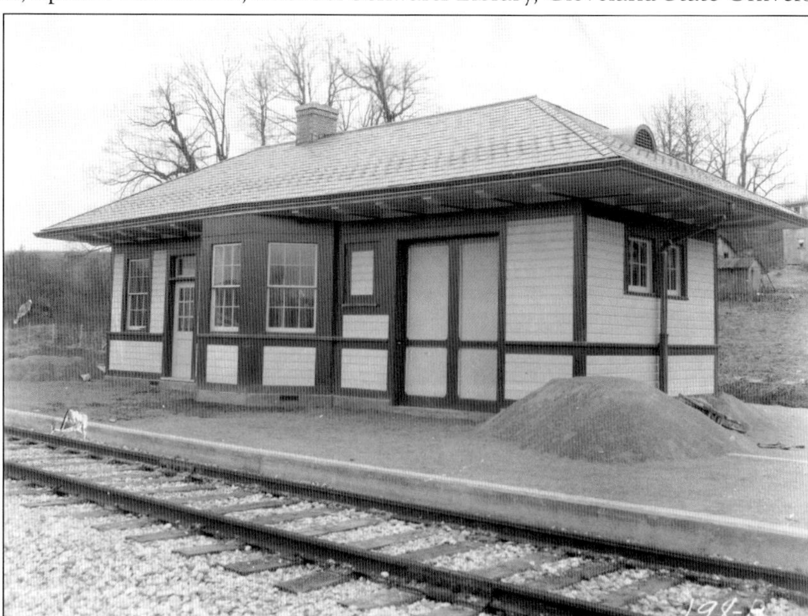

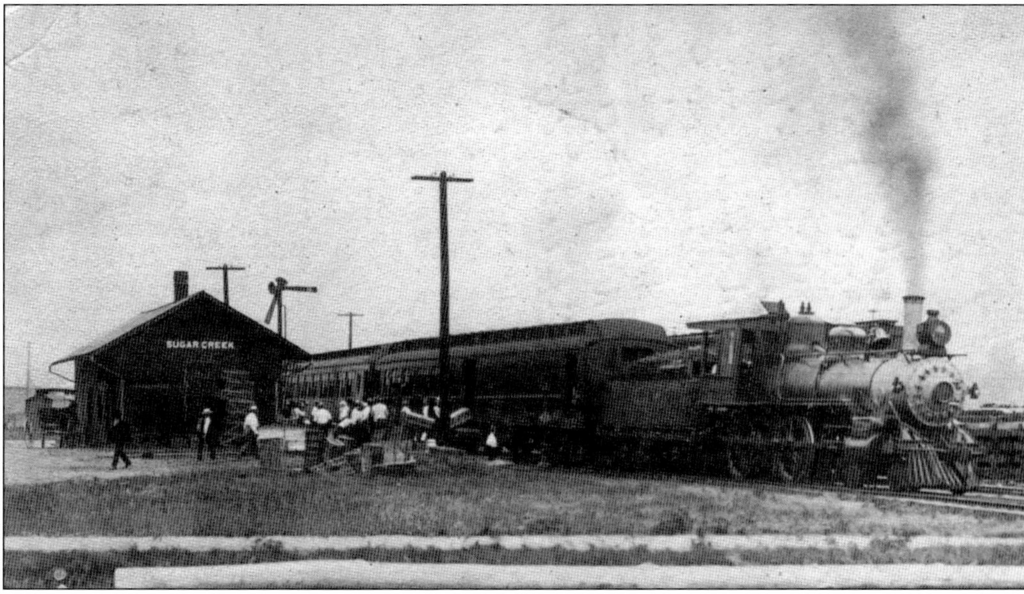

Around 1910, a southbound passenger train sits at the 1888 combination depot at Sugar Creek on the line to Zanesville. This line was completed by the Connotton Valley (later Cleveland, Canton & Southern) in 1888 as far as Coshocton. The depot was destroyed by fire on February 8, 1914. The W&LE used bricks from the local brick companies in the new 1916 depot, seen below. This depot continues to serve the Ohio Central Railroad. (Both, author's collection.)

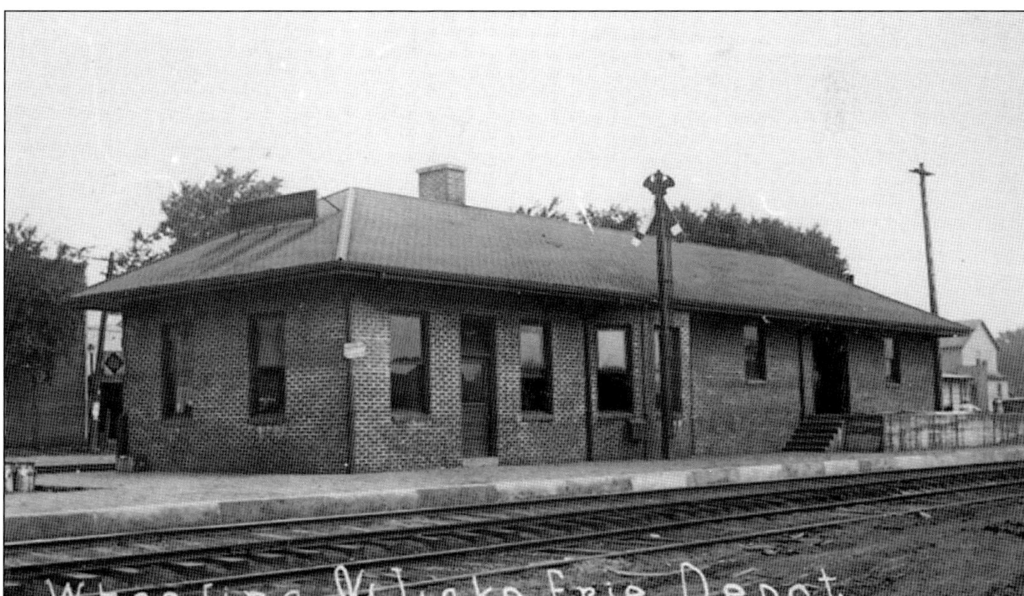

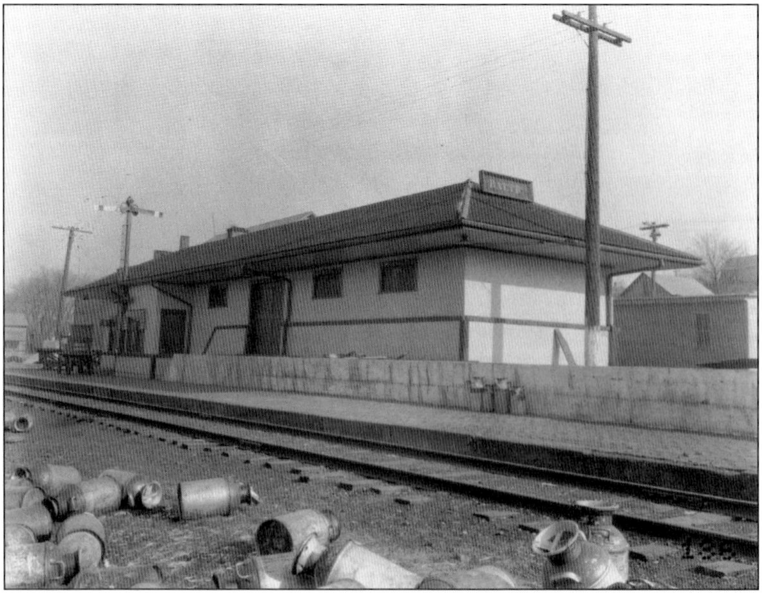

The stucco Baltic depot seen in 1925 had an extended freight room. The depot still stood in 1971. (W&LE photograph, Special Collections, Michael Schwartz Library, Cleveland State University.)

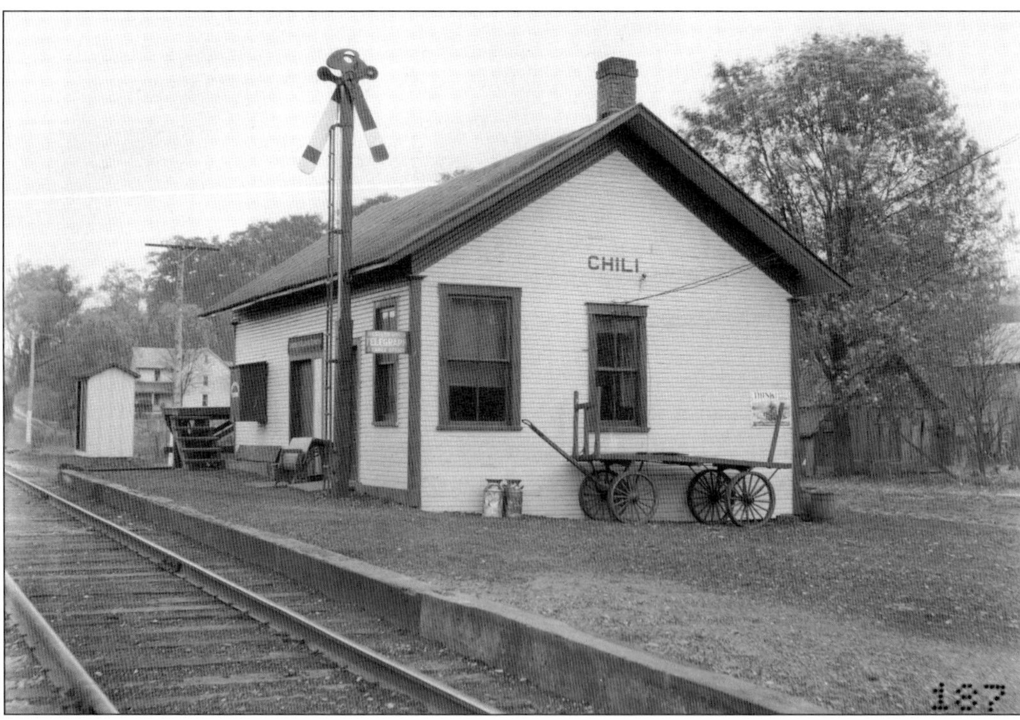

The Cleveland, Canton & Southern, standard-gauge successor of the Connotton Valley, built this combination depot in 1896. Chili, later Pearl, was also a water station on the Zanesville line. (W&LE photograph, Special Collections, Michael Schwartz Library, Cleveland State University.)

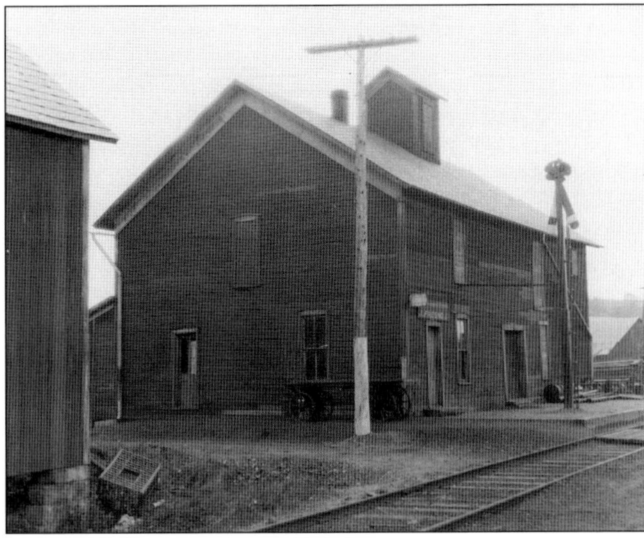

This unusual barnlike depot in Fresno was constructed by the Connotton Valley in 1883. The second floor may have been used for grain storage in lieu of a town elevator as was the case on the Lake Shore & Michigan Southern and Michigan Central lines elsewhere in the Midwest. The building was torn down in December 1948 and replaced by a metal prefab structure. By August 1969, only a concrete foundation remained. (W&LE photograph, Special Collections, Michael Schwartz Library, Cleveland State University.)

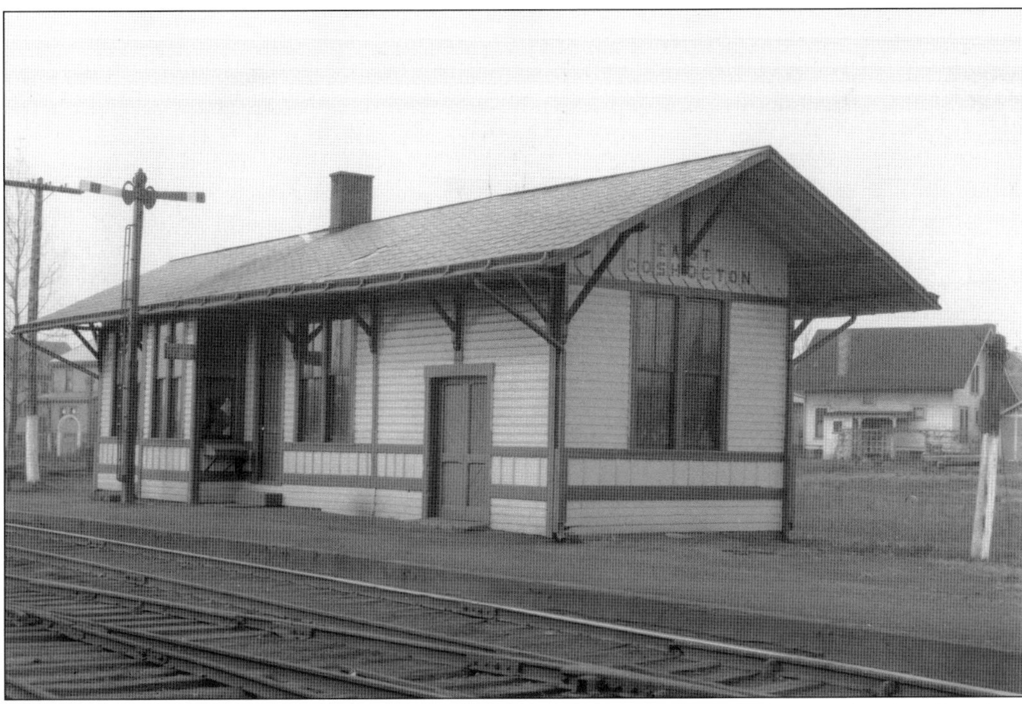

This passenger depot, originally known as Hill Station, was built in Coshocton by the Cleveland Canton & Southern in 1883 near the intersection of Cambridge Road and Orange Street. When predecessor W&LE constructed a downtown passenger depot, this depot was relocated south and renamed East Coshocton. It mainly served as a telegraph office until passenger service returned in September 1931 with the closing of the downtown depot. This did not last long as the W&LE terminated all passenger service June 1, 1932. The East Coshocton structure was razed around 2010. (W&LE photograph, Special Collections, Michael Schwartz Library, Cleveland State University.)

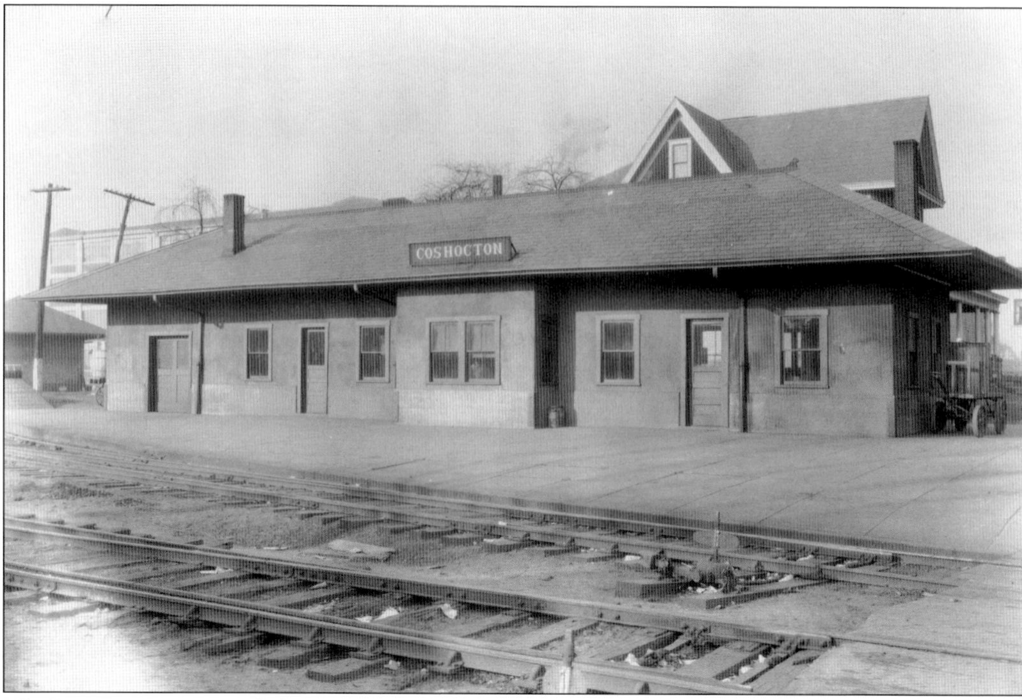

The W&LE constructed this stucco passenger depot at Sixth and Orange Streets in Coshocton, a block from the PCC&StL facilities, opening it in late August 1910. The W&LE abandoned the downtown depot in September 1931 and returned to the relocated Hill Station now renamed East Coshocton. The depot was still there in August 1969 but gone by April 1971. (W&LE photograph, Special Collections, Michael Schwartz Library, Cleveland State University.)

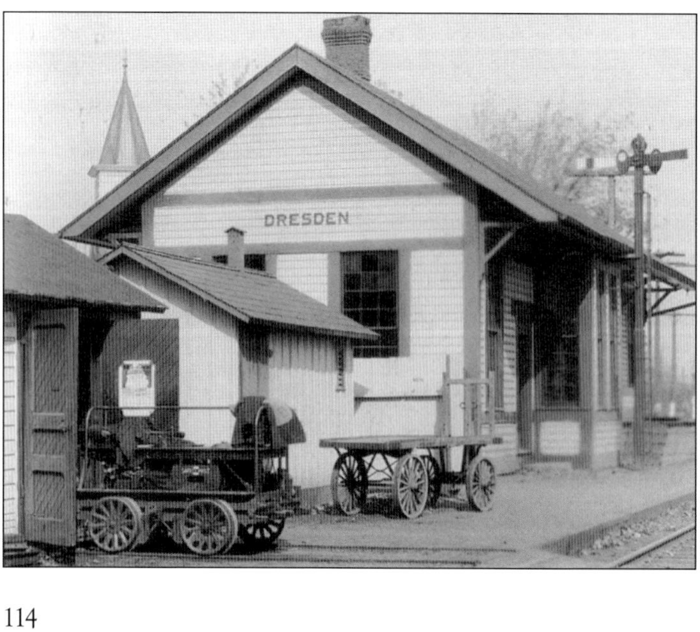

This combination depot was built by the W&LE in 1900 to replace an earlier Coshocton & Southern (later Cleveland, Canton & Southern) depot, which was located near the junction with the Cincinnati & Muskingum Valley (PRR) in Dresden. Railroad use ended in 1972. Both this and the C&MV depot have been restored and preserved. (W&LE photograph, Special Collections, Michael Schwartz Library, Cleveland State University.)

The two-story Coshocton & Southern (later Cleveland, Canton & Southern) depot was built in Ellis in 1888 with a second-floor apartment for the agent and family since suitable housing was not readily available at this country location. An old boxcar was placed as a freight house. Everything was razed in December 1938. (W&LE photograph, Special Collections, Michael Schwartz Library, Cleveland State University.)

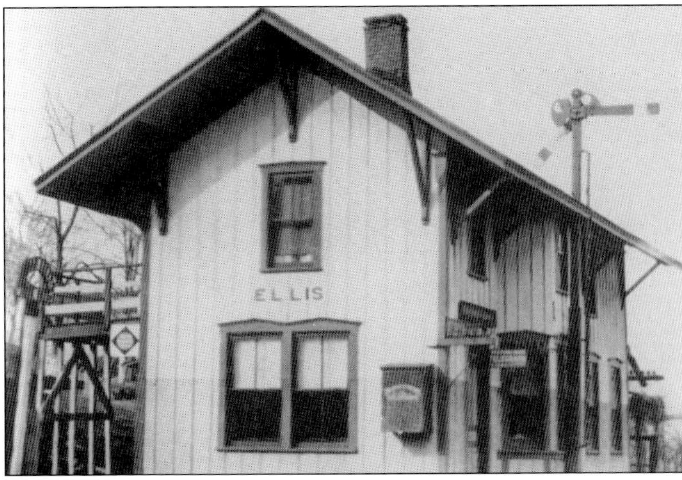

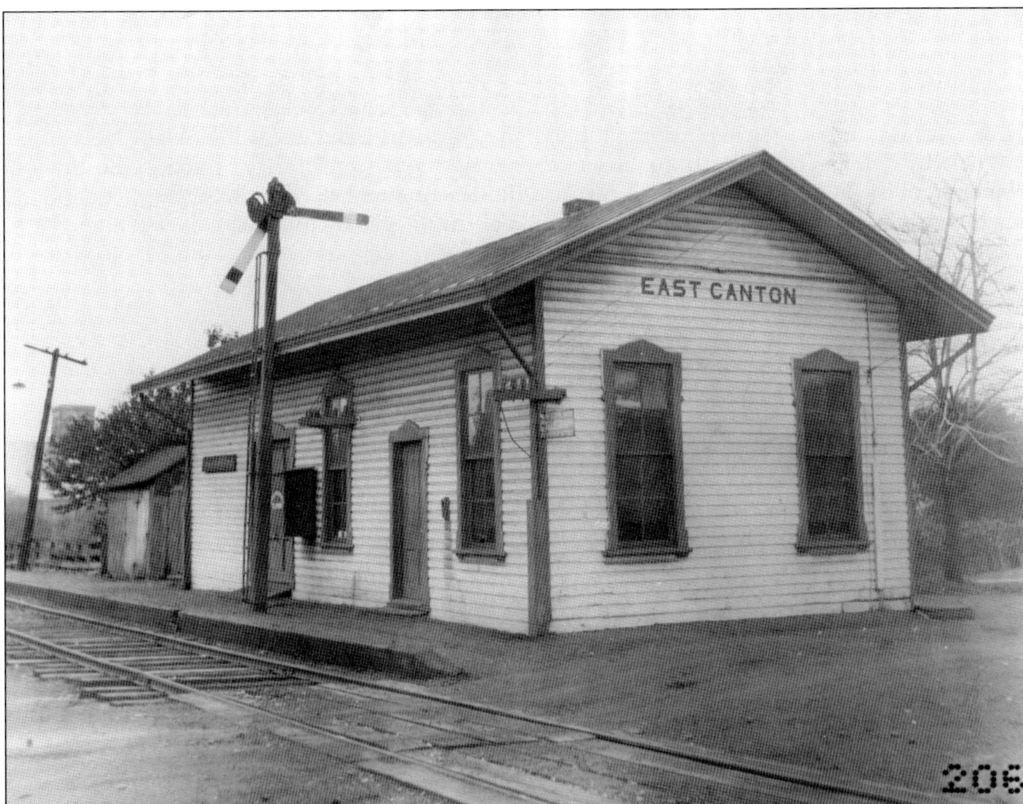

The Connotton Valley began serving Osnaburg, now East Canton, in Stark County in May 1880. This depot was built around this time, initially with copper roofing. Sometime in the 1930s, it was reportedly replaced with shingles. Spurs were extended off the main line to a number of coal mines. A local brick plant provided more business. The depot was a candidate for preservation but unfortunately was torn down around 2010. (W&LE photograph, Special Collections, Michael Schwartz Library, Cleveland State University.)

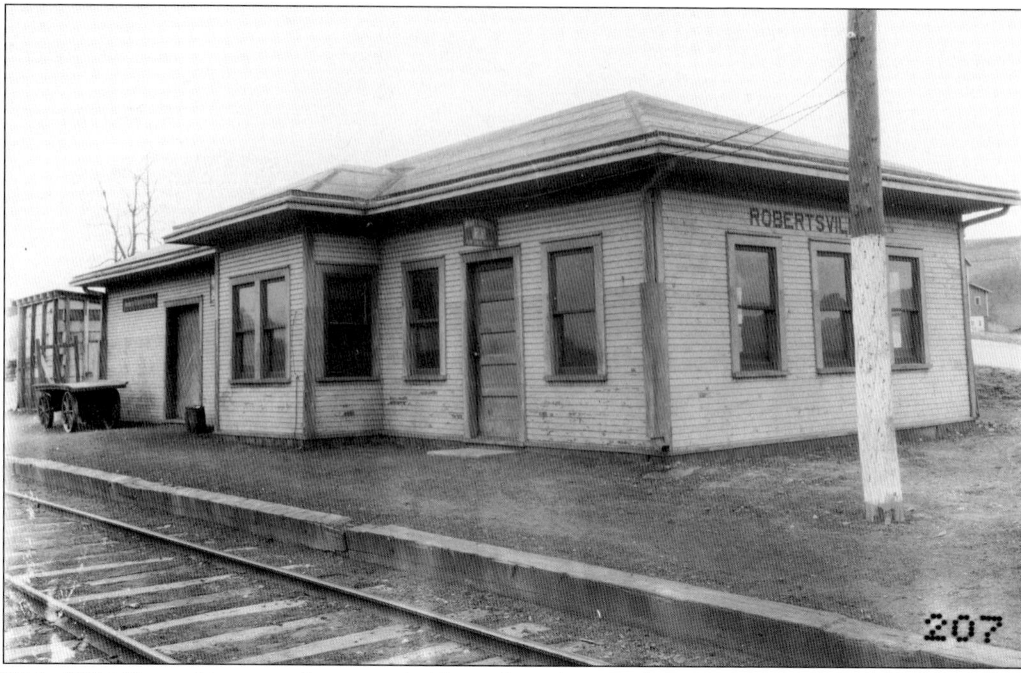

This W&LE combination depot probably replaced an earlier Connotton Valley structure in Robertsville. Nearby was the Robertsville tunnel dating to 1880. This valuation photograph dates to 1925. (W&LE photograph, Special Collections, Michael Schwartz Library, Cleveland State University.)

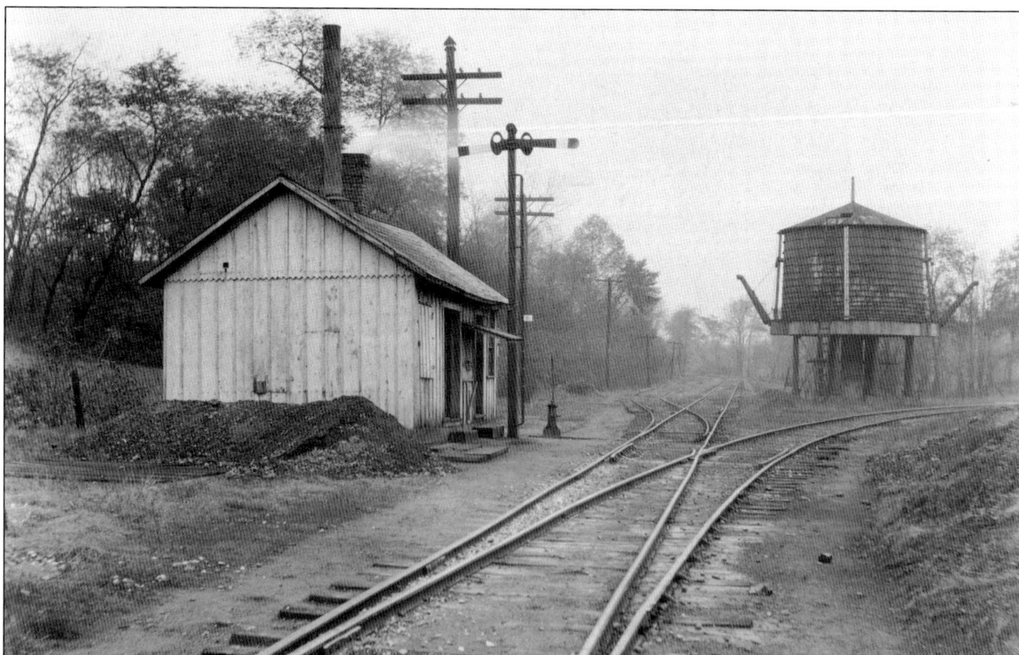

This view at Minerva Junction shows the pump house/train order station and twin-spout water tank. The view is looking north towards Canton. The branch to Minerva heads off to the right. (W&LE collection, Special Collections, Michael Schwartz Library, Cleveland State University.)

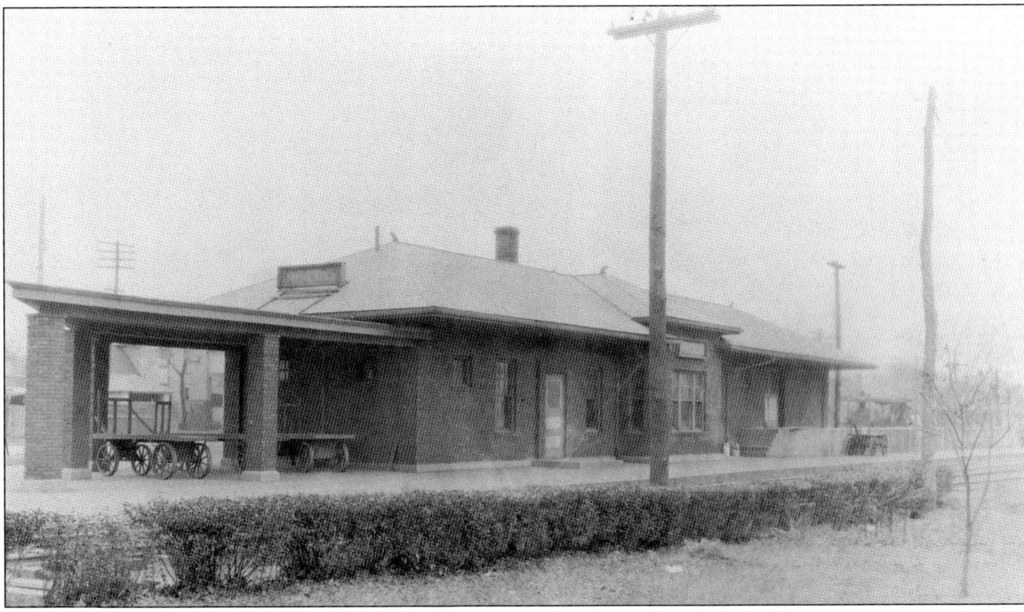

The W&LE replaced an earlier frame depot with this brick building around 1915. The Minerva depot closed in 1980 and was refurbished in the 1990s. A general store also served as the depot at Hibbets between Oneida and Carrollton. An old boxcar was used as a freight house. (W&LE photograph, Special Collections, Michael Schwartz Library, Cleveland State University.)

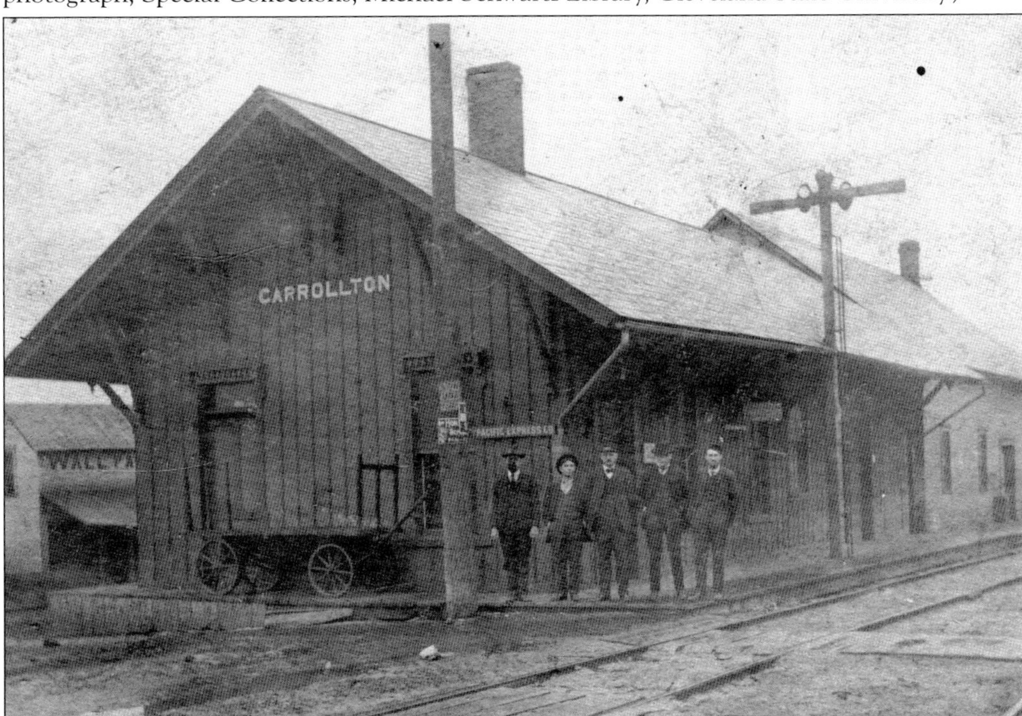

Carrollton was an early area of railroad development in east central Ohio. The first depot, built by the Carroll County Railroad in 1853, burned down in 1876 and was replaced by the depot seen here around 1908, built by the Connotton Valley in 1880. (Author's collection.)

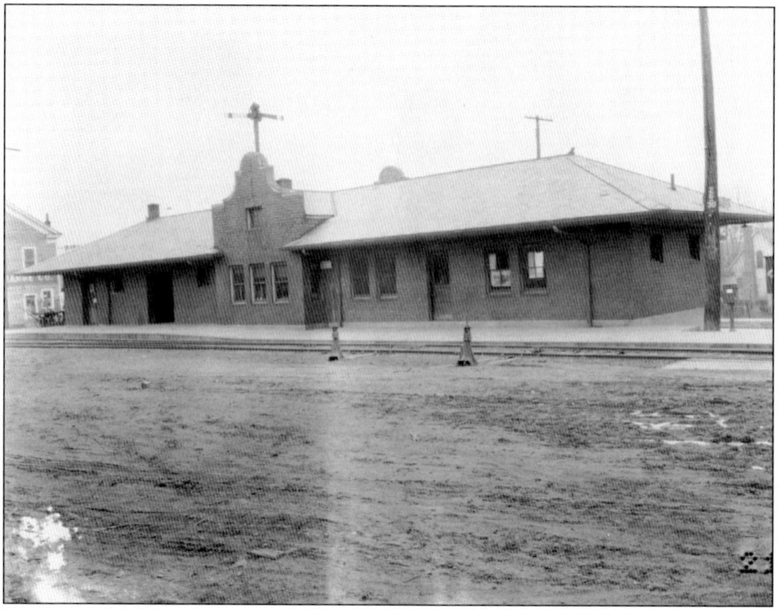

The W&LE built this Carrollton depot in 1913 of brick from local brick plants. Business was booming, with two local potteries being the largest employers in the area. (W&LE photograph, Special Collections, Michael Schwartz Library, Cleveland State University.)

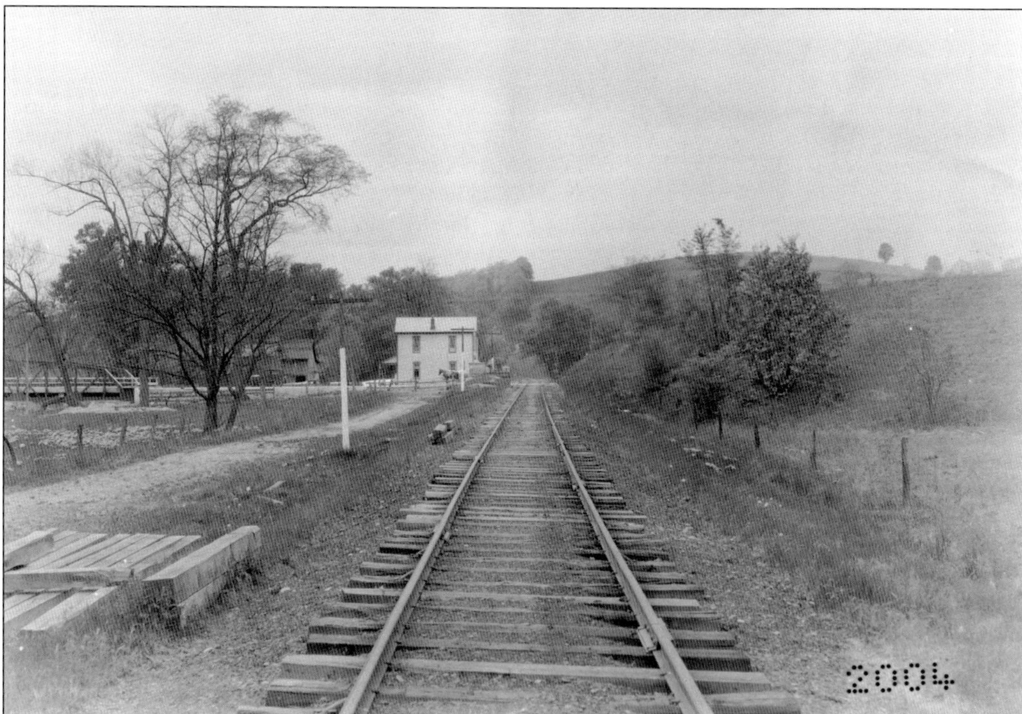

Tabor Station is seen in the distance of this W&LE valuation photograph. This station was originally called Scott's Station, but the name had to be changed because there was already a station of that name. The second floor was a boardinghouse. The first floor contained a kitchen, dining room, storeroom, and a blacksmith shop. The W&LE line south of Carrollton was abandoned due to another flood control project Atwood Lake in 1935–1936. Part of Tabor Station was relocated for preservation at the Algonquin Mill complex in Petersburg. (W&LE photograph, Special Collections, Michael Schwartz Library, Cleveland State University.)

Five

Other Lines

Passing through the northern reaches of Wayne County and the central part of Ashland County with a branch from Youngstown to Lisbon was the Erie Railroad. This evolved from the broad-gauge Atlantic & Great Western Railroad that opened across Ohio to Dayton in June 1864 and became the New York, Pennsylvania & Ohio Railroad in 1880. At this time, the line was changed to standard gauge. The Erie assumed control of the Niles & New Lisbon Railway, which had built a line between the Atlantic & Great Western at Niles to more rich coal beds at Lisbon.

Brick and tile was the main reason for the building of Millersburg, Jeromesville, & Greenwich Railroad in 1894–1895, linking Brown's Station on the PC&StL to Jeromesville. This line opened to Ashland in 1899 as the Ashland and Wooster Railway. After monetary woes, the line was connected with the Lorain & Ashland Railroad, which ran from Lorain to Wellington, creating the Lorain, Ashland & Southern Railroad. The line closed down in August 1925. Due to the early owner's brickworks, many of the depots were of brick construction.

The Pittsburgh, Lisbon & Western (PL&W) Railroad, incorporated in October 1902, replaced a series of earlier coal- and clay-carrying Pennsylvania lines. The New York, Pittsburgh & Chicago Railway was building west towards Rogersville (now Rogers) in 1882, completing it to Lisbon in 1888 as the Pittsburgh, Marion & Chicago Railway. Shops were located in Negley; offices were in Lisbon. The PL&W ran its last train in 1942.

Heading east from Pittsburgh Junction, a station on the W&LE, to a crossing of the Ohio River at Mingo Junction is the Toledo, Pittsburgh & Western Railway, incorporated in 1901. This late-bloomer, completed in 1904 as the Wabash Pittsburgh Terminal Railway, was a masterpiece of cut and fill and bridge and tunnel engineering between Pittsburgh Junction and Pittsburgh. After reorganization, it became the Pittsburgh & West Virginia Railway in 1917. Norfolk Southern trains use the route in 2017. Depots were built to a set of standard plans.

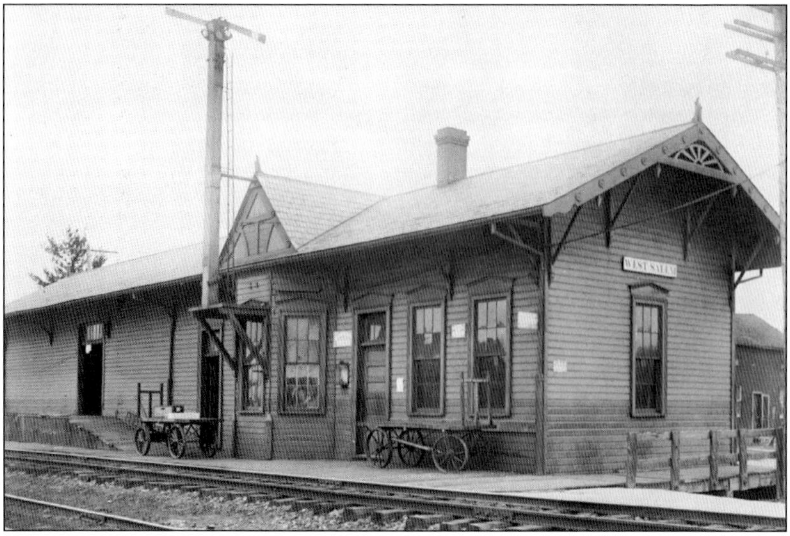

The Erie Railroad used this standard plan combination depot at West Salem. Note the unusual design of the orderboard. Most Erie depots had freestanding orderboards. The West Salem combination depot was still trackside in 1971. (Erie photograph, author's collection.)

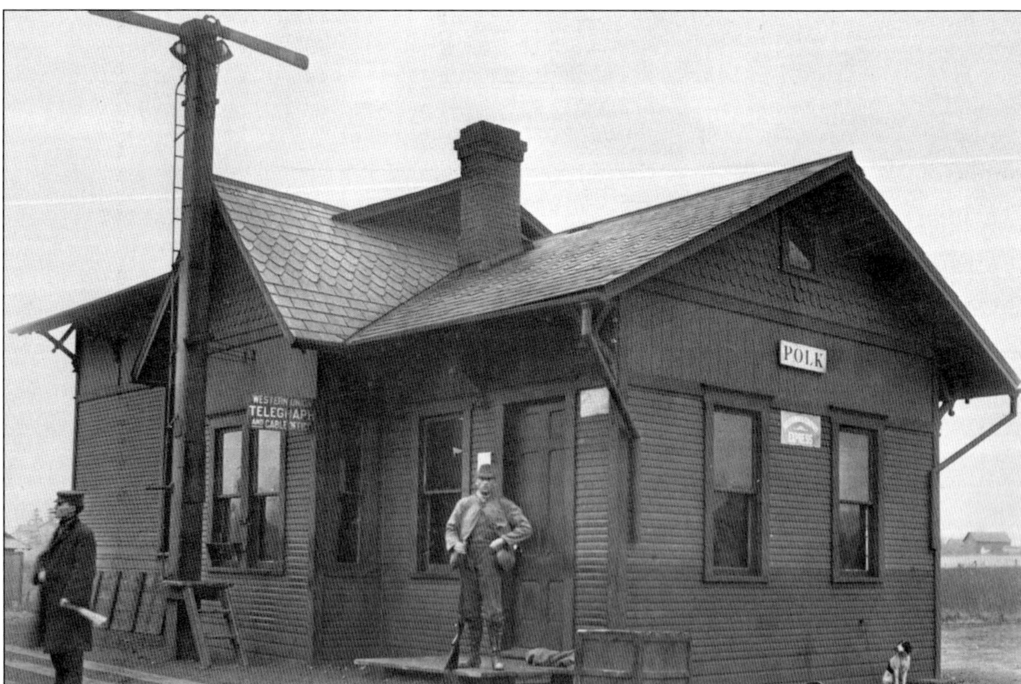

A second standard plan for Erie depots was used at Polk, the next station to the west. The agent, a lone passenger, and agent's dog await the incoming train. This depot was removed by the late 1960s. Passenger service ended in 1970. Another view of this depot appears on the cover. (Erie photograph, author's collection.)

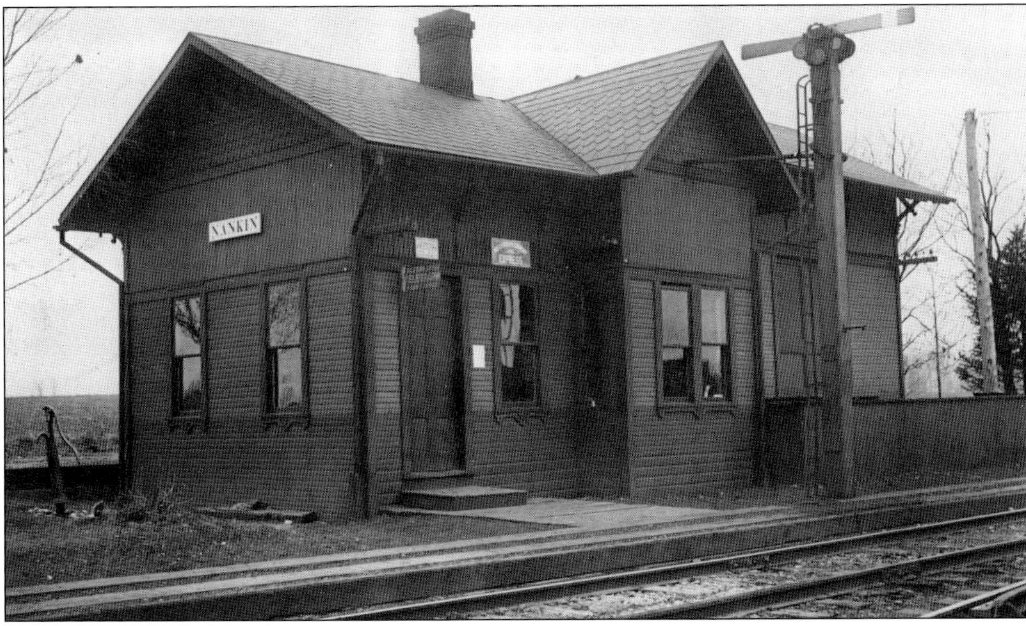

The Erie combination depot at Nankin was built to the same plan as Polk, but it was a mirror image. Nankin also had an elevated freight platform. Declining business led to its closing and removal by the late 1960s. (Erie photograph, author's collection.)

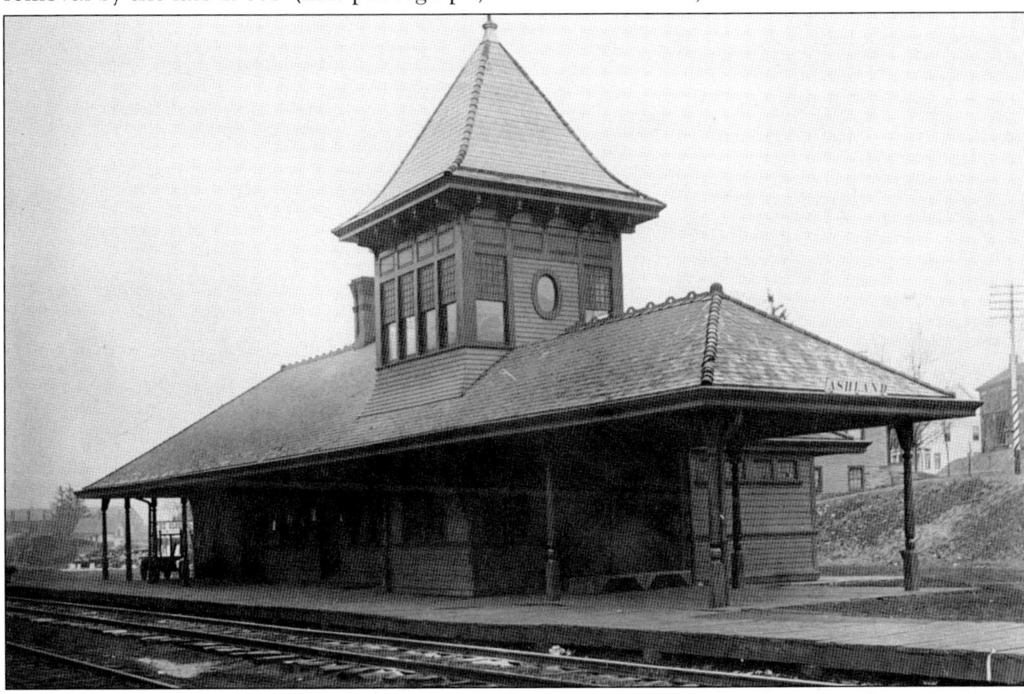

New York Pennsylvania & Ohio's original depot in Ashland burned on October 17, 1891. A temporary ticket office and waiting room were established in a former section house. Eventually, the Erie opened this $4,500 depot on February 9, 1893, to a crowd of approving residents and officials. After many successful years of serving the travelers of Ashland and the surrounding countryside, the depot was beset with two unfortunate events in 1943. (Author's collection.)

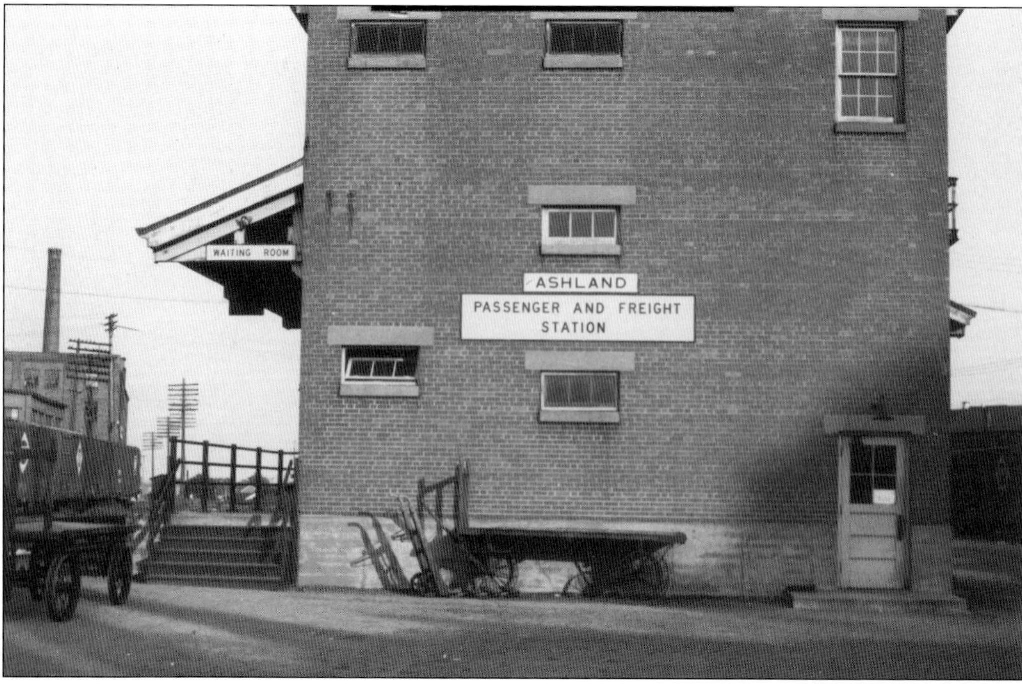

On June 23, 1943, a tremendous explosion in a boxcar near the Ashland passenger depot resulted in two deaths, serious injuries to three others, and major property damage. It also so damaged the second-floor tower that it had to be removed. On September 25, 1943, a couple of tank cars derailed outside the depot and crashed into the depot. An intense fire created havoc. In all, a total of 21 gas tank cars derailed. The Erie demolished the damaged depot and moved its passenger facilities to its brick freight house shown above in 1960. (Charles Garvin photograph.)

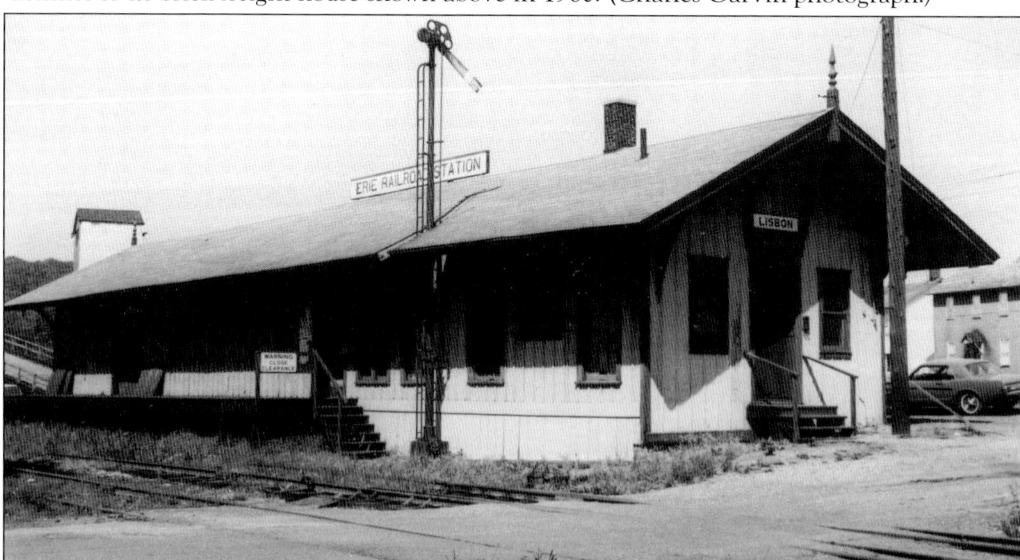

The Niles & New Lisbon, formed in 1869, became the Niles and Lisbon branch of the Erie Railroad. There was a joint passenger depot in Leetonia (see page 40) and a frame combination depot in Franklin Square. The line ended at this combination depot in Lisbon. The depot is now a museum. (Author's collection.)

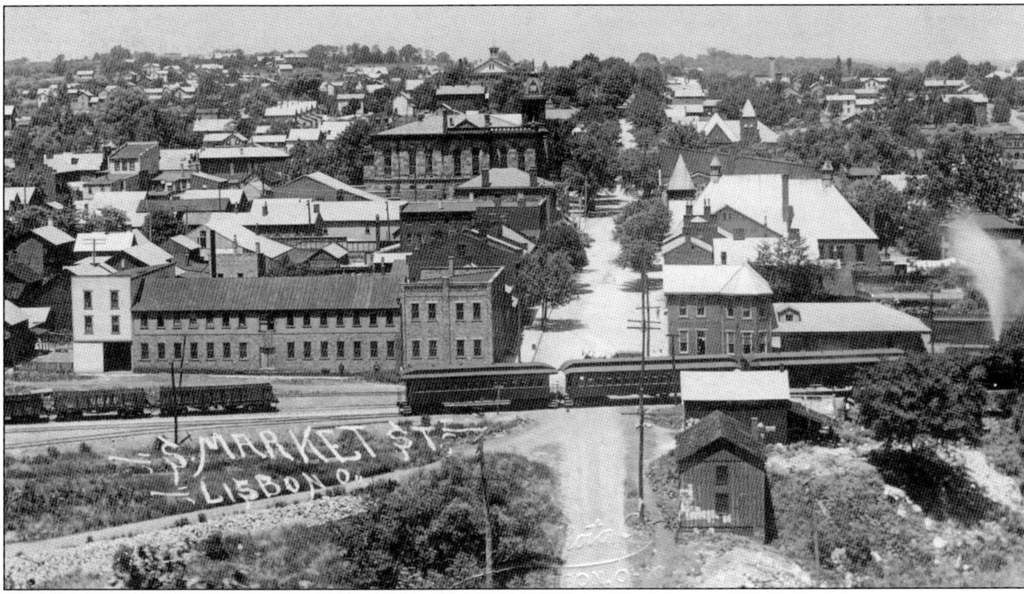

This brick depot-office building (left of center) on South Market Street in Lisbon was reportedly built in 1893. After abandonment of the Pittsburgh Lisbon & Western line in 1942, it was converted to commercial use. It was restored and, in 2017, is serving many uses including being the terminus for the Little Beaver Creek Greenway Trail. (Author's collection.)

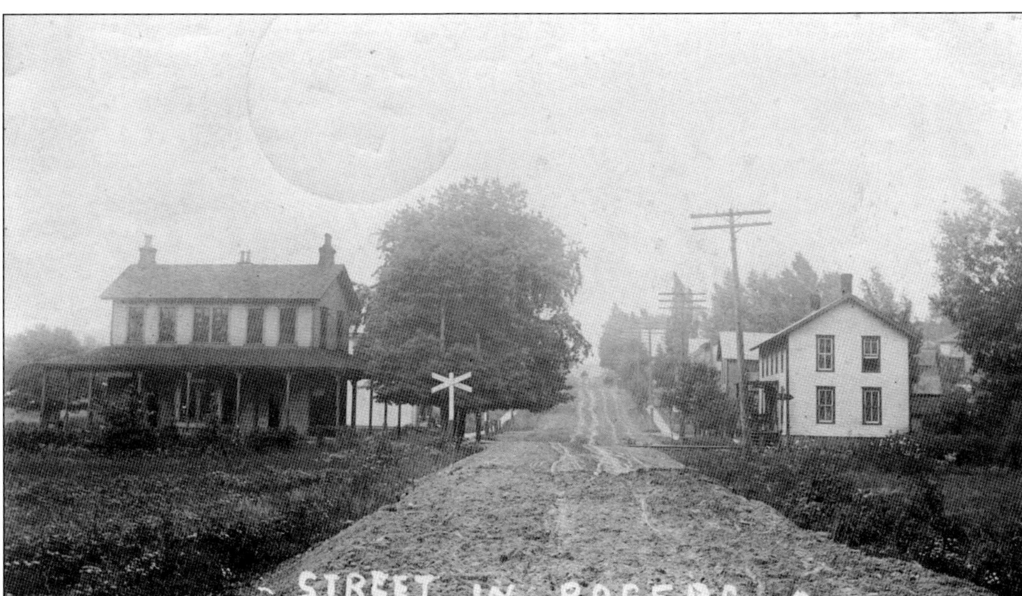

The combination depot of the Pittsburgh Lisbon & Western in Rogers had second-floor living quarters for the agent and family due to the remoteness of the station when it first opened. Rogers more or less began with the arrival of the railroad in 1883. (Author's collection.)

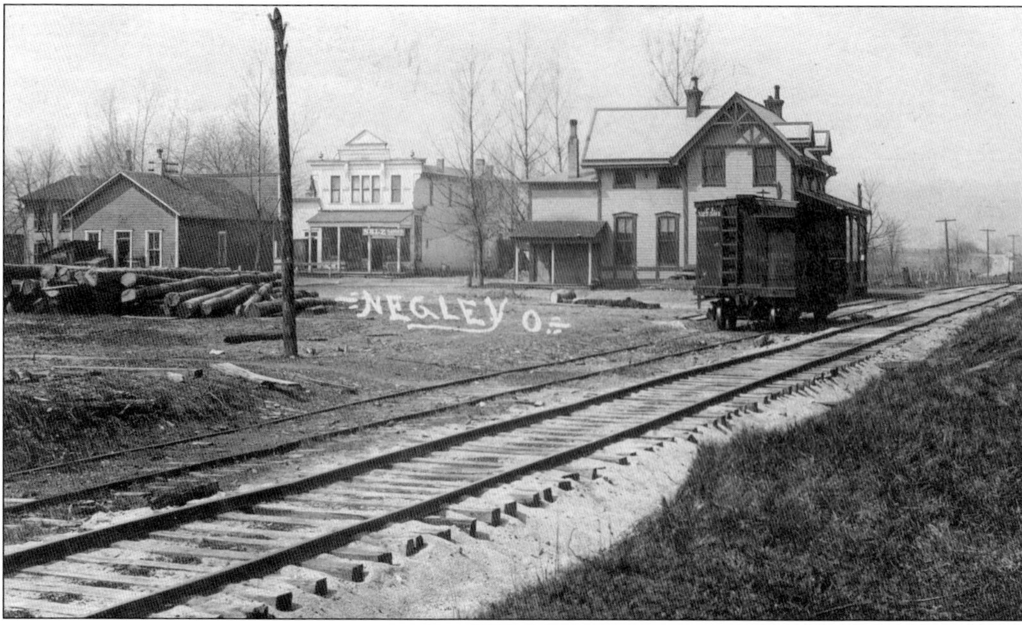

The PL&W had a similar depot to Rogers in Negley. The second floor also provided living quarters for the agent. The building behind the Negley depot was the home of Powers Moore and Company, which held the title of the largest general store in Ohio from 1910 to 1915. (Author's collection.)

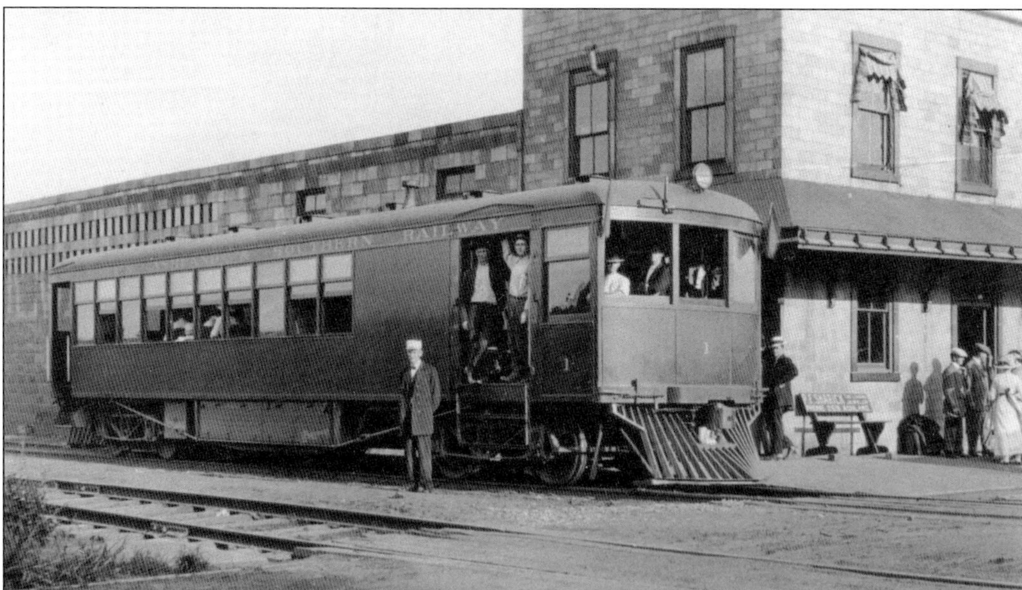

The Ashland & Wooster Railway depot in Ashland opened in 1901. This view shows it around 1913 with predecessor Lorain Ashland & Southern's Edison-Beach Battery Car No. 1. Conductor Theodore George and his train crew pose with the brand-new engine. The depot contained offices and waiting rooms in the two-story portion and a freight house and adjacent two-stall enginehouse behind. The bricks and glazed tile came from A&W owner Horace Camp's brick plants. (Ashland County Historical Society collection.)

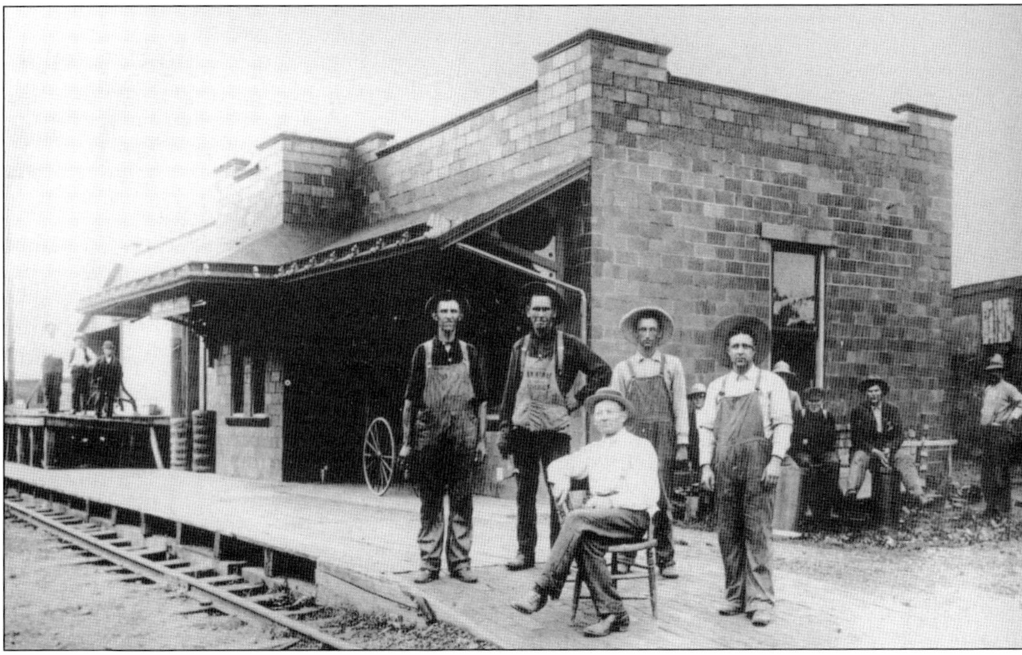

The Ashland & Wooster combination depot in Jeromeville dates to February 1902. This brick and tile depot, along with an almost identical one in Funk built in June 1902, replaced earlier 1895 structures. Again, the building products came from the A&W owner's clay plants. These depots were of a unique design and not found anywhere else in the state. Jeromeville was torn down in the 1970s. The A&W also had depots at England and Sprengs (an old passenger coach). It used the PRR depot at Custaloga. (Bob Lorenz collection.)

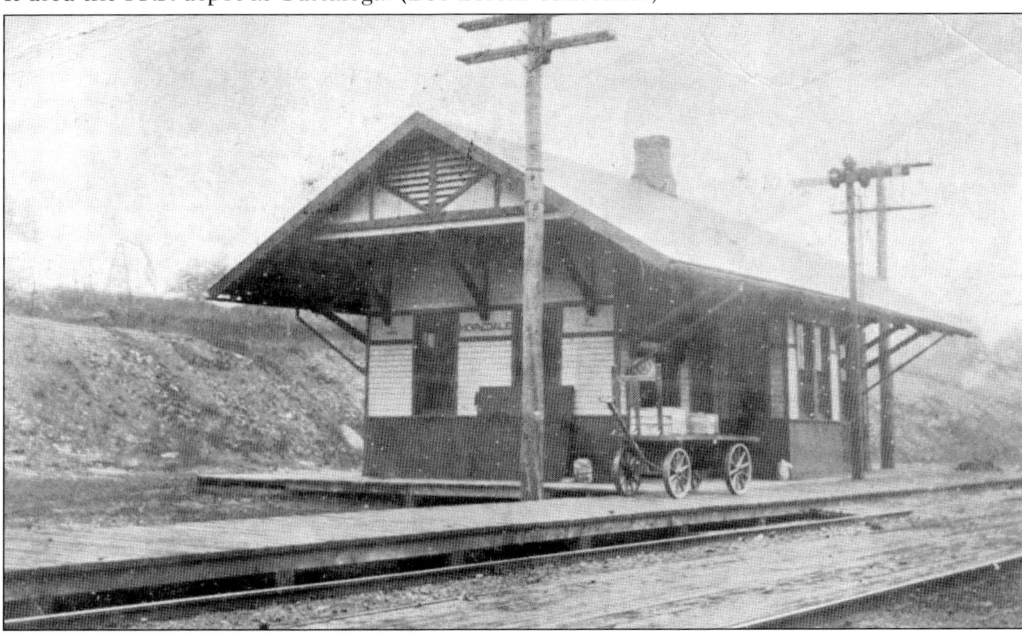

Hopedale was at the top of the grade on the Pittsburgh and West Virginia Railway. From here east, it was a descent into the Ohio Valley. The c. 1904 depot was still standing in 1971. The Lake Erie Alliance & Wheeling also served this community. (Author's collection.)

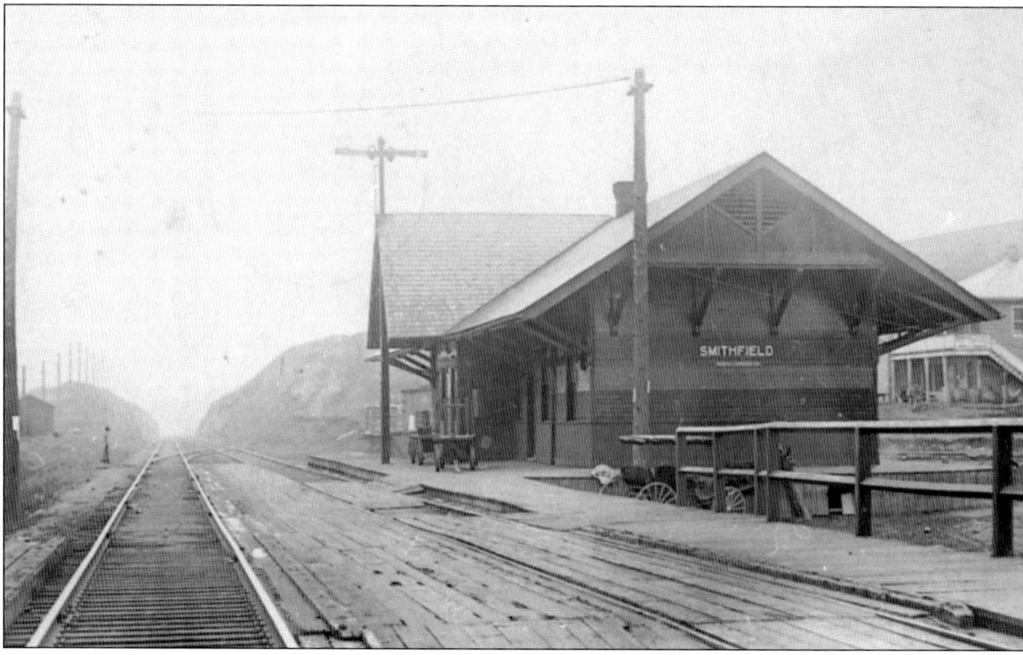

Smithfield's P&WV depot also dates to about 1904, when the line was opened for traffic. It also was still trackside in 1971. (Author's collection.)

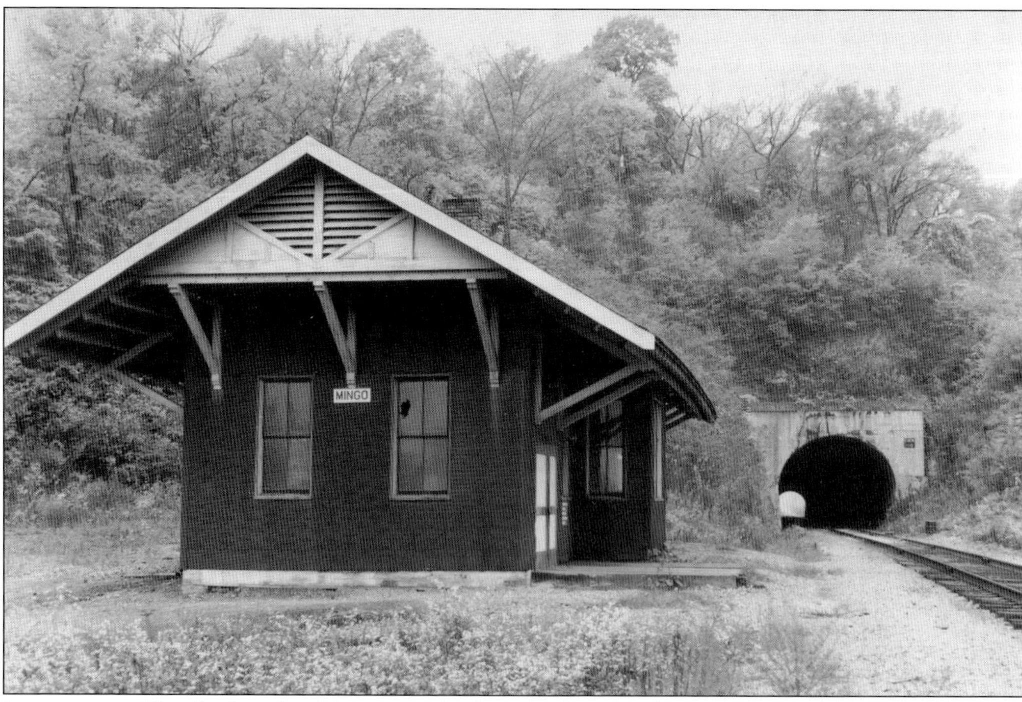

Last stop in Ohio before the Ohio River bridge was this combination depot in Mingo Junction. This c. 1904 depot sat just east of 845-foot Coen Tunnel. This image was captured in 1952. (Bob Lorenz photograph.)

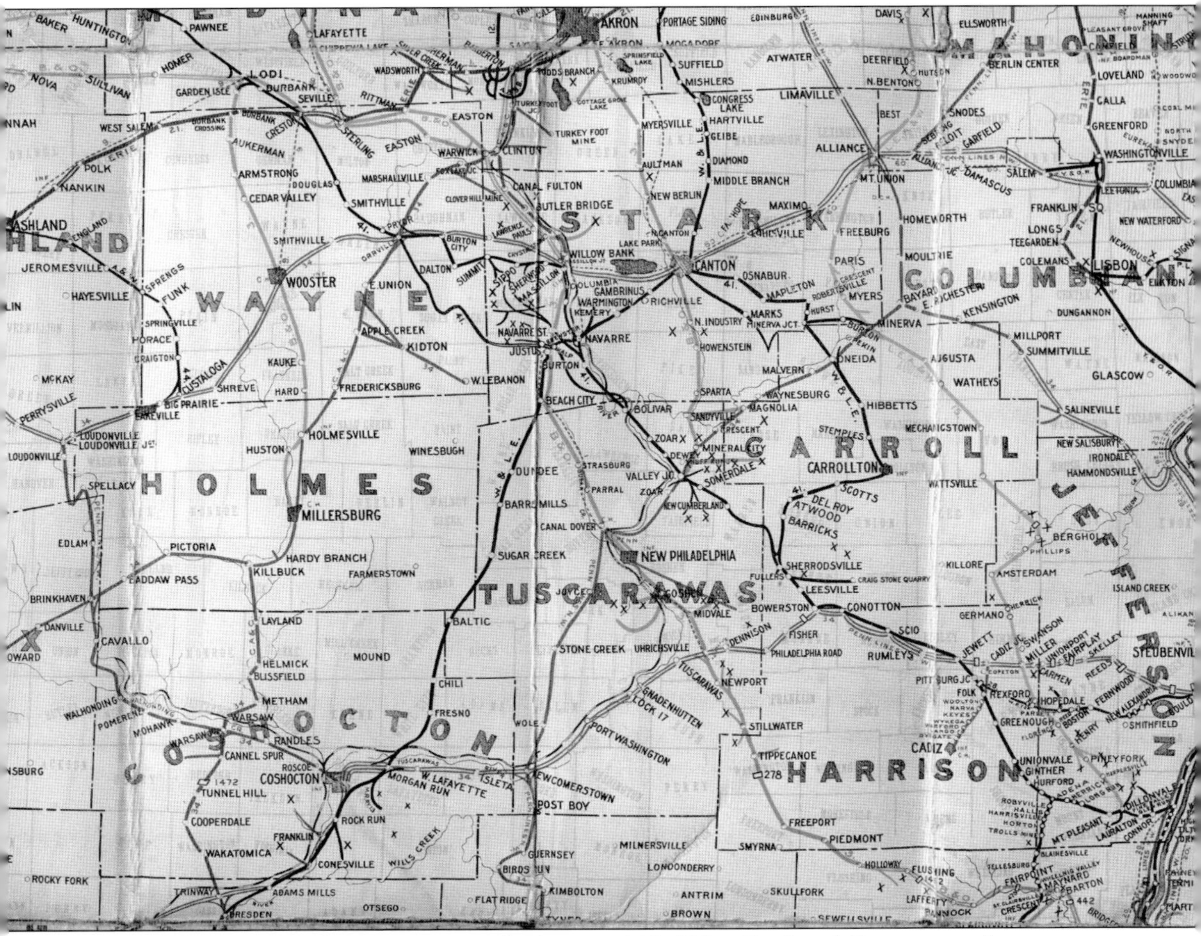

This map shows railroads in East Central Ohio in 1909. (Ohio Railroad Commission.)